DEDICATION

To my mother,
Edna Nightingale Kravette,
who during her 60's and 70's
became one of the
leading women life insurance agents
in the country
and whose Alternatives To Aging in her 80's
include her extraordinarily high degree of
commitment to serving all those in her life.

ABOUT THE AUTHOR.

Stephen Kravette is a professional writer, lecturer, seminar leader, creative advertising specialist, career counselor, stress reduction therapist, astrologer, and new age consultant who lives in Cohasset, Massachusetts. His previous books in Schiffer Publishing's Whitford Press line include Complete Relaxation and Complete Meditation. For the last 12 years, he has been working with, teaching, and proving out the principles of Alternatives To Aging. In the process, he has been privileged to have had the opportunity to share his unique and empowering personal perspectives with hundreds of thousands of people through guest appearances on more than 550 talk shows.

Currently, he is writing two new books and preparing an expanded Alternatives To Aging seminar series.

CONTENTS

PREFACE

Early training in scarcity has taught us that time and energy are finite. Aging in contemporary Western life is portrayed as a series of beliefs that: (1) We can expect to become obsolete in an increasingly youth-oriented society. (2) After (your choice of age), it's all downhill. Or (3) What else but adversity can we expect at our age?

Fortunately, alternatives do exist. However, they exist only for those of us who are willing to grow beyond the boundaries of our early scarcity-oriented reality. The key is that we have many more choices than we ever dreamed possible. And this unique book has opened my eyes to that key.

At the half-century mark, my personal and professional world views have been undergoing profound changes as a result of exposure to Stephen Kravette's work. He has supported me in creating a quite unanticipated openness to alternative views of aging and death, making possible an enormous expansion of self-determination in relation to both my own personal aging and my professional teachings.

This book has actually been responsible for transforming my negative 'poverty' view of health to a positive 'prosperity' view of wellbeing.

During my past two decades as a nurse gerontologist and a university educator, I had become heavily invested in learning and sharing the accepted bio-psycho-socio-spiritual theories about the 'normal process of aging'.   Making peace with the losses of aging while rejoicing in the gains, letting go of youth, affirming life while not denying death, creating intentional caring communities for support during crises of aging as well as life-threatening circumstances were all themes of my learnings and teachings.

All were based upon respect for the limitations posed by the aging process.   After all, cross-cultural research when Gerontology was coming of age suggested that all human beings would secretly prefer to live forever without growing old.   Although many of us engage in wishful thinking and costly measures related to avoiding the aging processes, in our secret heart of hearts, we believe in the finiteness of youth and life and we dread loss of control and other indignities of aging.   Thus we relinquish responsibility for creating a context for living as fully as possible, in health and with a sense of re-creation.

Exposed to rich Alternatives To Aging through the pioneering work of Stephen Kravette and others less scarcity-oriented than my traditional self, I have been opening up to an astounding number of alternatives in my own life and my life-work.   Never before have I felt so keenly the zest for surrounding myself with the whole range of healthful life-enhancing possibilities.

The fundamental theme is that we have many more choices about life and living than we ever dreamed possible.   We create our own reality even as we make these choices.   We can choose wellness and life over illness and death.   This kind of commitment begins with the powerful belief that we are up to making these choices and we deserve to age in healthful ways.

The extraordinary gift of this book's message is that it has empowered me to challenge all of the old myths about aging.   Since Stephen shared his original draft with me several years ago and encouraged me to consider applying the principles in my hospital and university work, I have been living this message for quite some time.

It has changed my reality to the extent that I can take great pride in my own age and the aging processes of those I love.   I no longer fear or dread old age;   I now have Alternatives To Aging's thoroughly enlivening message to sustain my positive health attitudes and practices.   I no longer blame aging for unwanted changes in my physical body;   I now know that I can choose to tune myself like a fine instrument. And I no longer have uncertainty about the contributions I am making to my gerontological patients at the hospital and my students at the university; I can now actually see the truly remarkable ways in which I am able to make an impact their everyday lives, simply by drawing on all of my own newfound insights and strengths.

Living in the realm of Alternatives To Aging has already opened doors to almost unlimited expansiveness for me and I am sure it will continue to keep opening these doors of growth and transformation for many years to come. I invite you to join me here!

Caroline Jo Dorr, R.N., C., M.S.

Associate Chief, Nursing Service For Education

Certified Gerontological Nurse
VA Medical Centers, Brockton and West Roxbury, MA

Adjunct Assistant Professor, Boston University, Boston MA

CHAPTER 1

THE COMING
OF AGE

There is a place where no one lives much past the age of twelve.

It is a playground kind of world. Populated by children. Run by children for children.

Every morning, the children leave their houses and go out to play. They play with trucks and erector sets and small machines and balls and electronic games and guns and shovels and doctor kits and marbles. Some of them play house.

Snacks and meals are provided automatically. So are clothes, sneakers and other necessities of life. No one goes without. No one lacks.

It is a well run economy with centuries of stability behind it, although no one seems to know how or why it works. In many ways, it is better than yours and mine. In many ways, it is somewhat the same.

The most important difference is that no one lives much past the age of twelve.

You know what happens when you turn twelve, don't you?

Your glands pulse with strange new secretions. Your biological clocks shift to a different rate of ticking and propel you down new developmental paths. Your body begins to lengthen out. Your proportions change. You grow hair on places that are not your head. Physically, you no longer appear childlike. Your emotional needs rise to unaccustomed levels of wanting and longing. And you are led in new directions by new dreams and new ideals.

Your mental perspective expands along with your metamorphosing body and emotions. So you see things in ways you never saw them before. And your intellect processes material differently than it did one or two or five years before.

Even time flows at an altered rate of speed than it did when each day stretched out like an eternity and each night became an endless struggle with shadows and terrifying hidden forces of adversity.

You know what happens when you turn twelve.

You change.

And when you change, the other children do not like it one bit.

They don't like it when you begin to think differently and look differently and act differently than you used to think, act and look. There is some scary substance that sticks to the notion of change.

At first, they good-naturedly make fun of you. They kid around about how your child-styled playclothes don't fit you so well. And how your hands are too big to manipulate the child-sized controls on the games. And how your mind no longer tracks clearly on childish chatter.

At first, it is so good natured that you even join in and make fun of yourself. But that stage passes quickly. Soon it is no longer funny at all.

The closer you get to the other side of twelve, the more serious a problem it becomes in the playground world.

The children will not allow anyone in the play areas past the age of thirteen. There is a special isolated section of benches where thirteen and fourteen-year-old people have to sit, if they live that long. All they can do is watch and wither away.

Those who live to the ripe old age of fifteen look and act so grotesque that they cannot come out in public at all where the children can see them. They are shut away in dark rooms because they are so close to death.

Naturally, they die there. Where the children don't have to be around them or deal with them. Naturally, it is better that way.

And in that merry little place of eternal spring and summer, sheltered and securely set in their youthful patterns, the peachfaced cherubic children play on and on and on.

The day that sperm met ovum and you were conceived, an interesting process began. You started to age. It's true. Before you were even born, your process of aging replicated in microcosm the entire history of life on the planet Earth.

Each human organism does it. So you were not alone as you passed through all the ages and stages of evolution as we know it. Ages and stages, after all, are simply periods of time in which aging occurs.

You experienced all of it, personally and profoundly:

The Age Of Single-Celled Protozoas, in which you engaged in life at its simplest level.

The Age Of Multicelled Creatures, in which you began to differentiate into cooperative families of cells, all working together in harmony.

The Age Of Fish, in which you actually possessed rudimentary gills and flipper-fins.

The Age Of Amphibians, in which your lungs and limbs emerged and you changed as tadpoles do each spring.

The Age Of Reptiles, in which your heart and internal organs developed into more efficacious instruments and your skin thickened into a protective coating.

The Age Of Mammals, in which you stabilized as a warm-blooded life-sustaining being.

By the time you were born, you had crossed over into the Age Of Man. You had already acquired billions of years of aging experience. In just nine months. Most people will never age that much or that dramatically ever again. Not in this life anyway.

But by then, another equally profound period of aging had begun. In the first five years of your life, you grew from a tiny baby who needed assistance to lift its own head to a small but perfectly scaled model of an adult human being.

Once again, a staggering amount of growth,

development, aging and expansion had occurred. You may not remember any of it but there are reminders all around you. Just keep your eye on any baby. And watch what happens.

Puberty and adolescence marked the next most profound cycle of aging in your life. Chances are, you remember a lot of it. Even more than the significant physical changes involved in becoming a mature sexual being, you may recall the emotional activity: All the loneliness, the alienation, the suppression of feelings and of personal identity. The struggle to become the next step in your life. And all of the differences associated with that step that seemed so awkward and strange to you.

Wherever you are right now in the chronology of your years, those three major cycles of aging are probably behind you. Each of those three huge waves of metamorphosis has smoothed out. Even the ripples are still. The fascinating thing is, you survived. In fact, you grew.

So you probably think all that upheaval is finally all over.

Not quite.

If you are anywhere between the ages of 16 and 60, a fourth wave is on its way. It is a cycle of aging that is just as massive and just as transformational as your prebirth, babyhood, and adolescence.

The problem is, unlike each of those previous cycles, this one is loaded down with consciously and unconsciously accepted belief systems, attitudes and evaluations that clog the gears of workable change. The coming of aging, for example, is almost universally considered to be a period of major slowdown and shutoff. A problem. Instead of what it actually is: just another phase in the process of life.

In other words, the problem is not aging itself. Aging is no problem at all. Aging is nothing more than another period of growth and development and change. Birds do it, bees do it; even uneducated trees do it.

The problem occurs when you begin to define aging as a problem. By doing that, you begin to create more than enough internal stress and trouble to cause the kind of disturbances that justify your definition. As you will soon see.

Take the next few moments to find out exactly where you stand regarding aging. Most of us are sandwiched somewhere between being somewhat fearful of it and being completely unconscious about it. Some of us watch furtively for each new sign of decrepitude. Others pay severe penalties for pretending that nothing is going on, nothing at all.

The following short exercise will begin to put everything more in perspective for you. With how many of the following statements do you agree or disagree?

1. Most older people are not able to take care of themselves.
2. Old people are more susceptible to colds and disease.
3. Old people are more fragile than young people.
4. As you get older, you lose your eyesight.
5. As you get older, you lose your hearing.
6. As you get older, you lose your desire for sex.
7. As you get older, you lose your ability to perform sexually.
8. Old people shrink and shrivel up in size.
9. Old people smell funny.
10. Old people cannot think clearly and lose their memories.
11. Old people cannot concentrate very well.
12. Old people need lots of medical care and drugs.
13. Old people should take more vitamins.
14. Old people tend to be emotionally unstable.

If you believe that at least four of these statements are true or more true than false, take another moment and do this exercise. Say the following sentence beginning to yourself over and over about 20 times. Fill in a different ending to it each time.

The older you get. . . (You finish the statement in your own words. Any words will do. They don't even have to make any sense.) By now, you may be beginning to see what you are up against when it comes to aging. You are pressing your nose against a tightly woven blanket of negative beliefs and attitudes. And it is literally smothering you and your ability to age freely, spontaneously and joyfully. It is also making it difficult for you to discover expansion and satisfaction. Instead, at every turn, you immerse yourself in depression and loss.

You will have an extended opportunity to examine and reconstruct your beliefs, attitudes, positions, evaluations and judgments about aging in Chapter 6. For now, just begin to notice the extent to which you have them. Also begin to become aware of the way they act like fences and boundaries that limit, suppress and contain your experience. Notice also exactly whose beliefs, attitudes, positions, evaluations, and judgments they are, who put them there, and who holds them tightly in place.

None of the twelve statements you read, by the way, is necessarily true or false. In terms of your own life, you will soon see that you get to choose which of them will become true or false for you.

And that, more than anything else, is what this book is all about. It will return to you a power that you have always had but may have failed to use. The power to choose how your life will be.

You will see that you have always had alternatives, whether you actually used them or not. And you will realize that you are the one who gets to cast the decisive vote about whether you will have:

- A face that is liver spotted and distorted or a face that is calm, clear, strong and attractive.
- A body that aches, weakens and dies a little more each day or a body that is strong, vibrant, usable, and able to support you completely.
- Emotional upsets and strain or a balanced ebb and flow of feelings coming from an overall sense of your own magnificence.
- Mental degeneration or expanding clarity and heightened perceptiveness.
- Failing health and persistent physical problems

or remarkable wellbeing and vitality.
- Disappearing sexual desires and capabilities or a constantly regenerating sex drive that leads you to new levels of satisfaction and a renewed cycle of potency and responsiveness.
- Alienation, shutdown and despair or powerful new abilities, evolving personal characteristics and expansive growth.

All the alternatives in each area of your life will open up for you in this book. You will then be empowered to take it from there. As a result, you will find yourself choosing responsibly to have what you want with each passing day and each advancing year.

A large variety of life-extending techniques will be revealed, some for the first time, about exercise, diet, vitamins, goal direction, and other physical, emotional and mental mechanisms for maintaining vigor and health at youth-like levels and for restoring capacities and appetites that you may have unknowingly let slip away. I have personally used, tested and proved each technique you will read about. I have also instructed many many others in their use over the last twelve years with consistent success. The techniques work. Absolutely. They provide dramatic and often instantaneously measurable results.

But more important than any techniques, tips or advice, my intention in this book is to provide you with an altogether new context in which to handle aging and to offer a powerful new way to align yourself with your experience of the passage of time. What this book is all about is how you can become older with style and dynamic growth; it is not about what to do to resist the processes of life.

Looking at it one way, there is no Alternative To Aging. You age from the moment you are conceived. You age from birth. You age until you die. And only then do you become ageless.

Looking at it another way, you can begin to get clear about how you perceive aging right now. Then you can open yourself up to a variety of alternatives to what you have always thought of as aging, to your pictures about aging, and to virtually all of the problems that you and most of contemporary Western civilization associate with aging.

Those alternatives are all here for you. And the principles behind each of them will hold true whether you are 14 or 140 or any age in between.

Much of the book's material will be especially relevant if you are on one side or the other of the decade of your 60s. Or if you are particularly concerned about that critical and perilous period and what comes after it.

What comes after it, if you catch the brass ring of the next cycle around the carousel of life, can be as many as 50 to 70 more years of vitality and adventure. All at new and more intense levels of mental and psychic expansion, power, control, and freedom.

That is the biggest and best alternative of all. For you, it begins to unfold right now.

CHAPTER 2

HISTORY AND OTHER MYTHS

'I had the strangest dream last night,' said Charlie.

The other children looked up, surprised. It was just about a week after his eleventh birthday and Charlie didn't talk much anymore. He usually just hung around on the edge of whatever happened to be going on. 'It was about another world. Or maybe this one either a long time ago or a long time from now.

'Kaka,' said Kathy.

'That doesn't make a bit of sense,' said Joan.

'What do you mean?' Freddy asked.

'Well,' said Charlie, 'the people in my dream lived to be very very old. Some lived as long as 70 years, a few even made it into their eighties. That's more than ten times older than you are right now, Joan.'

'Ho, ho. That's awesome,' said Kathy.

'You're talking like one of those weird old kids,' said Joan.

'What are you getting at?' Freddy asked.

Charlie continued his dream story. He told about a kind looking white-haired man and woman who befriended him and others that he had met. He described swashbuckling heroes and heroines of 20 and 30, powerful leaders of 40 and 50, gifted sages and teachers of 60 and 70. 'It seemed so familiar. As if I had seen it all before. And yet, it seemed very odd.'

'You're full of it,' said Kathy as she skipped away, dragging her yellow-haired dolly by the arm.

Joan frowned and shook her curly head. 'I think you are becoming an early candidate for the big kids benches,' she said.

Aw, it's only a dream,' said Freddy who was 9-1/2 years old, 'and yet, I wish ...'

'Come along, you little jerk,' said Joan. She tugged on the sleeve of Freddy's little yellow t-shirt with the cartoon of a moosehead on it. 'You know very well that everything we've been taught is true is really true. And that what everyone else says is right really is right. Well this sure isn't any of that, so it can't be true and it can't be right. And besides, haven't you been told you can never trust anyone over ten?'

Charlie listened to her voice fading away in the distance and went back to bed. It was at least a day or so before anyone wondered where he was.

Long long ago when the human race was very young, an impressive variety of tribal species of not-quite men and not-quite women roamed the face of the earth and coped with the challenges of a pre-informational, pre-industrial, pre-agricultural society.

They wandered, following gigantic herds of not-quite bison, not-quite deer and other long gone herbivores. As they hunted, so were they hunted. By enormous not-quite wolves, not-quite tigers and not-quite bears.

Even then, humans had a longer potential lifespan than other mammals. The only consideration was the difficulty involved in attempting to live it out. Few did. Nevertheless, each tribal subspecies had its own way of dealing with members of the group who aged beyond their physical ability to hunt or work or move quickly from seasonal camp to seasonal camp.

One group of neanderthalic people with stooped shaggy bodies and sloping apelike skulls revered and worshiped the elderly. Their oldest men and women knew more than anyone else about the earth, the nomadic herds, the everpresent dangers. They were the seers who could perform complex feats of ritual magic. They were the shamanistic wizards who could heal with herbs and restore life with their body energy.

Many of these oldtimers could draw back the curtains of a peculiar form of genetic racial memory and recall aeons of past events to provide a proven source for solutions to tribal problems, powerful rituals and incantations, and glorious sagas of heroic deeds performed by long-dead ancestors.

Younger tribal members were assigned to assist each of the aged. They served as apprentices, learned as much as they could, and willingly carried the much valued elderly along the yearly migrational routes whenever hands-on support was needed. Such work was considered a great honor.

Another group of near-humans long ago had large wedge-shaped heads with pointed ears and teeth, dwarfed hairless bodies, and disproportionately long muscular arms and hands. These fanged folk dealt with older tribal members more expediently. When tastier game was scarce, they ate the aged. They particularly savored the hearts, brains, livers, appendix and genitals of their former companions and believed that great powers and spiritual energy were transferred to whoever consumed these special parts.

According to custom, it was taboo to die a natural death. The spirit, when not elevated by battle, valor of the hunt or communal feeding, could not soar free from the body and remained earthbound where it could haunt the rest of the tribe.

Other groups of not-quite humans came in an almost unlimited assortment of sizes, shapes, colors and degrees of shagginess. Each tribal community handled its aging members in a way that fell somewhere in between these two extremes. Generally, early humans neither exalted nor ate the aged. Some adored them; some abused them. Some cared for them; some neglected them. Tribes with more-or-less average points of view simply accepted age as a phenomenon similar to youth.

Their old people died as they lived, without honor, dishonor or ceremony, and lay where they fell when the group moved on.

Similar patterns continued as humanity developed into its present model and, roughly 10,000 years ago, discovered the relative ease and stability of agriculture and the conveniences of writing and recording history. Here are some of the historical highlights from around the world between then and now.

In New Zealand, native tribespeople put most of their aged to death when they became useless or burdensome. However, older people who managed to survive achieved highest honors and were valued for their wisdom. They were looked upon as a symbol of preserving tribal experiences.

In Africa and also among the native Amerind tribes, widely diverging customs existed from group to group. For every tribe that preserved and cared for its older members, a neighboring tribe would cast them out to be killed by beasts or simply leave them behind in the brush. Notably good and notably bad examples of each are readily available in reference books.

Pagan Pacific islanders from Samoa to the Aleutians revered and respected their elderly and elevated them to positions of authority. So did the majority of tribes in the Caucasian Mountains of Central Asia, the Aborigines of Australia, the Mayans of Central America, the Peruvian Incas and many Mexican tribes. But with these few exceptions, attitudes about aging in the world's less known cultures remained negative at best for more than a hundred centuries.

Contempt and ill treatment were conspicuous in virtually all West Coast Amerind tribes from California up through Canada, Alaska and Greenland.

Voluntary death was chosen in more than a few tribal community settings. For instance, the North America prairie tribes, Payaguas of Brazil, African Hottentots and natives of the New Hebride and Fiji Islands placed their aged in open graves and buried them alive. These cultures believed that each person emerged in the future with only the powers and capabilities he or she possessed at the time of death. Waiting too long to die would only weaken the next life to follow. Another common belief held that natural death was the work of evil spirits. Those who escaped by voluntarily choosing death would fare better in future lives and the afterlife period in between.

The custom of eating the elderly did not stop in prehistoric times. It persisted well into the twentieth century in Sumatra, Tibet, Thailand, Central India, Northern Samoyed and Ostiak regions, and the Cachibo and Tapi areas of Brazil. In each case, cannibalism was not practiced because of hunger but as a religious ceremony to honor and preserve the physical attributes of an aged person by incorporating them into the bodies of those who lived on.

Examining the various remote and less known cultures can be useful as well as interesting. Traditions and customs among these people have been unchanged for countless years. Of course, by our standards, such examples are somewhat primitive. Therefore, we would expect to find unenlightened ways. Right?

Wrong.

Guess what was going on all this time in the more humane cradles of contemporary civilization.

More of the same. Occasional and noteworthy benevolence. Occasional horror. And considerable ground in between.

Several so-called civilized cultures stand out for their unusually humanitarian treatment of the aged among them.

Ancient China displayed a reverence for age that persists even today. Coming from a strong conviction that long life is desirable in every way, rulers who may have agreed about nothing else treated the aged with kindness and reverence.

Confucius was committed to securing rest and peace for the aged. His Book of Rites cites examples of how sages of earlier times proved their moral worth by their respect for venerable older people. Ministers and officials were granted special privileges based upon their years. Residents of each county took their places at community events according to their age, not their health or wealth. Pensions and retirement stipends were paid with useful articles like benches and walking staffs as well as money.

The unusual Chinese quality of respect for aging rested upon a premise that each stage of life contributes to the development of the complete individual. Life was divided into periods and it was not until a person reached the age of 60 that he or she could be described as a person of wisdom and experience.

In Japan, even before the influence of the Chinese, filial devotion was expanded to include the care of all older people. The divinely inspired emperors deferred graciously to the experienced judgment of their most elderly advisors. Artists glorified the longevity of the tortoise, the crane and the graceful thousand-year-old pines.

Ancestor worship and the moral benefits of revering the aged were significantly influenced and augmented to an even higher degree during later interactions with China. And the only exceptions to Japan's exemplary support of the aged came during civil war periods in which warlords and Samurai craved and admired power more than wisdom.

Egypt, Sumeria, Babylon and the Hebraic nations shared a strong spiritual reverence for age.

Egyptians cared for their elderly out of a multicentury preoccupation with immortality and a ceaseless quest for a bridge to the afterlife. The other Near East nations' attitudes were drawn from a fundamental regard for life and for the wisdom that accompanies long life. Among most Semitic people, old men have always been honored as patriarchal family and community leaders. The Arabic word for chieftain, 'sheik', literally means 'old man'. And God was thought of as a wise and white-bearded old gentleman.

According to the Jewish tradition, long life was considered to be a blessing despite its inevitable sorrows. In Proverbs 16, the hoary head is a crown of glory. And in Job 12, it is the embodiment and the symbol of abundant wisdom. All of the holy books exalt aging from the Torah to the Apocrypha where, in Sir 26, a passage reads, 'As the lamp that shineth upon the holy candlestick, so is the beauty of the face in ripe age.'

In Greece, attitudes toward aging were less consistent. Ancient Greeks respected the aged and rivaled rivaled the Chinese in their humanitarianism. But by the time of the Classical Period, social consciousness had been swept away by an infatuation with youth, youthful beauty, and youthful athletic skill, all of which were thought to fade rapidly with the passage of time.

Anything that destroyed beauty and marred enjoyment was looked upon with abject horror and treated accordingly. This shift in attitude may have been the result of an increasing interest in conquest and military expertise. Warmaking skills are not exactly enhanced by advancing years.

The Roman empire was largely middle of the road on the issue of aging. Caesars and senators who kept their wits and mental alertness were respected as authority figures. Otherwise, older people were more or less ignored and advancing years were viewed as a period of neglect and hardship.

Early Christian nations that emerged from the last years of Roman influence followed similar patterns. Through the middle ages and into the twentieth century, religion-linked concepts of charity and work-ethic productivity have kept an uneasily swinging pendulum in balance.

Throughout the history of the civilized world, nightmare-like treatment of the aged shows up with unfortunate regularity.

Ancient Persian cities were bounded by double walls. In between these walls, packs of killer dogs roamed wild. These vicious animals had been bred for the purpose of attacking and consuming the aged and infirmed who were thrown to them. Each metropolis was kept as meticulously clean and tidy as the streets of Disneyland, but the area between the double walls was littered with mounds of aged human bones. This practice was stopped centuries ago by Alexander The Great, after his conquering armies swept into Asia, but an almost culturally-based lack of concern with the value of human life has persisted in Iran even in modern times.

Albanians believed that vapors from a person who lived longer than 100 years were poisonous to the health of younger people around them. Graves were dug and filled long before that kind of harm could be done.

The Teutonic nations of the North extolled suicide and other techniques for killing off their aged, wounded or diseased.

Germanic people asked to be put to death upon aging. They were placed upon funeral pyres and stabbed repeatedly as the flames were kindled.

Swedes and Hyperborians were known to have cast themselves from cliffs and precipices when their time of usefulness was over. Reluctant individuals were assisted by thoughtful others. In Iceland, this custom persisted in times of famine until well after 1000 AD.

Long after Christianity had been introduced in Norway, a law allowing adults who could not support themselves to be disposed of was still actively enforced. Old or sick people who required excessive care were simply placed in holes dug in a graveyard and left to die.

Early Scandinavians, who held that it was a dishonor to die of disease or old age instead of in battle, would not be likely candidates for humanitarian awards for break-throughs in the care of the elderly. However, classic Viking sagas relate that in the most glorious days of legend, the aged were treated with respect and valued for their wisdom and experience. Odin, father figure of the gods, was thought of as old and he frequently advised his listeners to heed the words of the aged.

Worthy of note is the crossover legendry of the four ancient civilizations who most strongly have influenced our present day society. Each demonstrated a high degree of reverence for the process of aging and placed considerable value upon the attainment of a long life. Where both of these factors coincide, heroic figures tended to have incredibly long lifespans.

This certainly was the case among the ancient Greeks, Sumerians, Babylonians and Hebrews. In each of these nations, similar versions of the story of mankind evolved. Each civilization traces the event of human life from a point of intensely focused creative energy, through a period of extreme longevity, to a catastrophic flood of retribution from supreme beings. After these flood waters recede, the span of human life also recedes to an average of 70 years and a reported maximum allowance of 120 to 140 years.

Parallel pre-flood leaders or rulers from these four ancient nations and their lifespans, when known, are shown in Table 1. Curiously, each civilization has a line of ten long-lived key people before the coming of the flood.

TABLE 1.   LONGEVITY CROSSOVER MYTHS. FAMOUS LONGLIVED HEROES FROM 4 ANCIENT CIVILIZATIONS.

HEBREW Name	Age	BABYLONIAN Name	Age	SUMERIAN Name	Age	GREEK Name	Age
Adam	930	Galumum	900+	Alulim	-	Aloros	-
Seth	912	Zugagib	840+	Alagar	-	Alaparos	-
Enos	905	Aripi	720	Enmeluanna	-	Amelon	-
Kenan	910	Etana	635	Enmengalanna	-	Ammenon	-
Mahalalel	895	Pelikam	350	Dumuzi	-	Daozus	-
Jared	962	Enmennunna	611	Ensibzianna	-	Amempsinos	-
Enoch	365	Melamkish	900	Enmenduranna	-	Euedorachos	-
Methusaleh	969	Lugalbanda	1200	Ubardudu	-	Opartes	-
Lamech	777	Dumuzi	100+	Aradgin	-	Ardates	-
Noah	950	Gilgamesh	*	Ziusudra	-	Xisuthros	-

* Age in dispute. Varies in literature from 125 to 1000+ years.

In a more modern and researched version of these years of fable and myth, geophysicist Immanual Velicovsky asserts that during the time of Noah, Gilgamesh, Zinsudra and Xisuthros, the axis of the planet Earth shifted dramatically due to the nearby passage of a large comet which, when trapped by the sun's gravitational pull, became the planet Venus.

During the almost unimaginable upheaval of that event, almost all of our planet's surface was severely flooded, many species of life perished, the polar axis shifted by a factor of thousands of miles, and life-sustaining ions present in the atmosphere may have been diluted, burned up, or carried off by the pull of Venus. When everything settled down again, life on Earth just was never the same again. Particularly where lifespans were concerned.

Who knows? It is all history. In fact, if you have stayed with this chapter this long, that is all you have gotten so far. History. History does not make a lot of difference because all of it has all happened already. As a feminist friend of mine likes to say, 'His story? So what!'

That is not supposed to be funny. It happens to be true. All historical data, no matter how thoroughly researched or beautiful or inspiring or terrifying, is nothing more than someone's version of how they think it happened. Or how they hope it happened or how they conclude that it happened from whatever available evidence might be around.

How accurate are all those versions? Just think about it.

How accurate a picture of late Twentieth Century life in America could a Thirtieth Century historian create from the following materials: A copy of yesterday's Los Angeles Times. A National Enquirer dated July 1960. Richard Nixon's diary. Your last letter to a close friend. Any novel by Sidney Sheldon or Harold Robbins. A December 1979 Playboy magazine. Adolph Hitler's memoirs, translated into Spanish. A kinescope of an early 'Leave It To Beaver'. Videotapes of 'Friday the 13th VII', 'Hot Teenage Lust', and 'Snow White And The Seven Dwarves'. A Barbie doll, an antique piece of pottery, and your daughter's photograph album.

That's all historians ever have to work with. Shards, bits, pieces, and fragments. All of which are then strung together on the threads of strictly subjective attitudes, beliefs, hopes, wishes and biases.

Can you count on that? I don't think so. Would you want to bet the family jewels on it? I wouldn't.

And yet, in the most real sense imaginable, history exists. It lives in vivid three-dimensional splendor within each one of us. Often, it seems more exciting than the everyday reality of the present. I suggest that is the reason why people become so strongly attracted to the past that they choose to become historians, archaeologists and historical novelists.

Would you like to experience how history lives in you?

Clear your mind. Just close your eyes gently. Look at the backs of your eyelids and when you can see that nothing is there, think of Rome at the time of Julius Caesar. Stay in Rome, clear your mind again and think of the time of Michelangelo and the Renaissance.

Clear it again and think of England in 5 or 6 AD.

Clear it again and think of Egypt in 8015 BC.

Clear it again and think of a time when you were three years old.

Clear your mind one more time and think of everything you can remember that happened last Tuesday.

All of that is history. And each of your pictures is just as valid right at this moment as any written treatise. Any one of your pictures is infinitely more alive in your mind than it is ever likely to be on paper.

So history is merely his story or her story or your own story of what happened some other time or long ago. Unfortunately, when we use this kind of data conceptually, we form belief systems about the nature of things that can reach far into the future, distort our experience of how things really are, and immortalize whatever inaccuracies and opinions have been added to raw and undiluted past events. We believe, for example, that wars and famines are inevitable, forgetting that great periods of peace and natural abundance have always existed as well. Or we believe that people have an inherently evil side or a flaw that always shows up, overlooking all of the people who don't have anything like that at all. Or we tell ourselves that only the young can ever fully enjoy the many delights of life, ignoring the obviousness of the lie.

I will examine belief systems in detail in Chapter 6. For now, a glance at how historical beliefs and attitudes keep getting replayed over and over again on a cultural network will make one point absolutely clear:

There is nothing new about attitudes toward aging.

Things just have not changed much over the last 6000 to 10,000 years of recorded history. Things did not even change much in the infinite span of unrecorded history before that. And none of that makes the slightest bit of difference on any scale designed to measure the quality of life.

The biggest problem associated with our legacy from the past is that a lot of our present patterns relating to aging are no more than blind, unconscious, unthinking replays or updated variations of the same old stuff.

See for yourself.

In 99.98% of the world, here is what is happening as you read this page. In a few countries here and there, aging people are cared for, housed, fed and generally well supported by their communities. In a few other countries, aging people are thoroughly abused, left to die or even brutally killed by their families and neighbors. In still other countries including most major ones, a middle road is followed and the signals are somewhat scrambled. In this category, the United States is a prime example.

Against a background of government reforms and legislative advances that strongly favor the aged, neglect and heartbreak are apparent in every city, every neighborhood, every rural community. Negative nationwide attitudes about decrepitude and breakdown have been prevalent if unacknowledged for years and years. Accompanying negative beliefs have been further shaped, amplified, augmented and reinforced by even more years and years of seemingly innocent television programming.

You know what happens when you see and hear the same thing over and over. You begin to get the idea that it is true. At the University of Pennsylvania's Annenberg School of Communications, 1600 prime-time television programs with more than 5000 characters were analyzed over a period of 15 years. Consistently, senior citizens were portrayed negatively and unflatteringly. People over the age of 65 were cast as doddering, sexless, stubborn, eccentric, silly old fools. And that is only when they were cast at all.

Most of the time on television, aging people have been a nearly invisible segment of the population. Even though older people are increasing in number every year, according to the same University of Pennsylvania study, heavy television viewers believe they are fewer and more sickly than they were 20 years ago. Programming hardly

ever reveals the power that real older people have. Only
their frailties are shown.

We have all seen the few highly notable exceptions.
But the fact that we notice these rare cases as exceptions
because they stand out so strongly in contrast to normal
network fare only further reaffirms the findings.

So in 99.98% of the world, until now, neither
extreme reverence, respect and caring, nor abject cruelty
and abuse have led to any workable Alternatives To
Aging.

Bodies, minds and emotions continue to shut down
and fade away between 60 and 90 years of life. That
process is obvious in your own practical everyday
experience, isn't it? And yet, none of it makes any sense,
particularly when both religion and science are in
complete agreement that a normal lifespan of 120 to 140
years is both possible and attainable.

What about the missing 0.02% of the world?

These are the isolated pockets of unusual longevity.
The province of Georgia in the Caucasian Mountains.
The Hunza Region of West Pakistan. Certain provinces in
Tibet. The Abkhasian Region between the Black Sea and
the Caucasians, the Marquesas in the South Pacific, and
the Vilcambambam area of Ecuador. In these places and
other rare locations, longevity appears to be natural.
Natives in good health and highly active physical and
mental states claim to reach 150 to 170 years of age. And
beyond.

There has been some controversy about these
claims. In these geographic areas, birth records are not
precise and the cultural system of rewards and
acknowledgement favors age.   Therefore, researchers
have counterclaimed that many of the natives arbitrarily
add 20 or 30 years to their reported ages. For the sake of
argument, let's agree that is possible and that many of
the centenarians and double-centerarians lie a little.
Subtracting the claimed differences, we would still find
large numbers of 120 to 140 year old people getting
around as well or even better than they used to, living,
loving and thoroughly enjoying life at enviable levels of
satisfaction.

Certain patterns of diet, environmental issues and other variables appear to coincide even though the localities are widely separated. Each of the factors involved will be explored later in this book. Nevertheless, whatever these people may be doing is not nearly as important as their attitudes in achieving such a rich quality of aliveness and an abundant quantity of life.

In simplest terms, the aged in these regions expect to live long and active lives. In each case, the younger people who surround them expect and fully support the same. It is more than a self-fulfilling prophecy, however. Much more.

It is an ongoing act of creation. And it is based upon an idea that is large enough and powerful enough to sweep away the mists and myths of history and the demeaning, debilitating attitudes that swirl capriciously among them.

To discover your own Alternatives To Aging, I recommend that you do the same. Be willing to create the idea that you intend to live a long, active and productive life. Starting right now.

CHAPTER 3

ABOUT FACING IT

Set back from the play area are several rows of hard wooden benches. Given normal traffic patterns, the benches are where the children would not ordinarily pass too near. The benches are purposely remote, just outside the fringes of everyday awareness and attention. They are not really hidden in shade and long weedy grass. It only seems that way.

Often, the benches are crowded. Even when they are full, a silence hovers over them. Their occupants are as remote and distant as the hard structures themselves.

Today, however, only two elderly children sit at opposite ends of a front row bench. Each watches the little children at play, lost in private inner thoughts.

Marya will never see 14 again. Her face looks stretched out and worn with the experience of life. Gone are the round cherubic qualities that beautiful children possess. Her cheekbones are angular, prominent, strongly accented. Her nose is straight and chiseled with sensuously flaring nostrils. Her lips are red and full instead of chubby and puckered. Her chin is firm with just the slightest suggestion of a cleft.

Her eyes have a strange haunting quality. Their natural energy and vitality have begun to fade away. Large, but deeply set, they focus sharply and what they miss is hardly worth noticing. Their penetrating gaze is anything but vacuous. Green eyes like these demand attention and a direct response. Of course, the children avoid her piercing stare.

Some of them have nicknamed her 'Old Evil Eye'.   All of them will go out of their way to avoid her presence.

Eric is huddled over on the other end of the bench.   He sits with his face supported by his hands.   Idly, his fingers move over the surface of his skin.

He is 13 years old.   His cute little button nose is becoming thin and hawklike.   His curly blond hair has deepened to chestnut brown.   The silky facial hair that began to grow a year ago has become a problem.   He used his large jackknife blade to scrape it away because it embarrassed him so much, and now it comes back every few days as everdarkening stubble.   His fingers rest on another disturbance: a new pimple.   Pimples are the ultimate sign o f advancing age and the children will tease him unmercifully again.   He might as well be dead.   And he soon will be.

The warm summer sun beams down from an almost cloudless blue sky.   It is still bright, although the late afternoon shadows are beginning to lengthen.   An early chorus of crickets and cicada starts up in and under the full-leafed trees.   There are quiet, subtle manifestations of peace and abundance everywhere.

Oblivious, Marya senses that her recently emerging feelings of inner strength and self-reliance are only an illusion.   Already they have begun to retreat and each day she realizes that she is closer and closer to giving up.   Eric just feels lost and abandoned.

In their fear and depression and hopelessness, they overlook the one resource available to each of them that might have made a difference: Each other.

Whether you are now a 25 year old fashion model or an 83 year old great-grandfather, you are probably most reminded of the passage of time as it passes over your face. You may find that you are covering up your face more and more or looking quickly and painfully away as you glance at yourself in the mirror each day. There is a lot of cause for concern.

New lines. New wrinkles. New spots and blemishes. A possible return of acne as hormonal changes occur. Sagging areas under the eyes and along the jaw and neck. Widening pores. Warts. Discolorations and liver spots. Thinning, receding hair or baldness. A prunelike upper lip. Slowly enlarging nose and ear tissue. Massive shifting of all your favorite features. Maybe more.

Go and see for yourself. Put this book down. And for the next five minutes (time yourself), sit in front of a small mirror and check yourself out. Face to face.

Do you like what you see?

Does what you see look anything like the inner pictures you have of yourself?

What is different about you that you would not have noticed five or ten years ago?

What is still the same?

How do you feel about that?

Finish this process by being willing to acknowledge that the face you have right now is the face you have right now. But first notice whether you actually did the process or if you just read it, skipped over it or decided maybe to do it later. If you chose not to do it now, ask yourself why you made that choice. No mirror is no excuse; not when convenient bathrooms are always so close by. Find out what you may be hiding from yourself. And see what that is all about.

This book will include a number of opportunities to confront yourself personally and discover what is really going on for you about aging. From this kind of work and the honest and open self-disclosure that it demands, new Alternatives To Aging will appear as new evolutionary pathways open up. However if you decline these opportunities, nothing will change. Understand that your aging programming is at stake, not mine. And I can not possibly do all of the work for you myself.

As an old Rumanian proverb says: If you blindly keep on doing all the same things you did yesterday, how can you possibly expect tomorrow to be any different than today?

The point is to face yourself. Do this process. And do each of the other exercises that you will find in this book. Each one is a perfect place to start the rest of your life.

So get back to work!

After you complete the first process, remain at your mirror and continue to look at your face. This time, pretend that you are not looking at your own face but at a videotaped close-up of someone else's face. As you engage yourself, repeat the following sentence beginning out loud at least ten times. Each time you start the sentence, finish it off a different way.

Say: **If this face could speak, it would tell you...** (And invent ten or more endings as you go along. Don't worry if they do not make any sense.)

It actually does not matter what you say or how nonsensical it may sound. Just say whatever comes to mind first. Since there are no right or wrong ways to do this, you can't lose. On the other hand, you can make available to yourself more information than you may have ever been willing to make available to yourself before.

I repeat, it is a place to start.

Next, take out a piece of paper. Write a heading at the top that says: **Five Things I Like About My Face.** And list five things you like. When you are finished, make another list under another heading that says: **Five Things I Don't Like About My Face.**

Tell the truth. You may be surprised at what shows up. Notice which list may have been harder to write. Take a close look at what you said on each list. And notice who is saying those things.

Chances are, you have been hard on yourself again by being overly judgmental and critical. When you read about belief systems in Chapter 6, you will see what kind of effects your willingness to pick on yourself can cause. You will also see how to reverse those effects.

For now, if you don't like your face or if you wish that certain parts of your face were something other than what they are, ask yourself where you learned not to like those parts in the first place.

Somewhere, some other time, you got the idea from some external source that some things were beautiful and other things were ugly. Somehow, you accepted all that as the truth and it became an absolute scale upon which you could never measure up. Whose scale was it anyway? Was it a Miss America Pageant scale? Or a sitcom or Hollywood movie scale? Or was it something someone once said?

Whatever the source, you never questioned it. So it is time to question it now. Time to see for yourself how you really are. Time to find out what you want to do about it.

Consider this. When you were growing up, if someone had come along and told you that you were a millionaire, would you have believed them? You probably would have looked around and noticed that you did not have what millionaires have, could not buy what millionaires buy and never did the kind of things that millionaires do. You would then have had serious doubts that you were really a millionaire, no matter how sincere, well meaning or persistent your informer happened to be.

Maybe that never happened to you. But when you were growing up, someone did come along and tell you how and in precisely which ways you were not beautiful. They also told you which elements in life were not beautiful, like why an aging face was an undesirable face.

The problem is, you did not look around to see whether or not that was so. You did not doubt or question it. Instead, you became hurt or angry about it. Or you buried it all deep inside where it could fester and stew. Because you were holding on to it so tightly, it became part of you. And as you watched for confirming signs to appear, they did. Even today, you are still watching and the signs you are watching for keep on showing up.

It is too bad that you didn't hold on to the millionaire story instead of the what-is-beautiful story. If you had, at least you wouldn't have any money problems to worry about now.

By not choosing to cast your vote independently about what it is that makes beauty beautiful, you are probably facing at least one or more of the aging characteristics noted on pages 32 and 33. And you probably do not like it one bit.

A youth oriented society, such as the one we live in, categorizes wrinkles, spots and sagging features as not beautiful.   But that is only a cultural attitude or a collective opinion. If you do not agree that it is true, it will not be true for you. It never is.

It certainly is not true in societies where many people pass their 100th birthdays in what is considered to be a luminous state of beauty and grace. Neither is it true in nature, where many older animals, birds, reptiles, fish, trees and other life forms attain a serene richness and a quality of majesty. When I wrote this chapter, my son's schnauzer Bach was almost 18 years old. That is a ripe old age for a dog, but no one ever told him that so he was still very much alive. In his last days, he seemed to be most aware of changes in the weather, aches and pains in his hip, and whether or not he was fed on time, just like always. As I recall, he never spent much time thinking about how he looked.

All the varied signs that seem to show up as plain as your face are byproducts of aging. However, they are not natural byproducts. They are not even necessary byproducts, no matter how inevitable they may appear to be.

Scientists will tell you that wrinkles, age spots and loss of tissue elasticity are caused by chemically-reactive free radical molecules that damage proteins, fats and nucleic acids (RNA and DNA) in the body. Scientific data also indicates these common aging symptoms are caused by the same kind of molecular cross-linking activity that produces Jello and cured rubber products, and that the prime contributing factors are acetaldehydes in cigarette smoke, air pollutants and overexposure to ultraviolet light. In addition, the formation of brown spots is attributed to lipofuscin, an aging pigment produced by accumulating cellular waste matter.

The bad news is that these things are all true. The good news is that none of them have to be true for you. The best news of all is that even if wrinkling, age spotting and tissue damage have begun to show up, you can now begin to reverse them.

How do you go about that?

Begin by noticing your own face and all the faces of older people around you in a new way. Stop making the same old evaluations and judgments. Instead, develop your innate ability to observe what you see completely and impartially.

Notice especially how interesting and unique everyone looks when you really see them as they really are. Some older faces are wrinkled; some are not. Some have spots and blemishes; some don't. Some seem like carefully sculptured works of art; some seem like tragically neglected relics. Each one is different. Just like faces at any age. And each has something special to contribute.

Impartial observation will not be easy at first. In fact, it may never become really easy, even with practice. You will see a person's face and automatically you will begin to think: Ugly. Beautiful. Foxy. Pimply. Beefy. Incredible. Sleepy. Grumpy. Dopey. Worn. Wonderful. Witchy. Wow! Or whatever.

Whenever you notice you have started to do that, stop. Instead, describe exactly what you see as if you were writing a news story and not an editorial feature. News stories simply tell what you see; they state facts, not conclusions. Editorial features share your thoughts, feelings, attitudes, opinions and theories about what you see. There is a considerable difference in style between the two.

Your description can be as simple as this. Eyes, deep blue. Hair, blonde with light brown accents. Nose, long and thin. Ears, small and pointy with lobes connected at jawbone. Mouth, full and tense. Distinguishing characteristics: mole on left cheek, bushy eyebrows, pointy teeth, two small puncture scars on throat.

Be sure to stick to the facts and nothing but the facts. Facts are powerful, points of view are not. If you notice that your editorial opinions are chattering away inside of your head, quiet them by opening your eyes a little wider and focusing all of your attention directly on what you are observing. You will notice an immediate shift in your capacity for awareness.

Become ruthless with yourself whenever you do his exercise. The more you can avoid judgmental adjectives and phrases that package a person into a single, dimensionless conceptual box, the more you will free yourself from the false standards about beauty that you so blindly accepted from someone else and never questioned for yourself.

Disengaging yourself from those standards is the first and best alternative to an aging face. Because it does not directly involve doing anything specific to or for your face, it may not seem like much of an alternative to you. If that is so, notice whether or not you have the unfortunate habit of assessing or evaluating new ideas before you actually try them. And notice how a habit like that could close off new experiences and make you old before your time. So, I invite you to try this process before you form an opinion about it either way. And see the results for yourself.

In addition, there are many different types of techniques that you can use directly on your face to prevent or to diminish signs of aging. But all of them, from the simplest to the most drastic, require the following essential added ingredient to produce any noticeable long-range effects whatsoever: You must begin any facial exercise or process by completely accepting your face exactly the way it is.

Contradictory as that may sound, it is the truth. The face you have is the face you have. It is also the only one you've got. So you had better accept it. And after you accept it, you might as well like it. For precisely the same reasons.

If you do not like your face now, before you begin to work with it, I can guarantee that you will not like it better later. Even when it is clear, vital and glowing with life and beauty, you will still not like it because you will keep looking for and finding new flaws to complain about.

Are you willing to like your face just the way it is before you read any further? If you are not, take out your list of the five things you like most about your face and read it to yourself 300 or 400 times. If you are, any one or combination of the following things to do will produce the results you want.

Facial Relaxation.

As you become aware of older faces around you, it becomes more and more clear that stress and tension are the major sources of devastation and not the passing years. You see foreheads wrinkled tightly with confusion or bewilderment, mouths and jaws clenched with suppressed anger, lower eyelids sagging under the weight of unwept tears. After carrying all of that and more around for 30, 40 or 50 years, it is no wonder that we look exactly the way we look.

Here are seven relaxing alternatives.

1. Notice the spot on your forehead just above the bridge of your nose where your eyebrows come together. Notice how tight and tense it is.

Take a deep breath. And as you slowly exhale, focus on that spot from the inside out and tell it to relax. Sense how quickly it responds.

If you need to or want to, inhale again and as you exhale, focus your attention on the same spot, hold the second, third and fourth fingertips of your left hand together and use them to rub little counterclockwise circles on it.

2. Place the thumb and second finger of your left hand under your nostrils. Breathe in and pinch your upper lip together. Hold it tightly as you slowly exhale. Unless you are actively serving in the British Army, you no longer need to keep a stiff upper lip. Notice how it feels to let it go.

3. Hook each of your index fingers in corners of your mouth and pull your mouth open as far as you can. Hold your lips stretched apart for three long, slow breaths. As you release your fingers, tune into whatever emotions may rise to the surface of your awareness.

4. Focus all of your attention on the tip of your nose. Inhale slowly and tighten up your whole face into a little wrinkled prune-like ball with the tip of your nose at its center. Hold your breath in and your face tight and tensed for as long as you can. Then exhale slowly, allow your face to relax, let your jaw hang loosely open, and notice how refreshed you feel.

5. With your fingertips, gently rub little counter-clockwise circles over each of the points shown in the illustration. These are accupressure points and if you activate each of them once a day, you will increase your circulation and remove cellular waste matter from the tissues of your face.

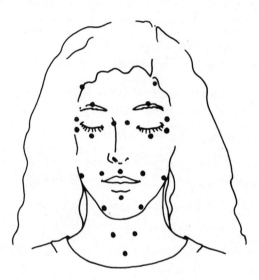

6. Allow your eyes to unfocus by shifting your gaze upward at a 45 degree angle and inviting your face to relax. Then using only your eyes, without moving or tensing your face, look up as far as you can and look down as far as you can. Up, down. Up, down. Rest a moment. Again without moving the muscles of your face, look to the left as far as you can and look to the right as far as you can. Left, right. Left, right. Rest. Finally, without wrinkling your forehead or tightening your upper lip, allow your eyes to make three complete clockwise circles. Look over to the left, up, to the right, and down. Again. And again. Rest. Then make three complete counter-clockwise circles the same way but in reverse. Close your eyes and cover them gently with the palms of your hands. When they are completely covered,

open your eyes and stare into the blackness of your palms for at least a minute. Sense how revitalized your vision has become.

7. Dig your fingertips into your scalp and move them together and apart until your scalp moves freely. Shift your fingers to other positions and repeat the process until your scalp can be moved at least half an inch in any direction from your forehead to the back of your neck and from ear to ear. Then rub all the fingernails of both your hands briskly back and forth at least 100 times. Feel your hair follicles re-energizing and returning to work.

Facial Massage

Touch works wonders. In your own hands is the power to balance the energy within you, stimulate your circulation, increase your flow of internal oxygen, firm your muscle tone, and reduce accumulated cellular waste material in your face.

Here is a eight-step Alternative To Aging characteristics resulting from oversight and neglect. Be sure to breathe slowly and deeply as you give yourself this short but complete facial treatment every day.

1. Start by placing the fingertips of both hands on top of your head. Knead and work over every inch of your scalp more vigorously and forcefully than you did in the scalp relaxation exercise to extend the movement of your scalp in every direction and encourage healthy hair growth.

2. Let the fingertips of both hands meet on your forehead, right at your hairline. Massage little counterclockwise circles all the way down to your ears, following the line of your scalp. Repeat this two or three times.

3. Let the fingertips of both hands meet on your forehead where your eyebrows come together. Follow the contour of the boney ridge under your eyebrows and massage little circles all the way across to the tops of your ears. Repeat this two or three times.

4. Place your fingertips under your eyes on either side of your nose. Massage gentle little circles all along

the length of your upper cheekbones up to your ears. Repeat two or three times.

5. Place the fingertips of each hand next to your nostrils and massage tiny counterclockwise circles along the hollow underneath your cheekbones as far as your earlobes. Repeat two or three times.

6. Let the tips of your third fingers meet on your upper lip where your nostrils come together and place the fourth fingertips of each hand together just under the center of your lower lip. Massage little counterclockwise circles all along the length of your mouth and follow the line of your jawbone as far as your earlobes. Repeat two or three times.

7. Place all of your fingertips together directly underneath your chin and massage slightly larger counterclockwise circles all along the loose skin underneath your jawbone as far as your earlobes.

8. Hold your chin firmly between the thumbs and forefingers of each hand and vibrate it until your skin moves freely and your lower jaw bounces gently up and down.

If you notice any tension anywhere else in your face, send your fingertips to that spot. Then let them loosen it and send it on its way.

Perhaps you have been wondering why the circular motions I suggest are always counterclockwise. When your goal is to reverse or set back the clock, is there any other way to go?

Nutrients For Your Face.

I will be discussing anti-aging vitamins and nutrients and offering my own guidelines and precautions in Chapter 7. For now, what I would like you to keep in mind about them is this: If you like and fully accept your fabulous face just the way it is and if you also believe that nutrients will contribute to your appearance, then go ahead and use them.

Current laboratory evidence is very much on your side if you want to try large daily supplements of Vitamins C, A, E, B1, B5, B6 and PABA; minerals like calcium, zinc and selenium; amino acids like L-Cysteine and L-Tyrosine; and synthetics like BHT or BHA and superoxide dismutase. On a strictly chemical level, all of these nutrients can slow down cross linking, support the break-up of free radical formations, and even retard the effects of smoking and air pollution.

Natural food sources like raw pineapple, raw papaya, grapes and bananas offer many of the same benefits and give you a way to condition your face while you are feeding it.

I will present several new insights about why these substances work later in this book. The point is that they really do work unless you have medical conditions or belief systems that get in the way of their effectiveness. At any rate, when used responsibly, they, will not hurt you.

The best conditioner for your face is still relatively plentiful and inexpensive. It is called water.

If you wash your face gently and frequently with plain warm water and rinse with cold, you will be able to handle dryness effortlessly. Just splashing your face in between washes every time you rinse off your hands will further provide all the moisture that beauty experts suggest you need. In addition, the liquid contents of a vitamin E capsule can be massaged into blemishes, scar tissue and wrinkles to help them disappear; aloe vera works well on such areas too. Either way, you will not need to carry around bagfuls of creams, moisturizers and lotions.

Heavy make-up users may not mind reapplying whatever they need after each wash or splash, especially when they see how refreshed and beautiful they are beginning to look underneath it all.

Surgery For Your Face.

A considerable amount of medical aid is available for aging faces from under-eye collagen treatments or silicone shots to complete face lifts and massive reconstruction.

If you are interested in this kind of Alternative To Aging and you can afford the services of the very best specialist you can find, then go ahead and have it done. But first, be absolutely positive that you have read page 38. And be even more positive that you can accept and like your face just the way it is.

That may sound like a contradiction. It isn't.

Cosmetic surgery is very much like getting your car repainted. When you love your car, plan to keep it a long time, and want it to look its best, repainting works. When, on the other hand, you are dissatisfied and upset about having such an old clunker to begin with, but you cannot afford to turn it in for a new model, repainting it is a waste of money. It is expensive, inconvenient and time consuming. And it does not get you what you really want. (Notice the importance of your own opinion in the matter. Your car doesn't care about it one way or the other. Neither does your face.)

It is a 100% certainty that if you don't like your face now, you will not like it later either. At best, you won't like it for very long. Furthermore, it is a 115% certainty that if you think your problems will disappear or your love life will improve or your self image will get better or people who don't care much for you now will be crazy about the new you, you will be tragically disappointed. Or worse.

Not liking what you see in the mirror has nothing at all to do with what you see in the mirror. The sooner that is clear to you, the easier everything else in life becomes.

It is only after you are satisfied with who you are just the way you are that a little nose job or necklift could be a lot of fun. Especially when you get to the other side of the cost, pain, puffy black-and-blueness, and time lost hiding out until you no longer look like a refugee from a motorcycle gang war. Then, reconstructive surgery can be like a new sweater or new suit of clothes that enhances the way you want to look.

I am personally acquainted with a surprising number of people who expected a lot more than that from their cosmetic surgery experiences. Not one of them is any closer to living happily ever afterwards than he or she was before. I don't want you to make that kind of mistake.

Instead, I am asking that you begin to enjoy the unique contribution your face is making just the way it is. Your face expresses your aliveness.   It transmits your inner vitality whenever you allow that to happen.   It is the primary visual statement of who you are and how you became that way.

Your face is never less than magnificent. And your own observations will prove it.

Here is the whole point. Your present attitudes about your face, the ones you may have encountered for the first time at the beginning of this chapter can do an abrupt about-face whenever you say so. You put those attitudes there to begin with and no one but you is holding them in place. Just as masterfully, you can send them all away.

Once you become aware that the solution to facial aging is as simple as accepting your face, liking your face and caring for your face any way you choose to care for it responsibly, your best alternative is to smile. And notice that the whole world smiles with you.

CHAPTER 4

EVERY BODY
HAS A CHOICE

The little swings swung wildly back and forth. Shrieks
and yells showed how closely the arc of each push approached
the scary point of no return, just this side of completely
looping the loop.

The chains holding the swings to the iron support bar
overhead were forged from solid steel links. Each seat was a
smooth rectangular piece of wood about one foot long, half a
foot wide, and perhaps two inches or so thick.

Just to the left of the swings, a group of little see-saws
teetered vigorously up and down. The children's legs and
feet usually took up the impact of each jolt, but every once in
a while some daring young wiseguy would put his or her feet
up on the board. Then the plank would crash into the
ground and the little bodies at each end would bounce up in
the air on impact, laughing.

The see-saws were built to last. Solid wooden handles
were bolted on to sturdy, dependable, long, hardwood
planks, approximately six inches from each end, creating a
perfect position for small bodies with short arms to gain a
reliable handhold.

Across the way, a group of boys played King Of The
Mountain on the monkey bars of a little jungle gym. The
durable structure was made of top quality steel pipe, about
one inch in diameter, arranged in squares just large enough
for the tiny bodies to snake through. It would last for years.
The children at the bottom gestured threateningly and

shouted at the boy on the top as he cruelly stepped on the fingers of those seeking handholds from which to displace him.

Just behind the commotion of would-be kings, there stood a glass and plastic building that housed row after row of video games with small stools in front them.   There were all kinds of games, each with its own compelling and hypnotic visual graphic display.   Space battles raged next t o demolition derbies.   Hamburger heroes battled centipede monsters and fanged wizards, while animated heroines eluded crocodile teeth and bat wings by leaping electronic pitfalls and swinging from LED jungle vines.

The games were similar in that each was controlled by cute little joysticks with three-inch hand and fingerholds. Lights flashed, displays turned, sirens wailed, space vehicles zapped, jets crashed, animals roared and dragons died as row after row of little children gripped those little joysticks for all they were worth.

That day and every day, there was nothing but fun, more fun, and even more fun than that to be had in the playground world.   As long as you were the right physical size to play there.

When you got to be too big to swing on the swings, teeter on the see-saws, monkey around on the bars or handle the electronic game controls, then you couldn't play there a n y more.   Quite literally, after a certain point of growth, you no longer fit in.   And a thing like that could be the death of y o u .

Did you ever notice how many structures, devices and things are constructed to accommodate healthy young adult bodies? And how their function is closely oriented to some preconceived ideal of an average healthy young adult form?

Think about that. It is just a small indication of how strongly enmeshed we are in the products of a society founded upon a young-old dichotomy. Observe how the balance point of that dichotomy is weighted in favor of youth and how being young is an ideal to be held tightly and maintained at any cost. Then see what the effect of all that has been on you.

Stop reading for a moment and begin to form a picture in your mind of whatever idealized image represents the physically perfect man or woman to you. Look closely at the physical characteristics of your vision and notice what they are.

Next, allow that image to fade. In its place, form another picture of an old man or an old woman. If this picture is not the same as your first, notice as many differences in actual physical characteristics as you can. See whether you can trace the progression of features from the first body that you visualized to the second more aged one.

What you may be looking at may well be a blueprint of your own aging process. As you will discover in Chapter 6, the vision of aging that you hold now is the model for the physical being you will become. However it is a model you can easily modify.

To begin, invest a little time in examining your body as it really is.

Find a room with a large mirror where you can lock the door and not be disturbed for at least 20 minutes. Take off all your clothes and really look yourself over. Observe the front of your body. Just let your eyes wander slowly over your reflection and take it all in without judging or evaluating anything. Raise your arms and lower them. Jump up and down a few times. Dance around a little. Most important of all, really look at yourself.

Then stand sideways to the mirror and repeat the process, at first standing still and then moving, jumping, dancing around. Notice yourself just like an impartial observer would. Observe yourself as you may have never observed yourself before.

Next, using a hand mirror, stand with your back to the large mirror and look at your reflection as you repeat the process once again.

In each segment of this exercise, pay particular attention to whatever parts of your body you do not want to look at. Also notice what you were looking at whenever your gaze quickly shifts away. If you find that you are experiencing a lot of difficulty or resistance or that you just don't want to do this at all, be aware of that and ask yourself what it might mean.   Then do the exercise anyway, only don't take it quite so seriously. Pretend, for instance, you have just arrived from outer space and have this very moment discovered a new life form. You. Make believe your job is simply to observe and record everything you can about this interesting but somewhat frightening life form for the first time in your galaxy's history.

When you really get into it, begin to move freely around the room. Follow each spontaneous movement in the large mirror. If any part of your body catches your eye or interests you, examine it more closely.

After you have completed each step to your own satisfaction without criticizing yourself, sit in front of your mirror for a few moments and allow all of your thoughts and emotions and insights to come to a state of rest. Then, and only then, take out one or two pieces of blank paper.

Set up a heading that says'**What I like about my body is...**'and list as many things as you can, describing each one briefly. Then, turn the paper over, write a new heading that says '**What I don't like about my body is...**' and start a new list. Be as complete as you can. And be sure to notice what you are leaving out or attempting to hide from yourself.

When you are all done, review each list and next to each item , write the following two words: 'Says who?' Or, if you prefer: 'Sez who?'

Begin to become aware of exactly who it is that says whatever is so about your body and who sets the standards you use to constantly evaluate it. It is essential for you to have that insight before you can begin to transform your blueprint for your own aging body.

Remember that perfect body I asked you to visualize a while ago? The biggest problem with trying to do that is, there is no such thing. Back in 1910, the so-called perfect body would have weighed 30 to 100 pounds more than the so-called perfect body does today. External consensus about perfection is only relative at best.

The next biggest problem with the whole idea of imagining a perfect body is that you don't have to imagine one. You have already got one. Only you probably have barriers that keep you from seeing it that way. Forgetting health issues and belief systems for the moment, and without the need to change a single thing, your body is absolutely perfect.

You can prove that very easily. Just notice that your body is alive and that it has carried you along for years at precisely the level that you have chosen to participate in life. That's perfect! For what it is worth, your body supports your purposes in life completely. Just the way it is.

In addition to being perfect, your body is perfectly miraculous. Given all the abuse and neglect you subject it to, it can still create and renew itself over and over, cell by cell, organ by organ, part by part, every six months. There is evidence that your brain and nerve cells may be exceptions and either do not replace themselves at all or do so at a much slower rate. There is also other evidence that this evidence is incorrect.

Either way, you are never the person you used to be. And you have the wide-open alternative to become any person you choose to be. In reality, the only constant point of reference you ever have is that you are always the person you are, at any given moment. That means, you never have to be stuck with or at the effect of your body. Unless you say so.

Consciously and openly examine your choices for the next few days and weeks and you will see what I mean.

As you work or shop or walk down the street, notice all the other people's bodies. Become aware of them as individual creations without comparing one to another. Resist any compulsion to evaluate or grade them according to whatever arbitrary rating system you may have. Simply become aware of them as the kinds of bodies other people have chosen to have and keep. In no time at all, you will begin to realize how many options you have. You. At your age right now. Whatever that age might be.

It's true. Every body becomes the way its owner chooses for it to be. The capability and capacity to choose is inherent in the programming and organic structure of each cell. All it takes for you to have the body you choose to have is a simple combination of diet, nutrition and exercise. Or the lack of them. On an even simpler level, all it takes is a clearing out of limiting beliefs and positions about yourself, followed by a commitment to create whatever kind of body you would like. On the simplest level of all, if you choose not to do anything about your body whatsoever, you still are creating the kind of body you will have, by default. And a body by default will be just as perfect for you as any other kind.

To find out just how perfect bodies really are, the first opportunity you get, go someplace where people are dancing and watch the dancers.

If you go to a dance attended mostly by young people, here is what you will see: Fat bodies. Tall bodies. Short bodies. Pudgy bodies. Skinny bodies. Bodies you think are beautiful. Bodies you think are terrible. And every conceivable type of body in between. Some bodies will be smokin' along, fast and loose. Some will be moving smoothly and gracefully. Still others will seem rigid, stiff and awkward.

If you go to a dance attended mostly by older people, here is what you'll see: Fat bodies. Tall bodies. Short bodies. Pudgy bodies. Skinny bodies. Bodies you think are beautiful. Bodies you think are terrible. And every conceivable type of body in between. Some bodies will be smokin' along, fast and loose. Some will be moving smoothly and gracefully. Still others will seem rigid, stiff and awkward.

Funny how that works out, isn't it. Actually, each one of those bodies is serving the person who carries it around perfectly.

It may surprise you to observe that aesthetically as well as functionally, there is no appreciable difference between the well-cared-for body of a 75 year old person and the well-cared-for body of a 25 year old person. Similarly, there are no appreciable differences between badly-cared-for bodies of 25 and 75 year old people.

Forget what your mind is telling you right now; go and see for yourself.

I have taught yoga and exercise classes to people in their 70s and 80s who were in much better shape and much more flexible than people in their 20s and 30s. Naturally, the opposite is also true. Bodies, like opportunities, depend on what you choose to make of them.

At any age and any stage of your life, you can choose and create the body you want to have. But first, you need to choose the body you already have. To do that, simply acknowledge yourself for being just the way you are. Avoid any tendencies to like or dislike the way you are. Just acknowledge, in fact, you are the way you are.

That is the only place to start because it explicitly recognizes the key to any successful bodywork exploration: You cannot change the way you are. That is the way you are. Done and complete. And you cannot change what already exists.

However, you can create the way that you intend to be, from now on. And you can do that powerfully and totally. It will probably require a little ongoing support or a little work. Although in many cases, it may not. Occasionally just knowing that you can do it is all that is required. To be on the safe side, I personally recommend a limited exercise program for everyone of any age, if only to give your body tangible evidence that you are serious about transforming it. Bodies always respond to that kind of evidence.

Limited to moderate exercise and healthy muscle tone tend to coincide. Healthy muscle tone is what you feel when you touch someone and their arm or leg or body feels good to you. Not-so-healthy muscle tone feels clammy, stringy or flabby, and your finger seems to sink into the tissue. One is not better or worse than the other. From a strictly subjective point of view, one simply seems more pleasant and more esthetic to the touch than the other.

If you were to lie in bed without moving for two days, you would experience a 50% loss of muscle tone.

That's right. Two days of neglect is all it takes. And in two weeks, the loss would pass the 80% mark. On the other hand, a limited to moderate exercise program can restore your muscle tone almost that quickly. If only in terms of your own desirability, this makes it well worth considering.

My approach to exercise as an Alternative To Aging has shifted radically since I began my own program years ago in my late 30s, after at least 20 years of neglect. Back then, I used to work out strenuously for an hour or more. Now, I can produce even better results in 15 to 25 minute sessions every other day, although I usually do more because I like it and I love the way I feel afterwards.

Over the years, I have developed a clear sense that physical wellbeing supports all other transformation associated with aging. By physical wellbeing, what I mean is the process of accepting and creating satisfaction from the act of physically being who you are, just the way you are.

It stands to reason that it works that way. In life as we all live it, we express our energy through the medium of a physical body. We bring forth who we are in physical form, set against the stage of physical reality. In other words, life shows up as a physical manifestation and our bodies are the only tool we have to work with for processing energy and expressing our selves in it.

Arising from that premise, my intention in this chapter is to assist you in taking care of the physical parts of your life. As effortlessly and painlessly as possible.

Traditional physical fitness exercises are all right, especially if you are in reasonably good shape to begin with. I enjoy running and sometimes include it in my program. And I enjoy rebounding on those little round trampoline-like things. Neither is the right answer for everyone, some days not even for me. I also enjoy swimming, and for almost ten years I did year-round laps in the chilly Atlantic Ocean off the Massachusetts coast where I live. This is not for everyone either. It's not even for exercise as much as it is for immersing myself in natural energy and checking out my now fairly well-developed temperature control capabilities. In addition, the effects are spiritual as much as they are physical.

In terms of pure Alternative To Aging benefits, however, traditional exercise programs may leave a lot to be desired. My most serious complaint is that each exercise form is limited to a specific result and not designed for over-all well-rounded body maintenance over a significantly extended lifetime. For instance, running builds endurance but not strength. Weights and weight machines contribute to strength but ignore cardiovascular conditioning. Racquet sports and golf don't work with all of the body as a unit. Long-lifers require the best of everything.

If you are happy with what you are doing now, don't stop it. Supplement it with your choice of the following Alternatives To Aging workouts. They offer complete body maintenance in easy-to-take 10 to 20 minute cycles which can be rotated every day or every other day to prevent boredom from settling in. They represent a creative exercise menu drawn from the varied techniques that I teach and use myself.

In each exercise process, I will share both the 'how-to-do-its' and the benefits or results you can expect. I will also include a maximum count to work up to and a minimum place to start that will probably be safe even if you are badly out of shape. I have instructed people ranging in age from children and teenagers to great-grandparents. Not one of them so far has been unable to do the exercises at the minimum suggested levels. Form occasionally leaves a lot to the imagination, but enthusiasm and excitement have more than made up for it. And everyone who practiced noticed almost immediate results in terms of wellbeing and satisfaction.

Since I am not working with you personally, I will leave it to you to become your own instructor and set your own limits. I am confident that I have chosen the right person for the job. As a standard precaution, if you have any question at all about your ability to do any of the physical processes, play it safe and consult with a medical authority that you trust before you begin.

There are only three recommended Don'ts: Don't attempt to do more than one exercise process a day at first. Don't do the same exercise more than two days in a row without switching to another. And, don't judge or evaluate the exercises or your performance of them. Just breathing and stretching your way through the directions can be an even more powerful anti-aging agent than an overly critical attempt at perfect performance.

Remember that no one technique alone can activate every possible muscle group in your body. All of them, though, will activate all of you on an ongoing basis. Count on them to revitalize and refresh you, trigger hormonal and chemical releases that can reverse destructive aging processes, and enable you to feel and perform at your physical peak regardless of your chronological years.

Stretching.

Start these simple stretches as complete exercises. When you can do them easily, incorporate them into each of your subsequent exercise cycles as warm-ups. One to ten minutes of stretching a day keeps you limber and flexible, prevents chronic stiffness, reduces tension, and prepares your body for more strenuous work.

1. Up And Down.

Stand with your feet shoulder-width apart and each foot pointing straight ahead. Raise your hands and reach as high as you can. Then let your hands drift down and hang loosely at your side once again.

Imagine that your hands have lead weights attached and let them pull you down until your upper body, head and arms are hanging loosely and your fingertips are approaching your knees or your ankles or the floor. Dangle for a moment.

Then repeat the whole process five or ten times.

2. Arm Swinging.

This is a popular Taoist yoga exercise developed in China more than 2600 years ago to reverse the effects of aging and restore youthful vigor.

Stand with your feet shoulder-width apart, your knees slightly flexed, and each foot absolutely parallel to the other without the slightest sign of turned out toes. Keep your back straight and your entire body as loose and relaxed as possible. Grip the ground with your toes and heels.

Let your arms swing freely forward and backwards as easily and naturally as you can. Do not let your body sway or change your posture in any way. Start with 50 swings to get the feel of it. Then gradually increase the amount each time you repeat the exercise until you can swing your arms comfortably for five minutes.

When you are ready to stop, let your swinging motion become smaller and smaller until your arms come to rest naturally at your side. Relax your feet and stand for a moment or two, noticing the tingling warmth of energy flowing through your body.

Then bring your arms up until they are rounded and positioned in front of your chest as if you were holding a gigantic beachball. Allow your palms to face each other without touching. Hold this position for two to five minutes. If you want, you may sit down while you are doing this. All the while, breathe slowly and deeply into your diaphragm (just below your rib cage and lungs) and allow the energy you have created to flow into whichever parts of your body have been the most negatively effected by aging.

3. Side To Side Swinging.

Stand in the same start-up position as before, with your arms hanging loosely at your side and your body relaxed and loose.

Begin to swing your arms from side to side. Twist your body gently as you swing your arms so that you can look over your left shoulder when your arms are swinging to the left and over your right shoulder when your arms are swinging to the right.

Swing your arms lightly and effortlessly at your own rhythm for two to ten minutes. Notice how your neck and shoulders and body are stretching out and how the tenseness and soreness in your back fades away. Then notice how deep and rhythmic your breathing has become, and how good you feel.

4. Pelvic Rotation.

Stand in the same basic position as before. Be sure that your knees are slightly bent and flexed. Place your hands on your hips with your thumbs pointing towards your spine. Allow your pelvis to sway gently back and forth with a slow sensual motion as you breathe in and out.

When your back and forth pelvic motion is smooth and fluid, add the full rotation movement to it. Tip your pelvis towards the back and swing it slowly around to the right as you inhale, then tip it forward and swing it around to the left as you exhale. Then start again. Make five or ten slow easy circles in a counterclockwise direction like that. And then reverse the direction of your circle and make five or ten more circles in a clockwise direction. Remember always to inhale when your pelvis is rocking towards the back and to exhale when it is tipped forward.

Pelvic rotation gently loosens and stretches the lower back and sacrum areas, strengthening them and preventing lower back pain or discomfort. It also reawakens and revitalizes sexual energy.

When you have completed a full cycle, be sure to notice how powerful you feel.

Breathing.

There is no life without breath. And there can be no longevity without the kind of deep complete breathing that lowers the pulse, soothes away tension and stress, and restores body tissue in need of healing. Eastern civilizations have perfected the art of breathing over centuries and centuries of study and practice. An opportunity for you to experience just a little of what they have learned follows.

1. Basic Relaxation Breathing.

Use this technique whenever you notice that you are tensed up or in a stressful situation and whenever you exercise or do strenuous physical work of any kind.

Practice it by placing your hands together just under your ribs with only your fingertips touching. Bend over a little from the waist. Then inhale through your nose and send all of the air right to your fingertips. Feel them separate as your diaphragm expands, as your ribs separate, and as your chest expands. Try to separate and differentiate each part of the process of inhaling. First you send your breath to your fingertips, then they separate as your diaphragm expands, then your ribs separate, and last of all your chest expands.

After you have inhaled, hold your breath for a few moments and then begin to release it slowly through your nostrils. As you do, notice how your chest contracts, your ribs come together, your diaphragm flattens, and your fingertips under your ribs overlap once again. Again, become aware of each of these elements as separate and distinct parts of each exhalation that flow together as one continuous whole. Notice also this kind of breathing is the opposite of the rapid, shallow upper-chest breathing that most people do, especially the shorter-lived ones.

Repeat this sequence and practice it regularly as part of your exercise routine or during the day whenever you sense that your breath has become tight and tense. When it begins to feel comfortable and natural to you, try it when you are standing up straight, sitting, or lying down, with or without your fingertips in place.

If you have ever watched your cat or dog breathing, you will understand why this is the appropriate and normal everyday breath for all living things except, perhaps, high school physical training instructors and drill sergeants. Eventually you will automatically sense when you are not breathing this way and you will consciously shift over to it. The benefits of basic relaxation breathing will become obvious and immediately apparent to you.

2. Regenerating And Healing Breath.

Since life flows in and out of our bodies with each breath we take, advanced breathing techniques can supercharge our lifeforce and provide specific benefits wherever we direct our breath to flow.

To experience the mechanical aspects of one of these techniques directly, stand or sit comfortably with your eyes closed and the palms of your hands facing each other about two inches apart. Breathe your basic relaxation breath, only imagine that you are inhaling through your palms instead of through your nose and that your breath is rushing up through your hands, arms and shoulders into your body. As you exhale, imagine that your breath is leaving your body through your palms instead of through your nose and that it is carrying all the toxins you have accumulated in your body along with it.

If you repeat this process several times, slowing each breath down until it takes at least 20 or 30 seconds to inhale and exhale completely, you will feel the supercharged healing energy you have created as it flows between your hands. You can enhance this feeling and the effectiveness of your hands as energy channels by rubbing your palms lightly together when you are inhaling every once in a while.

When you have your own solid experience of how this works, you can direct healing energy to any part of your body by breathing it there or by allowing it to flow through your palms as you breathe in and out of your hands.

Variations

To strengthen your kidneys, place your palms against your lower back, just over your kidneys. Breathe your basic relaxation breath directly into your kidneys so that you can feel your hands move away slightly with each inhalation and return with each exhalation. Once you have had the experience of how this actually feels internally as well as externally, you no longer need to keep your hands in place. You can kidney breathe directly and store energy there until you require it.

To strengthen any other part of your body, heal a wound, soothe an ache or pain, or improve your eyesight or hearing, simply adapt this technique to energize whatever part of you is involved. Just breathe directly into that particular part for a few minutes every day and allow each of your exhalations to carry all the toxins and tensions away. Place both your palms over the sensitive area until you have linked your breath to it and connected with the full experience of how that feels.

To energize or reawaken your desire and capacity for sex, direct your breath to the small sensitive hollow spot located midway between your genitals and your anus. First locate this point (or use your perineum if you can't find it right away) and place your fingertips on it. Then breathe your basic relaxation breath, imagining that you are inhaling into and exhaling out of the spot beneath your fingertips instead of through your nostrils. As you feel your breath flowing deeply in and out of your hollow spot or your perineum, contract it gently as if you were pulling it up into your body. Hold this contraction for as long as you can or for at least two or three minutes. After you have fully experienced the body sensations involved, you will no longer need to use your hands. You will be able to breathe regenerative energy directly into your sexual center and release any deadness that may be stuck there.

To cleanse the brain, restore memory, and revitalize neural connections, imagine that your spine is a hollow tube. Inhale your basic relaxation breath directly into the opening at the lower end of the tube. As you inhale, imagine your breath is like white mist rising through your spine and floating up into your skull. Hold your breath and visualize it swirling all through and around the interior of your cranium. Direct the white mist to any places that seem inaccessible or dark and watch it flow into, around, and through them, opening them up. When you are ready to exhale, release your breath slowly through your mouth and imagine that it is now a sooty grey mist, carrying away toxins, negativity and other debris. Repeat this same cleansing breath and visualization seven times and then return to a normal breathing pattern. As your breath passes in and out of your nose once again, imagine that your head is surrounded by a clear turquoise-blue cloud. Hold onto this image for a minute or so. And notice how alive and mentally alert you feel.

Salute To The Sun.

The sun is the source of symbolic vigor and vitality. Untold generations of yogis have drawn solar energies into their bodies by combining six classic postures into a unique rhythmically flowing sundance pattern that stretches, relaxes, and strengthens the body. Practice each part separately and slowly until you can easily coordinate the suggested breath with the suggested movement. Then weave everything together and repeat the entire sequence from a minimum of six to a maximum of 24 times whenever you include this process in your daily exercise cycle.

1a

Done slowly, the salute to the sun is a relaxing physical meditation that soothes and refreshes each nerve, gland and organ in your body. Done rapidly, it is Yoga's answer to jogging for an over-all workout with cardiovascular benefits.

1a.   Begin by standing straight with your feet together, facing the east if possible. Inhale and visualize the sun just beginning to rise above the horizon of your mind.

1b.   Exhale.   Bring your palms together at your chest in a prayerlike position.

2a. Inhale.   Stretch your arms overhead and tuck your pelvis slightly forward. Look up at your hands.

2b. Exhale. Bend over slowly from your waist until your hands are touching the floor in front of or beside your feet. (If you are out of shape and cannot reach the floor, bring your hands down as far as you comfortably can, extending your reach a tiny bit each day.)

3a. Inhale. Lunge forward by bending your left knee to a right angle and stepping your right foot back. Turn your right toes under for balance and straighten your body from head to heel. Then, as you hold your breath, step your left foot back with your toes curled alongside your right foot in a push-up position.

3b. Exhale. Drop your knees to the floor and lift your buttocks up. Then bend your elbows, bringing your chest and chin to the floor. Continue exhaling. Lower your whole body to the floor. Straighten your legs, but keep your toes curled under.

4a. Inhale. Push down on your hands and slowly lift your head as you straighten your elbows. Arch upward slowly as a cobra arches before it strikes.

1b

2a

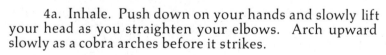

2b

4b. Exhale. Lift your buttocks all the way up and tuck your head down, forming a triangle.

5a. Inhale. Lunge forward by bending your right knee and stepping your right foot forward between your hands.

5b. Exhale. Straighten your right leg and bring your left foot next to your right. Lift your buttocks high until you are in a standing bend again.

6a. Inhale. Slowly lift your spine, unrolling it one vertebra at a time. Lift your head last. Look up, raise your arms straight overhead, and visualize an image of the rising sun once again.

6b. Exhale. Bring your arms slowly down to your sides and allow your image of the sun to become brighter and brighter.

3a1

3a2

3b

4a

4b

5a

5b

6a

6b

Cardiovascular Conditioning.

The whole idea behind cardiovascular conditioning is to improve the efficiency and stamina of your heart muscles and enhance the coordination of your heart fibers as they squeeze and pump your blood. The benefits show up in a significantly lower pulse rate, which means your heart rests longer between beats and fills more slowly and completely. This creates more of the kind of power that enables you to function with ease and facility, feel more alive and less susceptible to energy drain, and achieve a high capacity for action and activity. It also stacks the odds against heart disease in your favor.

The conditioning process involves exercising at a strenuous enough level to raise your pulse to your optimum level and then holding it at that level for a predetermined length of time. Your optimum pulse level is a function of your normal pulse and your age.

Your normal pulse, taken at rest, is a reliable indicator of your over-all physical condition. Normality, of course, is relative. A resting pulse rate anywhere between 40 and 90 beats per minute is considered normal. And the lower it is, the better it is. In fact, your chances of premature death are four times higher if your pulse rate at rest is 95 than it is when your pulse rate is lower than 65.

To check your normal rate, choose a quiet time of the day when you have been inactive for at least five minutes, and rest your fingers on your wrist or along the carotid artery on the side of your neck. Lightly feel around for your beat and when you have it, check it against the second hand or digital second counter on your watch. Count off the number of beats beginning with zero for six seconds; then add a zero to your total. That is your resting pulse rate. To find your active pulse rate, repeat the same process after or during exercise.

The active pulse rate you need to work with for cardiovascular conditioning depends on your physical condition right now. If you are in excellent shape, it will be 200 minus your age. If you are in moderate shape, it will be 175 minus your age. If you are out of shape, it will be 150 minus your age.

Whatever bodywork you do, you will want to perform at that level for at least ten minutes every other day. That means checking your pulse periodically as you exercise at two to three minute intervals and correcting as necessary. If your pulse rate is too low, you are coasting too much; step up your pace. If your rate is too high, you are pushing too hard; slow down your tempo. For the first few weeks of your cardiovascular conditioning program, be particularly responsible about taking care of yourself by zealously checking your pulse. You do not want to become one of those people who are just dying to look and feel better.

What can you do for ten minutes? Whatever you like. You can dance to lively music and swing your arms rhythmically. You can jog or walk quickly anyplace that is convenient: outdoors, on a pad in your living room, or on a bouncy rebounder. You can jump rope or do mild calisthenics at a fast pace or stretch vigorously and repeatedly.

The routine I prefer involves a combination of several of these elements.

1. For about one minute, stretch to warm up your body and loosen any tightness in your muscles. Any of the stretches already covered in this chapter are fine for these purposes.

2. For three to four minutes, alternate 21-second leanbacks with a series of 21 pushaways.

To do a leanback, sit on the floor with your knees bent and your toes hooked underneath a chair or sofa edge for support. Place your fingertips on the muscles of your abdomen and lean your chest and head backwards, as if you were going to lie back slowly, until you notice trembling and vibration. Hold that point for a 21-second count as you breathe your basic relaxation breath.

To do pushaways, stand two to three feet away from a wall. Extend your arms in front of you with your elbows straight and place your palms against the wall. Then bend your elbows to let your chest and chin approach the wall, and push away as if you were doing pushups from a standing position. If that is too easy, try pushing away from the seat of chair, the edge of a sink, or anyplace else where you can do 21 repetitions with moderate effort. If that is still too easy, try doing 21 classic pushups on the floor instead.

Do two sets of each in the three to four minute period: A 21-second leanback followed by 21 pushaways, another 21-second leanback followed by 21 more pushaways.

3.   With no break in between, except for pulse checks, for the next five or six minutes, jog in place, skip, hop, dance, jump rope, or just move around quickly enough to maintain your pulse at your optimum active rate. I usually hold and pump light weights in each hand for this part of the cycle and find that the upper part of my body receives a solid maintenance-level workout.

Keep extending yourself as your condition, strength, and vitality improve. Lean further and further back for your leanbacks or raise your arms over your head to change your center of gravity. Push away from more and more difficult starting positions. Move around faster and more strenuously.   One of the nice things about exercising like this is you are in complete control of the entire process. If you like, you can even extend the time or number of repetitions. Just remember to check and recheck your pulse frequently each time you modify your routine.   And never work out beyond your maximum rate.

Rejuvenation Yoga From Tibet.

Years ago, when I first began meditating, on one of my mental flights to strange and wonderful places I learned an ancient ten-step Tibetan yoga form that has the capacity to regenerate body, mind and spirit. I immediately began to teach it to my yoga students at that time and could track noticeable degrees of change in them from month to month. Several years later, I read about a similar yoga form with the same benefits being taught by Dr. Patrick Flannigan, a new age scientist in Arizona. His version of Tibetan rejuvenation yoga was slightly shorter but otherwise similar to my own. He also offered a story about its discovery.

According to Dr. Flannigan, a wealthy older man dedicated his last remaining years to searching for the legendary fountain of youth. After fruitlessly following up and tracking down myth after myth, he ended up in a remote monastery in the Himalayas. He was invited to join the order, and for several years he worked, meditated, and performed a daily yoga routine alongside the other monks. At the end of his fifth year, the Lama conferred with him and suggested that it was time for him to return to the western world. Tea was served on a lustrous silver tray in which, for the first time in five years, the man saw a reflection of his face. His sparse white hair had thickened and turned black.   His complexion was clear of spots and wrinkles. His body was firm, flexible and slender. His over-all appearance was that of a 35-year-old man or someone less than half his actual age!

I have practiced my own version of Rejuvenation Yoga from Tibet for more than ten years. My experience of it is totally positive and my own physical condition demonstrates that it works. I am significantly younger looking, more flexible and more mentally alert than I ever was in my 20s and 30s. If you would like to enjoy similar benefits yourself, give it a try.

Start practicing each part of the form slowly and repeat each section no more than seven times for at least a week or two. Do not leave out any of the elements. The parts that seem most difficult at first will eventually produce the greatest benefits for you.

When you are used to the flow of each sequence and can put them all together smoothly, gradually build up each step of the form until you can repeat it rapidly 21 times in combination with the other nine steps. The form moves quickly and should take no longer than 20 minutes when performed at its most proficient level. Once again, do not leave anything out. Some steps seem easy; some seem hard. All of them together, in the sequence I suggest, will add up to a complete experience that is also a completely nourishing and rejuvenating one.

1. Whirling.

Face north if possible. Stand erect with your arms outstretched at your sides and your hands just above shoulder height. Hold your left palm so that it faces up and your right palm facing the floor. Balance all of your weight on the ball of your left foot. Lift your left heel slightly and begin to rotate in a counterclockwise circle (to your left). To maintain your balance and prevent dizziness, keep your eyes focused and select one spot on the wall to use for orientation. Whirl around at least seven times.

2. Neck Extension.

Lie down on your back with your hands palm down under your buttocks or thighs and your thumbs touching. Lifting from the neck, raise your head off the floor as high as you can. Then slowly lower your head. Repeat at least seven times.

3. Pelvic Adjustment.

Stay on your back with your hands in the same position. Spread your legs until your feet are approximately shoulder-width apart. Keep your knees locked and straight. Point both of your big toes at each other and lower them towards the floor. Your feet will follow along until the inside edges of your arches are touching or almost touching the floor. Hold this stretch momentarily, then return your feet to their normal vertical position.

Point both of your big toes away from each other until the outer edges of your feet and ankles are resting on the floor. Hold the stretch momentarily, then return your feet to a vertical position once again. Repeat both parts of this stretch at least seven times.

4. Stomach Strengthener.

Remain on your back with your hands in the same position, palms down and thumbs touching under your buttocks. Bend your knees until your heels are almost up against your buttocks. Then exhale and slowly curl your spine, bringing your knees as close to your chest as you can. Hold that position and slowly lift your head until your eyes are looking directly at your bent knees. Then inhale slowly and as you uncurl your back, keeping your knees bent, lower your head and feet to the floor at the same time. Repeat at least seven times, exhaling each time you raise your knees and inhaling each time you lower them.

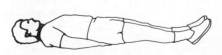

5. Chin Lift.

Kneel on your knees with your body straight and erect. Do not sit back on your heels. Join your hands behind your back. Then focus all of your attention on your chin. Rest your chin against your upper chest. As you inhale, raise your chin in an arc until it is pointed at the upper wall in front of you and observe how far behind your head you can see. (Note: Do not arch your back; just elevate your chin.) Hold your breath and extend the arc of your chin to its farthest point. Then begin to exhale and lower your chin slowly to your chest. Repeat at least seven times.

6. Torso Shaper.

Sit with your legs straight out in front of you and your feet about 12 inches apart. Place your palms down on the floor next to your upper thighs with your fingers pointing towards your toes. Notice how this pulls the upper part of your body forward. Exhale, and in one coordinated motion, lift your knees, thighs and pelvis off the floor and raise them until they are level with your shoulders and chest. Let your head fall back. The idea is for your body to form a table top, supported by your hands and feet. Inhale and slowly lower your buttocks, thighs and knees back to the floor. Repeat at least seven times.

7. Spine Adjustment.

Lie on the floor on your stomach with your elbows bent alongside your body and your hands under your shoulders, palms down. Be sure your legs are about 12 inches apart and that your toes are curled under your feet and pointed towards your upper body.

Inhale slowly, and without moving from the hips down, straighten your arms, thrust your chest forward, and slowly lift your chin as high as it will go. Lock your arms and elbows in place.

Exhale slowly as you tuck your chin into your chest and thrust your buttocks straight up towards the ceiling. Balance in this pyramid-like position for a moment or two, noticing the stretch in your hamstrings.

Then alternate these two motions, raising your head and chin as you drop your buttocks and then tucking in your head and chin as you lift your buttocks. Coordinate your breath with each motion, as described. And repeat the entire sequence at least seven times.

8. Breath Control

Sit on the floor in a crosslegged position or in a straightbacked chair. Hold your hands together so that your thumbs are crossed, then close the fingers of your right hand around your left thumb and close the fingers of your left hand around your right thumb. Imagine that you are smelling a fragrant flower and inhale deeply, filling your chest and abdomen with air. Exhale slowly. Repeat for at least seven breaths.

9. Energizing

Remain seated. Place your right palm up in your lap. Continue to breathe deeply and slowly. As you inhale, raise your left hand in a circular motion past your forehead. As you exhale, allow your left hand to rejoin your right. Repeat at least seven times.

10. Restoration

Remain seated. Place your left palm up in your lap. As you inhale, touch your right fingers to the center of your left palm and raise your hand towards the top of your head. As you exhale, turn your right palm up and allow it to float gently back down to your lap. Repeat at least seven times.

Remember to learn this unique yoga form by repeating each of the ten steps seven times. As you become familiar with the motions and the breathing patterns, and you can handle the more strenuous movements with increasing ease, work your way up to 21 repetitions of each step. Always do each step the same number of times as the others. Do not do one step more or less times than another.

Tibetan Rejuvenation Yoga is a complete daily routine unto itself. It offers cardiovascular stimulation, stretching, relaxation, over-all conditioning and limbering up benefits. You can count on it to provide a noticeable improvement in your appearance and a high level of vigor, vitality, energy and mental alertness.

Dancing.

For years, just about every Wednesday night from September to June, I used to attend a dancing class along with 100 to 150 other men and women, most of whom were in their 60s, 70s and 80s.

The class was led by Wini Hedrick, a former professional ballet dancer who once toured with world-famous international ballet troupes and who still moves with a style and gracefulness that any 20-year-old fashion model would envy. She teaches ballroom dancing and lots and lots of line dances like the Hully Gully and the Stray Cat Strut, many of which she choreographs herself. She has been working with classes like this for many years and radiates a beautiful and wonderfully ageless quality that exemplifies the dramatic benefits of choosing to handle your later years your own way.

If you have ever watched 150 so-called aging people dancing as energetically and uninhibitedly as kids at a Sophomore Hop, you have a slight idea of the really powerful nature of Wini's contribution to life on this planet. Especially since she teaches at least four classes like mine a week and thus manages to make a significant difference in the lives and physical conditions of a large large number of people.

I cannot fully describe the benefits of dancing because it has to be experienced to be believed. But even if you have managed to survive until your 50th or 60th birthday with two left feet, as I did, it is never to late to get out and dance anyway. For instance, after almost 50 years of wishing that I could do what Fred Astaire and Ann Miller used to do, I started to take Tap lessons. And I continued until I could create routines and improvisations on my own. Believe me, whatever embarrassment shows up at first will quickly pass. But the energizing effects of social, jazz, or any other kind of dancing on your system will go on and on.

Dancing is one of the only forms of bodywork that is no work at all. At the very least, find a class like Wini's in the city nearest you and join in. Just for the fun of it.

Gravity Inversion.

Once a day, your body will welcome the opportunity to reverse the effects of gravity that pull you down, distort your posture, and unbalance the internal relationship of your organs.

Chances are, you could learn to do a modified shoulderstand or headstand. I have taught versions of both to people in their 80s. Or you can just relax on a slantboard with your head below your feet.

There is a sophisticated mechanical device available called a Gravity Inversion System which gently and easily elevates your feet and holds you upside down for as long as you like. I use a simplified version of it: A chinning bar secured to a doorway and gravity inversion boots with metal hooks that catch on the bar and allow me to hang like a bat or do series of upside down sit-ups and pull-ups. If you try this yourself and notice any tension in your lower back, just tuck in your pelvis a little until you find your best position.

Two to five minutes of any inversion technique is all you need to stretch out, prevent compression shrinkage of your body and your spine, correct minor backaches and alignment problems, loosen neck fascia and calcification, and send a revitalizing rush of oxygen-laden blood to your brain.

Professional Bodywork.

The older you get, the more susceptible you may become to the irrepressible effects of gravity. Minor postural defects can worsen and devolve into functional impairments like dowager's humps, pot bellies and seriously misshapen shoulders or spines. While not inexpensive, a series of bodywork sessions with a professional specialist like an osteopath, a chiropractor or a rolfer can be a valuable investment in your physical wellbeing and in the attractiveness of your appearance and presentation.

I recommend Rolfing as an Alternative To Aging. The process realigns and reintegrates your body, once and for all ending whatever disagreements you may have been having with gravity. In ten sessions, it rebuilds you from the ground up and enables you to achieve a natural grace and balance that are a joy to experience and to observe. The process also eradicates emotional scar tissue that holds your body in a rigid, tense or unaligned position. It is one of those relatively quick solutions in which the treatment may be completed within weeks, but the results keep building and getting even better for a lifetime.

New Possibilities.

Everything you have read so far involves strictly physical principles that can provide practical alternatives for your body within widely accepted and easy-to-validate frameworks of thinking.

For the next few minutes, I invite you to pretend that everything you always thought about your body just may not be so. And strictly as possibilities, no matter how remote they may seem, consider the following premises instead. I suggest that you let this process be a game in which you let your mind flow gently around an idea that may be new to you and then file it away for future evaluation.

• **Possibility #1.**

At the beginning of this chapter, you read about the process of cellular recreation and renewal in which all the physical components of our bodies are constantly replacing themselves.

To take that one step further, keep in mind that our bodies are created continuously over the course of our lifetimes whether that lifetime is long or short. Our bodies, in other words, are not built up through the early years of our growth to one peak moment after which they fall apart piece by piece.

That means the energy our cells use to constantly rebuild and replace themselves, the energy that produces the actual content of our bodies is not just available for one period of time only, like a tankful of gas that gets used up as we drive along and is empty and dead at the end of the road. The energy that powers our life force is endlessly available for as long as we consciously or unconsciously wish to draw upon it. And we can direct and use it any way that we choose or simply allow it to trickle away.

● **Possibilty #2.**

The purpose of our bodies in an ultimate sense is to provide a learning experience. And that is all. As such, our bodies are simply vehicles through which all of our thoughts, emotions, beliefs, and internal as well as external experiences are materialized. Our bodies are perfect because they perform this function perfectly.

If only 'good' thoughts, emotions, beliefs and experiences were what we had to work with, our learning process would be boring and incomplete. We would never have the opportunity to live out the results of all of our infinite capacities for creativity in physical form. Moreover, we would never discover the true power of thoughts, emotions and beliefs as they relate to our own creative processes.

As long as we are learning something from our bodies, whether the lesson is painful or pleasurable, everything is precisely as it should be. And while the lessons of the past are complete, we have a lot to say about each coming semester's curriculum.

● **Possibility #3.**

As a physical form that contains our lifeforce, our bodies are always engaged in the process of becoming and evolving, in much the same way that each season is always engaged in the process of becoming and evolving into the next season. Because we live on the Planet Earth and draw upon space and time as frames of reference, the seasons of the year are actually mirrored in the seasons of our bodies. This notion will be developed in greater detail in subsequent chapters.

For now, consider the possibility that experiences we have in our 80s and 90s are as important, necessary, beautiful and desirable as the experiences we have in our teens and 20s. Each changing image of ourselves, as manifested in our bodies, communicates as eloquently as April, July, October, and December. Whenever we block or resist this communication, we lose contact with a vast number of interesting and empowering spiritual as well as biological messages.

And there you have a variety of readily available concrete and abstract alternatives to physical aging as you used to know it to be. With that in mind, try to recall the original picture of an aging body that you had at the beginning of this chapter.

Notice that it was only a picture and nothing more. Notice also all of the new options to that picture of aging that are now beginning to open up and emerge in your life.

In many cases, simply knowing that such alternatives exist may be all that is required to bring them about. If not, maintaining your body with regular care through simple ten to thirty minute daily routines will create the kind of physical miracles you may never have believed possible.

If anyone has the power to attain and produce those miracles for you, by now you can probably guess who it is going to be. And even here, the alternative is clear. As you grow older, especially in a world that appears to be designed and set up for youthfulness, you can still have your body just the way you want it. Or you can give up your vote and your body will have you.

The choice and the responsibility are yours.

CHAPTER 5

FEELING YOUR AGE

Freddy is angry today. He's mad at everyone. Not much is new about that. He is usually mad at everyone, every day. His jaw is tense as he stalks around the older children's benches with his left hand clenched in a kind of half fist. His life-force feeds on the thought that maybe a pudgy little seven or eight-year old will wander into his area by mistake so that he can beat the crap out of him or her. Everyone avoids him. Meeting rejection and imagined aggression at every turn, he carries a sharp rock in his pocket just in case he has to defend himself against one of the others, one of 'them'. He has fully accepted the story that it is all downhill after the age of twelve, and he is convinced there is no way out. When he thinks of the passing days, the onrushing months, the few remaining years, he rages at the circumstances that surround him. Someday he will find a way to fix them all. In fact, that is the only thought strong enough to keep him alive.

As he passes Patty Ann, he glares at her. Patty Ann doesn't notice. She sits dejectedly on her bench, looking considerably older than her 14 years. All her life, everyone always told her this would happen. They said life was like this. As it turned out, they were right. Now she is severely depressed all the time and has been for the last two or three years. Withdrawn to dimensions deep inside herself, the playground world seems cold and remote. It has become a place where no one shares and no one cares. The younger

*people ignore her.   Cherished friends of the past have
vanished.   Wherever she looks, she finds herself all alone.
Through a river of unwept tears, she wonders why this ever
had to happen to her.   Oh why, oh why, oh why.*

*She sits huddled in the bright warm sun and shivers.
Naturally she fails to see Marvin, hiding in the bushes just to
her right.   Hardly anyone ever sees Marvin.   He is so scared
that he hides from morning to night.   He has not always been
afraid.   Once he was an active outgoing child like all the
others, certain that the short bittersweet life-and-death cycle
of the playground would never overtake him.   Now he is
twelve, fearful and alienated beyond his years.   He is afraid
to speak and afraid to remain silent, afraid to reach out and
afraid to be alone, afraid to do anything and just as afraid to
hold back.   Almost paralyzed, the events of life threaten him
at every turn.   There is no safety, no refuge, no haven, no
hope.   When you are as afraid to live and afraid to die as
Marvin is, your choices are severely limited.*

*In fact, as far as every one of the older children on the
benches is concerned, the world is not much more than a
shadowy haze of mistlike red and grey emotional tones.   And
all alternatives have been cancelled.*

For most people living today, there is nothing more
powerful than the force of an emotion.

Love, hate, passion, jealousy, anger, fear, hurt,
greed, upness, downness, attraction, repulsion, longing,
loathing, horror and other feelings like that dominate
most forms of expression, trigger most activity, and
provide the underlying framework for most thoughts,
ideals, action and events.

Just look beneath the surface of just about
everything you think or do. Chances are, you will find an
emotional charge of one kind or another.

'I've got to have that new computer game.'

'I'm too scared to ask for the raise I deserve.'

'I wish I could meet that blondhaired man over
there.'

'I only did it because I was so angry at you.'

All those things and thousands more are everyday

examples of how emotions provide the fuel for thoughts and actions. If you strongly disagree, that statement will be particularly true for you. So look again. And again. Until you can find the connection. Your true emotionality may be suppressed or buried but it is always present.

In the classically accepted sense, emotions do not just happen. They are considered to be the results of an instantaneous, automatic, inner evaluative process that determines whether something is good for you or bad for you. Emotions, in other words, are internal reactions to external objects, actions or events. A snarling dog leaps at you and you feel scared. Something threatens your child or someone yells at you and you feel angry. Your sweetheart walks through the door with a flower for you and you feel love and joy. Or whatever.

In this context, emotions exist internally as floating wisps of energy just as chairs, grapes and kittens exist externally. And they are just as real.

In a somewhat different context, emotions serve as storage media for memories. We always remember life experiences which carry the heaviest emotional charges.

All emotions are appropriate and valid. But no emotions have to be acted upon or acted out. As we become more and more aware of our emotions and their effects on us, we can begin to choose which ones we really want to express and which ones we would rather hold back. We can then walk around less and less like loaded revolvers waiting to be triggered.

Most people think that some emotions like love, ecstasy and happiness are positive, while others like fear, hate, depression and anger are negative.

Actually that is not so. Emotions are neither good or bad; they are simply emotions. When we think one is better or worse than another, that thought is something we are adding to the experience of the emotion and not an intrinsic part of the emotion itself. Essentially, all emotions are perfectly all right. And when you let them be, they will let you be.

Left completely on their own, emotions will flow and ebb freely in, over and out of us in rippling wave-like patterns as new emotions flow in with our everchanging reactions to the different people, things and events around us. As long as we remember that we do not have to act upon our emotions or do anything because of them, it is never wrong or otherwise inappropriate to feel what we feel just as it is never wrong to see what we see or to know what we know.

All of our emotional problems and their associated anxieties, tensions and compulsiveness are the natural result of not allowing an emotion to live through its normal life cycle.

The problem starts when we suppress, repress or hold back an emotion we are feeling, particularly when we deny or disown it or lie about it to ourselves by pretending that it does not exist. How many times have you told yourself: 'I don't feel that way.' Or 'It's stupid to feel like this.' Or 'I shouldn't feel so strongly about that.'

Stop reading and take a moment or two to notice how this works with regard to your feelings about getting older. Find a blank piece of paper. And say the following sentence beginning to yourself over and over.

When I think about myself aging day by day, year by year, decade by decade, I feel...

Each time you say it, complete the sentence and write down exactly what you do feel about it. Do not stop until you have at least five different expressions of your feelings.

Then try another variation and say this sentence stem to yourself as many times as you want:

At the thought that my life will soon be over...

Again, write down whatever shows up for you. When you are all finished, notice what you wrote down. And afterwards, also notice what you held back. If that sounds hard for you to do, remember that you held back whatever you did not write down.

Emotions that we hold back have increasingly strong holds on the places in our body that we use to hold onto them. With the passage of time, those places begin to feel numb, tight and heavy instead of relaxed and alive. When we hold emotions back, the energy charge invested in the act of holding on also holds us back from spontaneity and aliveness. We fear that if we ever really let go, the emotions we have held back would break free and consume us.

Right now, if you close your eyes for a few minutes, breathe deeply, and scan your body from your feet up to your head, you may be able to become aware of places you cannot make contact with because they feel so dense or dead or frozen with tension. Those are the places where your withheld emotions are being stored.

You cannot afford to keep holding them there. In fact, if you do not let them go, they will surely make you ill. They will also accelerate the rate at which you age. And they may even kill you. Substantial medical evidence is accumulating that links cancer, heart attacks, ulcers and many other unpleasant physical problems to emotional causes. I will examine this more closely in Chapters 6 and 7. For now, just consider this: No one can make you hold back an emotion anymore than anyone can make you curl your fingers into a fist. You can only do it when you want to. If you did not hold on to it for whatever your underlying reasons may be, you could let it go as easily as opening your hand.

See for yourself.

Sit back and begin to breathe slowly and rhythmically. Send your awareness to the one place in your body that feels the most dense or difficult to contact and connect with. Then see if you can sense what you are holding on to there. If you find your heart is heavy, you may discover hurt. If your belly is numb, you may find anger. If your throat is unreachable, you may uncover sadness. In your hands, you could become aware of rage.

After you identify the emotion you are holding, look inside yourself for the sound that best expresses it. Perhaps a growl, a sob, a sigh, wild laughter or shouting, repeated over and over. Make the sound as loudly as you can. It is all right to feel shy or stupid about it. Feel as shy or stupid as you want and make the sound anyway. For your own good.

Keep releasing the sound and keep breathing as deeply as you can. You may experience trembling, vibration or tears as the energy of the emotion surges free and leaves your body. Trust your sensations and allow them to play themselves out. As you vibrate, you will begin to notice something new. Instead of the darkness of your trapped emotion, you will feel light and alive and free.

An even quicker way to release unwanted emotional patterns is this:

Identify whatever emotion you are feeling right now. Then stand up and give your emotion a voice by shouting a short phrase as you jump up in the air and reach for the ceiling six times.

If you feel terrible, shout 'I FEEL (jump for the ceiling) TERRIBLE!'

If you feel angry, growl 'I FEEL (jump for the ceiling) ANGRY!'

If you feel wonderful, yell 'I FEEL (jump) WONDERFUL!'

Be sure to repeat the shout and the jump six times.

The result will be a great new beginning. You will have noticed and identified an emotion. You will have accepted and acknowledged it. You will have given it a voice. And you will have released it.

Just one more element remains to be experienced. Repeat the exercise six more times with the following variation. This time, as you jump up, shout 'I *LOVE* FEELING (jump) TERRIBLE!' Or 'I *LOVE* FEELING (jump) ANGRY!' Or 'I *LOVE* FEELING (jump) WONDERFUL!' Or whatever it is that you do feel at that moment.

The benefits to be derived from this apparent foolishness are absolutely serious and as solid as a rock. Emotional repression drains the energy we need to propel ourselves through the act of existing. Releasing that energy in an appropriate manner always adds aliveness, enthusiasm, and years to our lives. That is quite a bit different, by the way, than releasing emotions in the kind of triggered inappropriate way that destroys more life than it creates. No one ever feels better when anger is released by punching out a supermarket checkout woman or sadness is released by a constant immersion in depression.

Appropriate emotional release involves three distinct and definable steps.

- 1. Become more and more aware of what you feel and what you may not be allowing yourself to feel.
- 2. Become fully accepting of yourself and give yourself permission to feel whatever you feel and be whatever you are all the time.
- 3. Become completely responsible for your choice to freeze emotions inside or to release them so that you can flow on to altogether new levels of feeling.

As you work with these steps, the power of your vote in the realm of emotions will become clearer and clearer to you, and your feelings will no longer appear to be so frightening or dangerously out of control. As a result, you will probably find yourself willing to let more and more emotions flow through you effortlessly and spontaneously.

Once you have mastered the alternative of identifying yourself with your emotions instead of just blindly feeling them and acting on them, a second alternative opens up. You can learn to peacefully detach yourself from your emotions. This can be an extremely powerful process that puts you in control without denying, stuffing, or suppressing any emotional content.

The idea is to notice that you are more or bigger than your emotions and that you do not have to be directed by them. Whenever you are feeling a strong emotion, stop what you are doing and sit as still as you can. Let the feeling wash over you and acknowledge its presence as separate from yourself by identifying it.

If you are angry, sit quietly and say 'Anger is present' or 'Anger is here'. Say it over and over for a few minutes.

If you are sad, sit quietly and say 'Sadness is present' or 'Sadness is here'. Say it over and over for a few minutes.

If you are afraid, sit quietly and say 'Fear is present' or 'Fear is here'. Say it over and over for a few minutes.

That is all you have to do.

You will have the full experience of the emotion as something detached from yourself. And the emotion will simply flow away without getting stuck inside or compelling you to do anything about it.

If you can learn to let your emotions flow through you and release themselves naturally, you will have achieved a near major breakthrough and you will be way ahead of the game. Without a doubt, releasing emotional blockages can add ten to forty years of aliveness to your life. But there is more to it than even that.

Maintaining the original premise that emotions are both internalized value reactions to external phenomena which we automatically judge to be for us or against us and storage media for life's experiences, the next step involves taking a closer look at the external events and actions that actually trigger emotional responses.

External events can only be perceived in two ways: As primary firsthand experience. Or as passive secondhand experience.

Our firsthand experience of external phenomena includes everything we actually see or do that directly involves our bodies and our own sensory organs. Firsthand experience includes opening our eyes in the morning, driving a car, being late, being early, watching someone abuse a puppy, disagreeing with another person, falling in love, feeling too cold or too warm, seeing your baby, getting mugged or raped, standing in line, winning the lottery, and at least a million other things that can happen directly to us and around us or that involve us personally in any way.

It is not difficult to see the principles in action. Firsthand experiences trigger emotions as instantaneous value reactions to whether something out there is good or bad for us. The relative strength of the emotion then locks the experience in the hierarchal storage banks of our memories in order of impact and importance.

It also is clear that these processes occur automatically and without conscious thought.

Somewhat less obvious at first is the correlation between secondhand phenomena perceived by indirect or secondhand experience and the just-as-real emotions that result.

Secondhand experience includes everything that we hear about from other people, read about in the newspapers, watch on television or in movie theaters, listen to on the radio, or otherwise become involved in without actually being physically present.   On strictly emotional levels, secondhand experiences generate feelings that are identical to those produced by direct firsthand experiences.   It does not even matter if the secondhand event is fact or fiction, true or make-believe. The emotional effect, as far as we are concerned, will be the same.

Such events might include reading about war in the Middle East (assuming that you do not live in the Middle East where the battle is raging), seeing a news special about the slaughter of baby seals, watching *The Exorcist* or *The Sound Of Music*, hearing for the first time how Little Red Riding Hood escaped the clutches and jaws of the wicked wolf, thinking about an incident from your unhappy childhood or a speech you have to give to a national conference of business associates next month, learning that a missing child in Kansas was reunited with her parents after two years, finding out that your wife or sister was raped or mugged while you were having a Happy Hour drink after work, and at least four million other things that are not happening to you, around you, or involving you directly *right now* in any way.

By monitoring your breath and the relative tightness of your jaw, chest and stomach, you can see how triggered secondhand emotions are identical to and just as powerful as the firsthand ones you generate from direct interactions.

Your emotions spring forth automatically. They do not know the difference between what is real and what is not real for you. That is why you can get just as upset, just as angry, just as fearful reading your morning newspaper as you sit in a warm, cozy kitchen drinking coffee or papaya juice as you can get when you realize that someone is trying to break into your apartment in the middle of the night.

Here is the problem.

Your emotions are biologically intended to produce chemical and hormonal changes within your body that mobilize and ready you for action.

The upset, fear and anger activated by a would-be

prowler find immediate release. You jump up fully awake and alert, make noise, phone the police, hide, or do whatever your proper course of action seems to be. Your emotions feed your ability to handle direct experience, when they are allowed an open flow of expression.

On the other hand, the upset, fear and anger activated by newspaper stories about impending nuclear war, energy depletions, rising prices, or fullscale unemployment have no such outlets as you sit at your kitchen table, warm and comfortable and serene. As a result, the purpose of these emotions is blocked and thwarted. No direct action is possible.

Blind to the differences between firsthand and secondhand data, your emotions continue to do their job, calling forth chemicals and hormones that alert your body for danger and arm it accordingly. Because there is no immediate danger present in your environment, your body becomes confused and disoriented. And the contradictory danger signals, when persistent, keep you in a constant state of anxiety and prebattle tension.

At best, your only recourse until now has been to train yourself to ignore your emotional feedback and the physical call to action that it generates. But in the process, your normal emotional flow is blocked and dammed-up fear, anger or upset build to alarming proportions deep inside only to splash out when you may least want or expect it.

While understanding how your emotional mechanism works may be interesting and informative, it will not change a single thing. It can't, any more than knowing how your motion-detector burglar alarm works will prevent it from blasting off at two o' clock in the morning when your cat runs across its field of activation.

It may possibly support you, however, to remember two overriding facts.

First, our bodies can only act in one framework of time and space: the present moment. Emotional alerts involving other places, other times and other versions o f what really may or may not be occurring there can only lead to a diminished sense of personal power and result in chronic anxiety or depression.

Second, gloom and doom, like hurricanes in Hartford, Hereford and Hampshire, hardly ever happen. When an unpleasant experience actually crosses our paths, a free and unrestricted flow of emotional energy will empower us to handle it just as easily as we can handle uninvited early morning visitors.

The truth is that it is well within our current capabilities to become consciously aware of our emotional responses to secondhand experiences and to reject them totally. Please note that what must be rejected is not the emotions but the validity of all nonexperienced experiences.

How can you ignore or reject everpresent reports about the presence of destructiveness and negativity all around you? By simply noticing that in direct firsthand terms, you and your world are as safe as your immediate personal perception indicates. Naturally and physically, you are completely safe. Threats are only threats; reality is reality; the two are not the same. Even if the worst were to happen and everything began to crumble all around, you would only experience your particular share of the reality of it. And you would be able to prepare yourself to take whatever direct action was open to you at the time.

No one wins imaginary battles. Especially on emotional battlefields.

What then, you may ask, can you do about poverty, starvation, disease, murder, treachery, corruption, holocausts, nuclear destruction and other issues that threaten your world if not your direct personal experience?

You can do a lot. In fact, you can make more of a difference than you ever imagined possible. You will find out exactly how to address issues like these in Chapter 9. There, however, you will see that in order to produce truly transformational results, you must work in a realm that excludes triggered emotions altogether.

For the present, strictly in the realm of emotions as we have defined them so far, I want you to know that there is no way for you to react appropriately to imagined dangers. And that is true no matter how real those dangers may be for someone else who is somewhere else. Because no authentic reactions are possible for you, all you can feel is frustration, which totally disempowers your capacity to act in areas that are fully open and well within your primary experience.

On an emotional level, if you allow the threat of wars, starvation, or global pollution to cloud your vision of life as it really is for you in your own relatively calm and serene personal environment, you give up your only valid anchorhold on reality. Accordingly, you begin to speak and act from positions about firsthand reality that are not your own and you deny others the benefits of your own version of reality as you are presently encountering it.

If, on the other hand, you remain exclusively within the boundaries of your firsthand experiences where your emotions can rouse you to the right action at the right time, you can take care of your fundamental social responsibilities and have a profound effect upon everyone else around you.

It seems paradoxical. And yet, your own version of reality is the only firsthand contribution you are able to make.

In simplest terms, the certainty that it is possible for you to feel warm and safe and comfortable as you sit at your cozy kitchen table this very morning has an immensely beneficial influence upon the rest of the world. It adds the peace and security that comes from knowing that constructive and harmonious events are many times more plentiful than destructive ones. In this way, each small moment of emotional satisfaction can have more impact on a global scale and on the future than the most insidious barrage of secondhand stories and threats.

Because it requires a steadfast commitment to sustain and share your own firsthand serenity in the midst of a storm of secondhand chaos, it is a contribution of the highest order. And a contribution you can make whenever you choose.

Take just a moment to think about that before reading on.

Weigh it against your fears or upsets about aging and begin to notice that the source of your fears and upsets is not firsthand and not in your immediate present.

The fact is: You are not aging. You simply are. Are what? Are what you are. And that is all. Whatever you choose to call what you are is something else entirely. It is a label that you stick on yourself and on your experience of yourself and it is no more important than you say it is.

In truth, every moment of your life is absolutely complete unto itself and fully centered in the present. When you are in the present, in each of your experiences from moment to moment instead of in your mind, you cannot age. You can only age when you think about some other moment and make a mental comparison or an evaluation based on that thought. Every single one of your emotions associated with aging is triggered by thoughts about the past or future or based upon some idea you may have picked up and internalized about other people's versions of what could happen someday. Either way, such emotions come from secondhand data and not your own immediate perceptual base. Therefore, there is no physical outlet for them. And they can serve no useful or valid purpose in your life.

Until now, I have been confining my examination of the emotional process to a commonly accepted psychological model that defines them as reactive processes. Naturally, there are other ways to view them as well. Because your emotions can profoundly influence aging, it is well worth considering these alternatives.

For the next few minutes, just forget about or ignore everything you already know about emotions as value responses which instantaneously follow and assess your perceptions of external reality. Consider instead, the possibility that emotions precede experiences, and that in some manner your emotions create and bring about everything that you actually do experience.

This may require a little stretch of your imagination but just pretend, if you will, that it is so. Then look at it this way.

Emotions are quite possibly the most highly concentrated form of energy that we possess while we are in physical bodies. Mystics and other explorers of the occult have held this to be true for many centuries. Strong emotions probably carry enough energy to heat, with ease, every home in New England during the coldest week in February. However, instead of providing power to run furnaces, they provide power to propel thoughts, beliefs and moods from our inner subjective states out into the physical objective world.

Over and over, with no chance of a shortage or crisis, our emotions bridge the gap between nonphysical and physical reality as each of us experiences it. You can test this by watching everyone draw back the next time you enter a room radiating silent but raging anger. Or seeing everyone ignore you when you enter shyly and fearfully. Or noticing them rush over when aliveness and joy beam from your eyes. It is a direct way of measuring how powerfully you are broadcasting internal states in highly explicit terms.

Speaking strictly experientially, everything is usually brought forth from the emotional energy that we generate. This means whatever we project from inside is likely to be what we will encounter outside. So when we are sad or hurt, we find tragedy and tears at every turn. When we are afraid, we discover one after another good reason to be fearful and our lives begin to be about surviving threat after threat after threat. When we are filled with joy, love and serenity, we create safety, acceptance and affection wherever we go.

Getting all this to work on an individual basis involves some of the alternatives coming up in Chapter 6, where I will discuss some of the ways that beliefs can attach themselves to emotional energy and dominate our entire experience of life. For now, the opportunity is to keep stretching your imagination and continuing to look at all the ways you constantly create external experiences using your emotional energy. Notice from day to day, for example, whether the weather is affecting you or whether it is you who might be affecting the weather.

Notice also whenever any event appears to be a classic case of cause and effect where the true cause actually resides.

Perhaps you are wondering why things do not always seem to go so well for you if you are the cause of all your experiences. If so, ask yourself who decides what is going well and what is not, and who says which is which anyway.   Then ask yourself who is always around whenever one or the other is going on.

The only reason it might not be more obvious that your world and everything you find in it originates inside of you is that you have been taught to keep your attention focused outside of you.   When only external physical events are considered real or authentic, your emotions (and your thoughts, beliefs, imagination and dreams) take a back seat and are looked on as not real and not important. When that happens, they dissolve and atrophy, becoming valid only as responses to external phenomena.

Whenever we choose alternatives, it is useful to consider big alternatives like the possibility that the way we are conditioned to believe everything is may not be the way everything is at all.   The notion that emotions might well be primary phenomena and external objects and events mere responses to them is that kind of really big alternative.

Purely as an exercise, in your imagination, allow it to be so if only for the purpose of experiencing what a true alternative is like.

Get the idea that your feelings and emotions are the hardcore reality base from which all external objects and events emerge.   Look at the world from the inside-out and notice the differences.   Then pretend that what you have always called physical experience actually originates from your inner reality.   Imagine that there is no longer any cause and effect, no triggered reactiveness, no stimulus-response. Imagine there is only cause and cause and cause and more cause.

Finally, begin to observe how all normal physical data might just possibly be your own concrete creations in time and space, drawn somehow from your own internal material. Close your eyes for a few seconds and do that right now.

I suggest that both of these alternative points of view about emotions are true: That our feelings cause or bring about the events we experience. And that our feelings then become the emotional assessments and evaluations with which we react to those events.

If this is so, notice how it could change the rules of the game of life by personalizing them to a very large degree. We could then have our emotions instead of our emotions having us.

You see, as long as we believe our feelings are automatic reactions, we are stuck with them and with the circumstances we constantly encounter that produce them. Once we open up to the possibility of alternatives, we can begin to become responsible for everything. That's right. Everything.

For instance, the next time you find you are stuck in an emotional pattern you do not like and you see yourself constantly blaming external conditions or events for it, do this instead:

1. Notice exactly what you are reacting to and what you think is the truth about it.

2. Remind yourself that what you are reacting to is only a notion you have about reality and not really reality itself. (If it were really reality, everyone would have identical reactions and there would be no differences in interpretation from person to person.)

3. Playfully take the opposing position about the issue or situation by turning your imagination in the opposite direction and willfully choosing to reverse your previous point of view.

4. Consciously create an appropriate opposite emotion to go with your opposite point of view. Then feel that emotion fully.

5. Watch what happens next.

Whenever you look inside yourself, you are sure to find an unlimited variety of subjective states, choices and available possibilities. None of them are right or wrong. In fact, any decisions about rightness or wrongness will never occur until long after whatever it is has happened externally.

Sometimes depression or sadness and periods of intense hurt or longing offer refreshing changes of pace. They can lead to times of quiet reflection and a slowing down of your body so that it can rest and be nurtured. Fear can blast your body from physical or psychological ruts and zap you out of lethargy or being stuck. As you learn to trust yourself, you can trust your emotions, allowing them to follow their own patterns and rhythms. This frees them to flow on and leaves open space for new emotions to flow into.

No discussion about emotions could be complete without acknowledging one last alternative: It is entirely possible to simply have them without dwelling on them, analyzing the reasons for them, or paying any more attention to them than you would pay to your socks, your keys, your wallet or your toothbrush.

While emotions may be extraordinarily powerful forces in the realm of experience, they have absolutely no impact at all in the realm of action. In this altogether separate domain of distinction, your purposes and your intentions and your goals can be realized no matter how you may happen to be feeling at the moment. You have probably noticed that whenever you are totally engaged in something, your attention is never on yourself and your emotional state simply goes along with you just the same as your hand or your nose. None of these appendages, however useful they may sometimes be, will ever account for much of anything in terms of your capacity for actually producing results.

I am not implying that emotions are not important; they most certainly are. I am simply pointing out that whenever you are where the action is, your emotions are usually somewhere else. And I am asserting that it is therefore possible for you to operate entirely independently of any emotional considerations whenever you so choose. It is interesting to be aware of that, especially since it opens up an entirely new level of options and choices.

As you can see, playing with emotional alternatives

is easy. The difficult part always seems to be accepting the existence of them in the first place. Once you cross that particular barrier, you will discover all the wonderful ways in which your experience of your own lifelong physical journey through time will never be the same.

CHAPTER 6

BEYOND BELIEF

Every night when the children are tucked and nestled snugly in their beds, all over the playground world the wallsized vidscreens light up. For a brief magic time, stories unfold. The stories are told by a mysterious voice that sounds cheerful, friendly, nurturing and deeper than most of the children's voices.

Someone, one of the children long ago, called them 'bedtime stories'. The name stuck.

In these bedtime stories, the content ranges from global fantasy epics to simple narratives about good triumphing over evil. But regardless of the plotlines, a few common threads hold true.

Good people are always young. Very young. In fact the younger the better. For the most part, they are sweet cherubic children who always do what they are supposed to do. Sometimes they rebel or act up in small or mischievous ways. Sometimes they even leave the group to seek fortune or adventure. But they always do what is right, which means they never never grow.

Bad people, on the other hand, are big, old, bad complexioned, and angular or stubble-faced. They break rules. They grow away from the good children. And the more they grow, the worse they get. So it is always a big old wolf or a big wicked old witch who causes all the trouble .

Magic forces invariably intervene and save the good little children from evil, just in the nick of time. No matter what else may occur or how scary it sounds in the telling, something or someone always comes along to save the good people

Bedtime stories have other magical qualities too. Sometimes the little hero or heroine has three wishes. Whatever he or she wishes for comes true. Sometimes a tiny pair of glass or pearl or ruby slippers grant special powers to the child whose little feet are still small enough to fit them.

Occasionally, the older children doubt that the stories are true. Of course, everyone knows that doubting is a well-known sign of advancing age so no one who matters at all pays any attention. All the good little youngsters know for certain that the stories are true stories.

What often happens is that the smarter doubters pretend that they still believe the simple bedtime tales. They go along with the good-against-evil sagas and the make-believe morality no matter how much their own experience says it can't be so. Only the dumber doubters speak out. Then everyone realizes that they have crossed over to the dark side and must be purged from the safe little world of good little children.

Every night when the children are tucked and nestled snugly in their beds, the bedtime stories come on and repeat their compelling dramatizations of the way things are. Over and over. And over and over. And over and over again.

By now, you may have opened up to the possibility that our emotions act as the fuel with which we propel our internal reality out into the external world where it is projected as our individualized version of external reality.

If emotions are the fuel, the actual substances that are thrust out into external reality are thoughts and the by-products of thoughts. These by-products include our attitudes, the positions that we hold to be true, our considerations, our judgments, our evaluations, and other fixed or heavy thought forms, all of which I will refer to from now on as a single group of internal substances called beliefs.

There is an enormous difference between a thought and a belief.

A thought is light and wispy like a dandelion seed floating on a breeze. It blows gently across the mind, is briefly noticed and disappears only to be replaced by another thought or a little cloud of thoughts.

A belief always begins as a thought. But instead of letting it blow by on an internal breeze, we attach some significance, importance, density or mass to it. So it sinks. Then, it remains stuck in place wherever it lands like a heavy weight. Unmoving and unyielding, it begins to attract and gather similar thoughts to it, which keep adding to its significance, importance, density and mass. Like a conceptual cancer, a belief grows and expands until it consumes one or more entire areas of subjective reality.

Most of our beliefs and the clustered belief patterns or belief systems that they form are firmly fixed in place by the time we are five or six years old. They are based on thoughts we had, decisions we made about our early experiences in reality, and things other people told us that we accepted without question.

Unfortunately, children from birth to six years old are not the best qualified people to evaluate the way things really are. That is why we go through life with so many unusual personal conclusions like the one that says we get more attention by getting sick or by being loud than we get by quietly having our lives work. That is also how we pick up lots and lots of pass-along beliefs about how life really is according to mothers, fathers, kindergarten teachers and other equally well-known experts on the subject.

If you pause for a moment and consider how life really turned out for your mother, your father, your kindergarten teacher, and all the others on your panel of experts, you can begin to get a rough idea of what some of those picked-up, passed-along beliefs may be costing you. Ask yourself: Are your experts genuinely happy? Are they fully self-expressive and overflowing with aliveness and enthusiasm? Are they aging in a way that allows them to expand and grow each year? Are they physically fit and in fabulous health? Maybe they are. If so, more power to them. But much more likely, maybe they are not.

The important thing to remember about beliefs is the same as the important thing to remember about emotions. When we have them inside, we will keep running into experiences outside that support and reinforce them.

Beliefs are always self-fulfilling. Driven by the power of our emotions, we create experiences which prove that reality really is the way we believe it is. In other words, we keep creating our lives in a way that proves our beliefs are right. Major survival issues result.

For instance, for more than 12,000 years of recorded history, beliefs like 'My God is better than your god' or 'Our country is better than their country' or 'This tribe is better than that tribe' have kept killing people off at an incredible rate.

Moreover, because it is the nature of beliefs to be self-fulfilling prophecies, if you believe that you are the product of an original sin or that you have uncontrollable, animalistic, destructive unconscious tendencies or that you have done terrible things in the past and will have to suffer now or in the future as a consequence, then suffer you will.

If you have such beliefs, they will appear in your day-to-day reality as suffering, limitations and barriers to fully experiencing many exciting and expansive facets of your life. And if enough other people share them, your beliefs will appear as conscious or unconscious cultural reality and society as a whole will suffer, experience limitations and generally fall short of achieving its full potential.

On a simpler scale, our beliefs that life is tough and filled with struggle and effort create a life experience proving that life is tough and filled with struggle and effort. Our beliefs that wellbeing depends on someone else so someone had better come along and save us soon will manifest themselves in a life of dependency, longing and unfulfilled expectations. Our beliefs about old age will just as surely create the kind of old age we believe in.

And we will experience a process of aging that mirrors our particular beliefs. Instead of aging as it could be and can be.

In every way, we go out into the world actively creating a reality that accurately supports and reflects each of our internalized notions. Out of the unlimited number of events and experiences that are possible, we unerringly call forth and participate only in the ones that mirror our own world views.

Usually, we are not aware of all the beliefs that form our personal realities. While they are held consciously and are fully available for examination, they are sometimes below our normal levels of immediate perception. To reach and examine your own beliefs, you will have to stretch your awareness. It is not that hard to do. First, you need to believe that you can do it. Then you need only to sit back and relax, imagine that your consciousnessis tuned to a certain station on a vast UHF television dial, and gently shift the tuner to another station where belief systems and their sources can be perceived with complete clarity.

Take a moment to focus on any belief you now have. Close your eyes and playfully tune in to its source before reading on. If you have difficulty doing this, try it again just before you fall asleep tonight or right after you open your eyes tomorrow morning. These are the times when so-called subconscious material is most readily available to you.

Here are three ways to identify a lack of conscious awareness about any particular issue involving beliefs.

1. Whenever something feels a certain way to you and always has felt that way, whether you know why or not, that is a belief. Beliefs are not facts. Beliefs are only something that you think are facts.

2. Whenever you know that you are right and someone else is wrong, that is a belief. It is definitely and absolutely not the truth. The truth is that no one is ever wrong about anything. Some people, especially the ones you think may be most wrong, simply see reality from a different perspective than you do. They see one part of it and you see another part of it. It is not until you add up

what everyone saw that you begin to get a picture of reality as it really is: A sum total of everything. That's right. Everything.

3. Whenever you have an ongoing internal dialogue with yourself, that dialogue is about a belief you have that someone or something has challenged. The dialogue invariably has to do with arriving at a defensive position or justification for your belief. Where there are no beliefs, there are no endless or constantly recurring internal dialogues. Instead, what you have is an endless internal monologue in which you hear a little voice in the back of your head chattering constantly at you. (If you just heard a little voice say 'But I don't have any little voice in the back of my head', that is the little voice I am talking about.) You can sense the difference between a simple monologue about a thought and a relentless internal dialogue about a belief issue by the weightlessness of the tone and the degree to which your mind remains stuck on that one fixed thing or one particular issue.

That is the way it works.

Using beliefs and the attitudes and expectations that tag along with them like heavy thread, we weave the material of our lives. Beliefs affect our thoughts, our emotions and our experiences. And because they seem so obvious, factual and self-evident, we take them as truths and never question them.

But here comes the trap. By taking on beliefs without question and incorporating them internally, we tend to forget that what we have accepted as personal dogma is merely a collection of beliefs about reality. And we mistakenly begin to think these beliefs represent reality itself. Examine your own beliefs about religion or sex or politics and you will see just how ironclad they are. Did you support Ronald Reagan or did you criticize him? Do you love the PLO or hate them? Tell the truth, is gay sex wonderful, or okay if that's what someone likes, or a blasphemy against God and Man?

Strong surface beliefs like these may be obvious and easy to recognize. Deeper beliefs about ourselves that we carry in subterranean caverns inside ourselves are no less insidious. We may be completely blind to them and never notice how we refuse to let certain types of ideas or experiences into our lives because they contradict cherished   but unrecognized or unacknowledged premises.

Three belief systems in particular totally disempower and rob us of more than ninety percent of our options in life. As you read what they are, notice your reactions to each of them. Strong reactions are sure signs of underlying beliefs about basic reality issues that limit self-confidence, diminish self-esteem, destroy self-assertiveness, and break down any capacity you have to shape and create your life the way you want it to be.

The first is the belief that we are limited in any way including physically, racially, intellectually, economically, genetically, genderally, or any other possibility that comes to mind.

The second is the belief that we are separate from everything else and merely observers of reality or that we have separations within ourselves like mind and body and emotions or conscious and subconscious components of awareness.

The third is the belief that we merely participate in reality or that we are victims of circumstances, fate or destiny instead of being the primary causal agents responsible for everything that ever happened, everything that is happening now, and everything that will happen in the future.

Just to see what comes of it, say each of the following sentences to yourself or out loud and try them on for size:

> * I have no intrinsic or extrinsic limitations
>   of any kind.

> * I am whole and complete and fully
>   networked with everything inside
>   and outside myself.

> * I create everything that I experience
>   and I am the cause of it all.

Pause a moment and let each sentence trickle through your consciousness whether you accept and agree with it or not. Notice whether you can feel a shift of internal substance or state of mind. It may take the form of a heightened sense of clarity, a tingling feeling of aliveness, a solid confident sureness or a momentary excitement. You can reproduce that shift and the feeling of certainty about yourself whenever you like by simply remembering and repeating these three statements. They reflect a certain kind of universal truth that can support you in a widely diverse variety of ways.

You may not believe that. In fact, you may right now be thinking something like: 'But I'm a woman and men get all the breaks.' Or 'But I'm a man and women get all the breaks.' Or 'But I only have one leg.' Or 'But I was an abused child.' Or any number of other similar 'Buts'.

For now, I am asking you to take my word for it. By the time you complete this book, you will no longer have to do even that. Given who you are and what you have to work with, each of the previous three statements is true. They are true for you. They are true for everyone. Without exception.

So why is life so difficult and nasty? And why does it seem to get even worse the older you get?

I don't know. But I can tell you where to look to find out.

Without thinking too much about it, take out a few pages of blank paper. Begin to list everything that you believe to be true about yourself in each of the following categories:

Your life.
Your helplessness or efficacy.
Your health.
Your money or lack of it.
Your sexuality.
Your own process of aging.
Your emotional stability.
Your ability to participate.

Your body.
Your relationships with others.
Your communication ability.
Your lovelife.
Your work.
Your family.
Your psychic awareness.
Your capacity to have it all.

The list you create will probably have to be an ongoing process. You will find it extremely difficult to finish it up in just one or two sessions. In fact, you may never finish it at all. Each belief that you write down may trigger three or four more in the same or a completely different area, so your list is likely to go on and on.

Fortunately, once you overcome your initial resistance to doing this exercise at all, you will get the point very quickly. And as each new session with your lists opens up more and more internal material, you will begin to see where most if not all of the difficulty and nastiness in your life is coming from.

Would it be the way it is if you didn't believe it was the way it is? Not a chance!

Would it be the way it is if you didn't use your beliefs as prime assumptions for your assertions about reality? Absolutely not!

'So what,' you may ask, 'can I do about it?'

To start with, work on your list. And notice how many of the beliefs you write down agree with or contradict the three statements you read on page 103. Areas of conflict are areas that you will want to look into more closely. Those are the areas in which you are likely to find yourself trapped in chains of beliefs which are linked to other chains of beliefs which are linked to still other chains of beliefs.

It will all show up on your list.

Something else that will show up is a tendency to want to change some of the beliefs that you notice you have. Too bad. It is too late. You can't change a belief that you already have. All you can do is look at it, acknowledge that you have it and recognize that you are responsible for creating it and sustaining it. Then you can allow it to dissolve and consciously implant a new and more productive belief in its place.

Here is an example.

Maybe you believe that you are unpopular or that other people do not like or understand you. You can't change that any more than you can change a letter after you have dropped it in the mail. That is what you believe, so it is what you will keep running into over and over everywhere you go. Until now, that has been the truth. And you cannot change the truth.

So simply look at that. Notice what you believe. Notice also, who believes whatever it is and who is saying they believe it. Acknowledge the belief and acknowledge its source. And, after that, just to see what happens, choose to believe that you are lovable and acceptable instead. That isn't hard to do. All you have to do is say it over and over a few times. Then, from time to time during the day, remind yourself that from now on you are choosing to believe that you are indeed lovable and acceptable. As you pass people in the street or at work, look each one directly in the eye, smile, and affirm silently to yourself: 'I am lovable and acceptable. I have a right to be loved and accepted.'

Maybe it sounds simple or dumb. But you truly cannot imagine what will happen in less than a week. See for yourself.

The best way to dissolve a chain of lifelong beliefs that keep getting in your way is to go after it link by link. Carry your Belief List with you for a few weeks and every time you become aware of a belief that you consider to be true, write it down. Sort out beliefs that work for you from beliefs that don't work at all. Then play with the latter group one at a time. If you use the exercise you just read or any of the others in this chapter you will see results and sense new dimensions of personal freedom at every turn.

You may observe that you believe you have an unconscious self and a conscious self. When this issue comes up, be particularly careful to check it out. Look in a mirror and try to see your unconscious self. You'll find you can't do it because it does not exist. All that it has ever been is something like a ghost or a superstition, unable to survive without your sanction.

What exists in place of an unconscious self is a fully developed capacity to experience your life on a variety of interconnected multidimensional levels. And if you have not yet experienced your life this way, it is only because you believe it is not possible.

Many scientists and serious psychiatrists support the belief that you have an unreachable subconscious and that it is the source of a lot of your badness and trouble. That is their belief; nothing more, nothing less. Your personal badness and troubles arise from your own personal beliefs or their external projection as personal experiences in everyday reality.

Be particularly watchful if you notice that you believe you are locked in a struggle between conscious and unconscious parts of yourself instead of engaged in a constant ongoing process of communication between inner and outer levels of your being. It can cause you considerable unrest and anxiety because you will never be able to trust yourself totally or act on your impulses.

When you become aware that you have a conflict of beliefs or that you hold two or more dissimilar beliefs, how can you tell which is the right one?

Usually the answer is self-evident. Just ask yourself which one allows you to expand, to experience ongoing challenges, and to enjoy your awareness and aliveness. Also ask yourself which one limits your experience, diminishes the vision of your consciousness, or holds you back. You will always know which beliefs to allow to dissolve and which to hold onto when you measure them on that kind of scale.

Most false beliefs are simply beliefs you have not examined. Once you bring them up into the light, the process becomes easy. Your thoughts, feelings and impulses will merge into guidelines for action.

Left to your own natural flow, you will always act in an integrated and cohesive way, checking and blending inner and outer sensory material, signals and other data, and forming beliefs that accurately reflect reality and fully support your life. These natural beliefs are easily accessible for examination. There is no conflict surrounding them. Therefore there is nothing to bury, hide or tuck away.

But even your most hidden beliefs can be hauled out and examined if you believe that they can be, if you are quite certain that you can interact with them and transform them, and if you are willing to actually plunge in and do it.

It is a lot like playing the piano by ear. Your fingers brush over the keys without differentiating one from another. When your fingers strike a discordant note, they instantaneously switch to another more compatible one. It is fairly automatic. If you believe that your limiting beliefs are fixed and immovable, it is like believing a wrong note is frozen in reality and can never be restruck correctly.

Once you commit to consciously examining your beliefs, many negative and limiting ones will dissolve by themselves to make room for the new ones you will choose to hold in their place. That's really the good news about all of this. As soon as you know that you are responsible for bringing forth the events and circumstances that you experience, you will never be stuck with them. You can move on to the next event realizing that, even if you put an obstacle in your own way, it is merely so that you can watch yourself respond to that particular challenge or just see what would happen.

Only when you immerse yourself in the external end-product of a belief such as loneliness, bad health or an overdrawn checking account without examining the internal cause will themes of that nature become fixed or stuck in place. Such themes sometimes hang on for a lifetime largely because of the weight of the assumptions that become an integral part of the mass of the belief system involved. These assumptions closely follow your beliefs and lead you to the false conclusion that what is so right now has always been and will always be so.

One assumptive belief involves time. Because we accept and actively participate in the belief that we exist only in terms of years, months, days, hours, minutes and seconds, we base a lot of personal day-to-day operating conclusions on it. Our perception becomes structured according to whatever time or day or month it is supposed to be. We usually eat our meals, go to sleep and take our vacations when we are supposed to, instead of when we may actually want to. And our focus remains fixed on only one of many possible ways available for measuring the content of our lives.

As a result of our collection of assumptive beliefs about time, we think of our experiences as a straight line progression from birth to death, thereby screening out vast arrays of experience that are fully accessible on other multidimensional levels. For example, we may observe that time passes at a differing rate of speed now than it did when we were children. Or that time rushes by when we are completely immersed in an activity that we enjoy, but drags on endlessly when we are bored. Unfortunately, we tend to choose not to question the implications of such observations. And so we allow many useful and valuable insights to slip away unnoticed.

Many native cultures do not count the passing years, automatically eliminating many stereotypic patterns of aging associated with numbers like 45, 65, 80 or 100. As much as I love birthdays, there is a lot to be said in favor of this practice. It avoids arbitrary and artificial divisions in a naturally unbroken stream of experience. Once free of any beliefs to the contrary, it becomes clear that all of our power rests exclusively in this flowing succession of moment after moment of primary personal experience. From where each of us intersects in time right now, we can draw on capabilities that we have had in the past and on possibilities that may open up to us in the future.

Consider, for just a moment, how useful it could be to have immediate recall of and access to your past and future knowledge, talents and accomplishments. It is an odd notion. And it is offered simply as an alternative to whatever other odd notions about time you currently claim to be true.

Actually, time is nothing like everyone thinks it is. That's why animals, who have no beliefs about time at all do not deteriorate very much before they die. The only exception are pets who somehow pick up and play back their owners' beliefs. When a puppy is treated differently than an adult or older dog, the animal responds appropriately and acts accordingly. In very much the same way, our own beliefs about time and aging become facts of reality.

When we are willing to suspend these assumptive beliefs and become open to other possibilities, an almost limitless variety of choices begins to show up. For instance, you could choose volitionally to take on the physical and mental characteristics you would have if you were ten or fifteen years older or younger than you actually are. If you are 25, you could draw upon the knowhow and experience of 40; if you are 60 or 70, you could have access to physical strength and energy that you never realized was so readily available. You would no longer have to feel youth was wasted on the young or that old age demanded a trade-off of vitality and joy for wisdom.

Does that sound hard to do? Here is a way to playfully make it easier.

Just use your imagination. Pretend that you are any age you would like to be right now. Then, let your eyelids close and for the next few minutes, see yourself as you are at that age. Visualize, if you will, a simultaneous period of existence in which you are actually that age. And follow yourself through whatever episode or scene or situation emerges.

You can do this whenever you want. Each time, be sure to notice and make use of whatever overlapping skills and abilities remain available to you when you open your eyes. You will find yourself accessing an internal network of ageless and timeless capabilities and talents. And many of the artificially imposed barriers of time as we mistakenly believe it to be will disappear.

Time is only one of many common assumptive beliefs. Another involves the whole idea of scarcity.

Instead of simply being aware that one thing or another appears to be lacking to some degree right now, we believe that a condition called scarcity exists as one of the givens of life. So we act as if we never have, for example, enough money or time or love or opportunities, even when we may be surrounded with an enviable surplus of each. We believe that we have to protect and hold onto what little we do have because time, money, love, opportunities and other things are in such short supply and so hard to come by or to replace. And even when we have enough, we act as if we don't.

Look at your own relationship to any of these examples. See how your natural tendency is to parcel each of them out with great care and give them only to other people who are particularly deserving of your meager supply or who will trade you back something in return.

Hitched tightly to the back of all assumptive beliefs is the concept of inevitability or the belief that things will always be the way they are or else they would have changed by now. If you ask yourself whether or not it is possible to end war, prejudice and inequality, or whether you could go through the rest of your life without ever losing your temper or hurting someone else, you will see how deeply rooted your belief in inevitability is. Everyone knows that war, prejudice, inequality, losing our tempers and hurting other people are inevitable.

Of course they are!

But what if they weren't?

And what if we had the power to handle all of them just by reassessing our own patterns of belief?

It sounds unlikely, doesn't it. So let me remind you that anything that ever sounds unlikely is nothing more than evidence that you have an opposing belief system. Otherwise, you would have no yardstick to measure likeliness or unlikeliness against. And everything would take on the neutral quality of being just another possibility to explore.

Finally, if you ever thought that external reality existed independently of you or that you were separate and apart from everything else that shows up outside of your skin, that is another major example of an assumptive belief. As you have seen with other beliefs of this type, it prevents you from experiencing other, more satisfying possibilities. Unfortunately, it closes off the distinct possibility that since you are an integral part of everything that exists, you can draw unlimited quantities of strength and nourishment from your relationship to all-of-it and never have to succumb to loneliness or alienation ever again.

Now that you can see how belief systems set us up for the actual experiences we encounter in our lives, it is time to get to the point and begin to take a long hard look at your own personal beliefs about aging.

For openers, notice the images that come to mind as you think of the words 'young' and 'old'. In this culture, youth is believed to be alert, aware, beautiful, strong, able, capable, resilient, energetic, creative, healthy, with-it, physical, and sexual. Old is considered to be the opposite of young, with a variety of opposing images automatically triggered, if only by association. Check this out for yourself and see whether it is true for you.

These and other beliefs that automatically follow an image or a key word are triggered beliefs. You pull a trigger and they all shoot out, long before you can consciously appraise or think about them. Spontaneous as they may appear to be, they are powerful forces in your life. They can hurt you severely. And you are loaded with them. Watch for triggered beliefs whenever you notice contradictions between your desires and your actions or between your emotions and your thoughts. Like any beliefs, triggered beliefs are fully available for your inspection although they often tend to hide beneath internal pockets of stress. If you are at all intellectual about your feelings, start with your next strong emotional outburst and see if you can trace it back to the triggered belief associated with it.

You can always trust your emotions to lead you to beliefs that cause you difficulty. In the chain of processes leading to action, emotions follow beliefs and precede events and actions. Once the belief is uncovered, a free flow of natural feeling invariably emerges and emotional explosions tend to diminish or disappear.

There is little doubt that no one deliberately wants or intends to grow rigid, inept, unattractive, unathletic, weak, debilitated, sickly, stodgy, and otherwise unappealing as they grow older. That so many people do and that so many more believe they have no other alternative is a major byproduct of triggered beliefs.

I assert that our massive cultural tendency to condemn aging and try to remain young can be directly linked to beliefs of this type. Perhaps, because they are so closely linked with invalidation and the covering up of authentic experience, triggered beliefs about aging are particularly well hidden and unusually stressful to uncover. That may also explain why it is so easy to believe they are reality itself without question or doubt, rather than to write them off as nothing more than a collection of beliefs about reality.

It is particularly important to remember never to repress or hide from our experience of life. When we refuse or pretend to refuse to accept certain aspects of physical growth and change, we also deny aspects of spiritual development that are linked to physical growth and set in motion by simultaneous hormonal and chemical activity.

Since our bodies exist within a physical framework of space and time, our experiences when we are 50, 70 and 90 are as necessary as our experiences when we are 18. Each new interaction with our environment has essential data to communicate. When we block these messages by hiding out or attempting to hold on to earlier phases of development, we miss the very biological and spiritual messages that would most support us through change and voyages into unexplored territory.

One such message involves the nature of cycles. With the arrival of old age, our entire organism concentrates on rebirth. Body, mind, emotions and spirit mirror the ending of one season and the beginning of another. If unblocked communication from within were possible, we would greet each cyclical passage not only with acceptance but with excitement, joy, and enthusiasm for new adventures and new experiences. To resist the experiential reality of time in this particular sense only keeps us stuck in it and obsessed by it to the exclusion of everything else.

You see, by freeing ourselves from erroneous beliefs about the nature of time and by allowing ourselves to participate in the basically balanced state of integrity of transformational growth, we would give our bodies the option of functioning in complete health and harmony for many decades longer than we now believe possible.

Another Alternative To Aging, powerful enough to completely transcend our current distorted notions, would open up.

All you have to do is be willing to give up whatever beliefs you may now have that youth is it and aging is all downhill. This, by itself, can release the unnecessary and unnatural stress on otherwise normal patterns of growth that cause your aging process to be one unpleasant experience after another. Concurrently, you need to notice and examine the implicit stands you have taken based upon all of the beliefs you have been dredging up and tracking down on your list. Finally, you must identify exactly who agreed to set it up that way in the first place, by choosing to buy into or otherwise accepting that particular set of beliefs. After that, everything gets to be a lot easier. And a lot more fun.

So who said that it had to be hard in the first place?

That's right, you will find whoever said so in the nearest mirror. And it does not lessen your personal responsibility to point out that you had a whole lot of cultural agreement or that our entire society has been saying the same thing for centuries.

In most parts of the Western world, it is true that men and women are taught to fear old age from childhood. The fully functioning mind is believed to grow from youth to its most highly developed form in young adulthood, a period that is highly acknowledged as the prime time for success, physical prowess, and worldly grace.

Certain circumstances seem to support this particular belief.

In young adulthood, the mind develops its most critical and penetrating powers of differentiation. The art of identifying and discerning differences and distinctions is raised to new heights and this faculty becomes the standard for evaluating existence and experience. Accordingly, intellect and intelligence are measured in terms of their critical and diagnostic skills by scientists and educators, and adult consciousness is primarily directed toward manipulating the physical environment. Those abilities are well and good. In fact, they represent an important evolutionary accomplishment. But that's not all there is to it.

Equally unique assimilating, merging, and correlative facets of our minds are just as important, as evolutionary capabilities and as contributions to the complete development of the human psyche.

Left to a normal process of development, as we approach the age of 70 or so, our minds would shift from one set of measuring tools and standards to the other. Freed from the straight and narrow task of determining what's different and evaluating what the differences are between ourselves and everything else or between this and that, as we grew older we could become more integrated, more creative, more assimilated into our environment, and much more in touch with the rhythm and flow of the universe around us.

Instead, just as we approach the pivotal balance point of true mental maturity, we are warned over and over against straying from artificial boundaries of the differentiating mind of young adulthood.

Betrayed by the differences inherent in a normal process of growth and expansion, we begin to fear and suppress them. We personalize, however unwillingly or unwittingly, the consensus of cultural beliefs that any transition into another realm of experience is a sign of mental and physical deterioration instead of a primary step toward the acquisition of new skills and new dimensions of consciousness. If you took an otherwise normal healthy baby and ferociously slapped it to the floor each time he or she attempted to stand up and walk, the results would be much the same.

We end up condemning ourselves for each new sign of emerging transformation to higher levels of development. We block or repress each sign of growth, seal off each new doorway that threatens to burst open.

And as a result, if we ever did trust the inherent integrity of our bodies and minds, we lose that essential sense of being at peace within ourselves. Instead, we voluntarily accept and begin to play out tragic stereotypic cultural scripts in which we act our age, according to the now internalized beliefs of others.

It is a sellout on a massive scale. And the price of selling out and rejecting our firsthand experience of aging is enormously high.

Quite literally, it costs us the rest of our lives. And since the rest of your life could be up to 120 to 140 active healthy enjoyable years or more, it is definitely worth whatever degree of effort may be involved in transcending the belief systems that now stand in your way of attaining them.

There is a lot that you can do about it. Strictly on your own.

Start with your ongoing list of beliefs. Notice your own patterns and write them down. Notice the deeper beliefs that your top layers tend to cover up; write them down too. Review your list at least once a day and allow five minutes of introspective time afterwards to give your hidden, assumptive and triggered beliefs a chance to emerge. They will emerge. You can count on it. Remember that your list is a passive opening-up process. You don't have to do anything about it. By simply noticing your belief patterns, acknowledging them without judgmental evaluations, writing them down and looking at them, they begin to lose their mass and density and they dissolve all by themselves.

Maybe you are as active and impatient a person as I am. And the idea of just making a list does not seem as if you are actually doing enough. You would rather jump into some really active technique for exorcising limiting beliefs and creating fully-supportive positive ones in their place.

Jump into your list. Do it actively. It works.

Concurrently, you can also do either of the following two exercises. Choose only one of them and practice it regularly for at least three weeks before you stop or switch to the other. Then you can switch back and forth at three or four week intervals, if you like. Just don't attempt to do them both at the same time. The overlap will confuse or otherwise inhibit the startling effectiveness of the results.

Exercise 1. Creating Beliefs.

Choose an area of beliefs from your list that you can readily connect to one specific unwanted condition in your life. For example, maybe you are always short of money and have stacks of unpaid bills, a history of overdrawn checks and never enough cash to buy the things you really want. If you examine your list, you will probably notice that you believe money is scarce or there is only a limited amount of wealth available or some people have too much so others have to go without. You may also notice you believe that money corrupts or that rich people are shallow and snobbish or that only poor but spiritual folk can attain enlightenment or enter the gates of heaven.

When you can clearly see the connections between underlying beliefs and unwanted conditions in this or any other area of your life, create your own simple belief in the form of a sentence or mantra of ten words or less, or a series of simple visualizations that you can see behind your closed eyelids. A sentence of affirmation might be ' I am surrounded by abundance and rich and happy' or 'I am crawling with money'. Appropriate visualizations might include opening your pay envelope and discovering a large raise, piles of checks arriving in the mail, your hands stuffing lots and lots of money into your wallet or a winning lottery ticket and all the prizes and new things you will surround yourself with when they give you the money.

For five to ten minutes a day, sit in a private place where you will not be disturbed and repeat your sentence aloud or silently to yourself or view your visualizations over and over. Take no more than ten minutes a day with this part of the exercise and then forget about it . Do not keep doing it or dwelling on it.

In addition, every day for the period of the exercise, treat yourself at least once to a small token gesture of newfound affluence. Buy a pack of 30-cent gum or mints instead of the 25-cent generic brand. Choose a slightly more expensive lunch or dinner selection for yourself. Or get the $55 sweater instead of the $50 one, if you like it a lot better.

You should experience noticeable results showing up within three weeks. Often, it takes less time than even that.

Exercise 2. Suspending Beliefs.

Working from your basic list once again, select a group of beliefs that you can clearly connect with an unwanted condition in your life. Maybe, in this case, you are lonely and you would like to become more popular or experience true love or find your ideal partner. At the same time, you may notice you believe that love is scarce, particularly when you are over 50 or under 20. Or you believe that you are overweight or homely or otherwise unappealing. Or that people who fall in love always get hurt and end up alone in worse shape than ever. Or that sex is bad or nasty or sinful or stupid or anything other than just plain sex.

Given that you can see connections between your beliefs in this area and a painful, difficult or distressing external situation, here is what to do.

Find a place where you can sit quietly without being disturbed for about ten minutes. Close your eyes and repeat to yourself several times the following sentences, substituting your own words for the parenthetical statements: 'For the next ten minutes, I agree to voluntarily suspend all of my previously held beliefs about (my unworthiness to be loved, the difficulties of being in relationship, my unattractiveness and overweightness, the scarcity of appropriate people, and the nature of sex). Instead, for the next ten minutes, I will consciously choose to believe that (I am worthy, attractive, 135 perfectly proportioned pounds, and an irresistible magnet to dozens of gentle, loving, warm, self-sufficient, unattached and unmarried potential partners, all of whom I will drive wild with desire). I will also choose to believe, if only for the next ten minutes, that (love and sex can be rewarding and enriching experiences in which I am willing to participate fully for my own pleasure and satisfaction, without fear or shame)'.

You get the idea. Specifically set up these initial statements to handle whatever area of beliefs you are willing to suspend. Be as specific and concrete as you can. And then, for the remaining part of your ten minute session, visualize yourself actually involved in the manifestation of the new beliefs you have chosen to accept for the remainder of the exercise. Sticking with the example, you might see yourself as you would look as a highly attractive 135-pound person, surrounded by a wonderful variety of eligible people who are wild at the thought of being in a committed relationship with you. You might visualize yourself buying exciting new clothes for your exciting new body, having your hair styled, going out, being the center of your lover's attention, caressing and making love just as you always imagined it could be, all of that and more.

When the ten minutes are up, tuck everything away until the next day and forget about it. If any of the material surfaces as a daydream or fantasy later in the day, let that be all right with you. Just do not consciously bring it up again.

If you do this exercise every day, in three weeks or less you will definitely produce a noticeable shift in your belief patterns and in many of the related circumstances in your life.

It is easy to prove these exercises produce results because within weeks you can watch the intended results show up on their own.

More work with belief systems as they relate specifically to health and aging issues will be found in Chapter 7. And in Chapters 9 and 12, you will encounter technologies that bypass beliefs altogether. Because so many life issues are hopelessly quagmired in self-imposed swamps of beliefs, whatever time you invest in clearing them away will ultimately prove to be a foundation for many previously unavailable Alternatives To Aging.

CHAPTER 7

A
HEALTHY
OUTLOOK

Molly was scared. Really scared. Although still in the golden prime of her young life and well on the carefree and socially-acceptable side of her tenth birthday, something severe was beginning to become physically wrong with her.

Until this week, she could only vaguely detect signs and symptoms of the dreaded disease in her system: A bittersweet pang or two. A sharp sudden surge of loneliness and longing for something unknown and undefinable. A recurring sensation of some wild and uncontrollable growth building inside, spreading, consuming her with an extraordinary momentum all its own.

That was bad enough. But at least that didn't show. She could hide her inner pain and discomfort from the others behind a dimpled smile. Now, though, she could begin to feel the awful disease spreading to the surface of her body, breaking through her resistance, betraying her, exposing her, humiliating her. They will say, she thought, 'Tough break! Too bad! She was so young and beautiful and had so much of her life ahead of her!'

Yet, in her heart she knew that no one would really care. Once she was put away in isolation, she would quickly be forgotten.

She had been able to track the progress of her disease with surprising expertise. Of course, posters pasted all over strategic locations in the playground world made all that relatively easy. While standing on line for dinner, everyone could see the Seven Suffering Symptoms poster with each miserable malady to watch for in large easy-to-read type and with cute little cartoon animals and flowers with happy faces playing in-between each line. On the community bath-house wall, as everyone toweled their little bodies dry, Dreyfus Duck headed a list of Deadly Diseases And Defined Debilities. Almost at every turn, everyone was reminded to check themselves regularly and to go to the infirmary at the first sign of any one of a number of distressing indications of sickness and ill health.

So, of course, Molly knew from the very beginning. And now that the outward signs were becoming obvious, she found herself with the nearly impossible task of never again exposing herself, no matter what, in her community dormitory or that once-friendly bathhouse.

There was no place to turn. She was absolutely certain that a simple trip to the infirmary for help could only mean she would never see her little friends again unless they came to visit her, which hardly anyone ever did because it was so depressing.

Molly was really scared. The problem, arriving so early and uninvitedly, was here to stay. There was no longer any way to hide the awful fact that two ugly round cancer-like growths were insidiously emerging on her flat little chest just behind her tiny nipples. And her life was as good as over and done forever.

If belief systems can profoundly influence external events that we experience, their effects at their source or on our own internal processes are even more impactful and even more likely to show up either as problems or pure existential joys.

This chapter will explore fundamental issues of health, well-being, nutrition, diet, and physical and emotional/mental illnesses as they relate to aging. However, instead of looking at these issues as products of circumstances or conditions that originate somewhere outside of ourselves, I will be inviting you to consider exactly how you are directly and personally responsible for creating and maintaining each of them.

You may not want to do that. Especially if you think you tend to be sickly, chronically in need of medical care, seriously overweight, rigidly positional about the foods you eat, hospitalized or terminally ill. However, if you promise merely to maintain an open mind as you read on, the alternatives you encounter will not only make you feel better. They will almost certainly make you feel wonderful.

A quick look at some of the actuarial numbers involved is an appropriate place to start. Most health-and-aging statistical reports draw sharp distinctions between two separate issues: maximum lifespan potentials and average rates of survival.

Throughout recorded history, the maximum lifespan potential has remained fairly constant at about 120 to 140 years of age. This means only that theoretically, anyone can live to be 120 or even 140 if he or she manages to stay alive that long. Somehow no one ever seems to exceed that limit.

On the other hand, quite a lot of observable action and progress has occurred in the statistical area involving the average rate of survival. This reflects the average person's average age at death based upon his or her susceptibility to various prevailing diseases and other environmental factors like plagues, famines, droughts and wars. For instance, the average person between 1900 BC and 1900 AD survived between 25 and 40 years. By 1900 AD, the average person lived about 60 years. And by 2000, it is likely that the statistical average rate of survival will be between 75 (where it is now) and 80 (assuming that no major breakthroughs and advances in longevity occur between now and then).

During these same 3900 years, the maximum lifespan has become available to an increasing percentage of the world's population. In olden days, less than 0.5% of the people ever lived to see their 120th birthdays. By the year 2000, as many as 5% to 10% of us or more are expected to be alive and kicking up our heels when our so-called biological timeclocks wind down and stop. If you are wondering why I said 'so-called' in the last sentence, I suggest that you either find a real biological time clock and send me a photograph of it or that you examine your beliefs about biological timeclocks and inevitability. Then I suggest that you consider the possible consequences of holding on to beliefs of this nature.

There is a staggering amount of worldwide agreement and support for every single one of the hundreds, maybe thousands, of unworkable beliefs you have, not only about timeclocks and inevitability but also about health and disease. Let's take them on, one topic at a time.

Inevitability has already been handled in Chapter 6, so there is no reason to be repetitive.

Biological timeclocks are a concept developed by gerontologists to explain the aging process. As you get older, the theory goes, a series of internal clocks slow down one at a time. This slows down the body's production of hormones and initiates other internal and external processes that result in the symptoms and manifestation of advancing age.

Is that true? And, if so, is that all there is?

First of all, more and more geriatric research, as reported in a variety of recent nonfiction articles and books about aging by Durk Pearson and Sandy Shaw, Ray Walford and others, has been invalidating both the fixed, rigidly programmed nature of the biological timeclock concept and many of the basic principles of the concept itself. This can only mean that the scientific community no longer agrees about internalized clocks and their effects on us.

Second of all, let me remind you that a concept is nothing more than a belief. Therefore it cannot and does not exist in reality. Only the consequences of blindly accepting a belief can ever show up in the real world. There is, by the way, an easy method for proving whether something is actually real or merely a belief. If you can see it or touch it or hear it, chances are it is real. At least it is real for you, and that is what counts right now. Someday, someone may come along and show you a biological timeclock or give you one for your birthday or anniversary. That is the day you will know that it is time to go along with the idea. Until then, simply remaining open to other alternatives makes sense. As always, it is nice to have a choice.

And now, on to health.

The more clearly you can see what is making you sick, the more clearly you will know what is making you age in a manner that you neither like nor choose to fully accept. Both conditions stem from similar sources.

Just take a look around.

The morning newspaper arrives, bringing with it headlines about a brand new disease, a rapidly spreading epidemic, a particularly virulent strain of flu. Symptoms are described in lucid detail. Explicitly or implicitly, a warning shrieks at you. Watch out! You're next!

All day long, wherever you go, people are sneezing, coughing, complaining about their digestions, their colds, their sleeplessness, their bad backs, their aches, their pains. Even more than complaining about relationship problems or lack of money, everyone loves to complain about their health. If you call your parents, you are certain to find out what's wrong with Mom and Dad this week. Maybe you will also learn that a childhood friend has just come down with something incurable. Besides making even more of an unfortunate occurrence, all of this negative preoccupation serves as a constant reminder that all is not well in the world. And if you don't watch out, you will surely catch some of it.

Each night, there is more of the same. You can go out to a movie and see someone heroically or not-so-heroically handle cancer, loss of a limb, or some other heavy-duty medical problem. Or you can stay home and watch the same themes played out on the tube. With your television programming, you get bonuses: Four out of five kindly doctors will recommend which chemical combination of ingredients to stuff into your nose or mouth when you want to mask and repress a physical symptom or minor discomfort instead of experiencing it, noticing why you may be producing it, and curing it. Well-meaning public service announcements will alert you to which diseases are in style this year so you can have them too. Still other commercials will remind you that you require some external remedy or outside authority to maintain your health because you are certainly incapable of handling it yourself. Finally, you will even be advised to bet on the inevitability of becoming seriously ill at some future date by buying a health and hospitalization insurance policy now.   After you have one,   in order not to lose out on your investment in premiums, you will have to get yourself really sick. So, naturally, that is exactly what you will do.

You can easily see what is going on. Living in an environment in which you are constantly bombarded with reminders of disease, it is very difficult to create a belief system that focuses on wellness.   Unless you consciously and conscientiously commit yourself to setting it up that way.

Since thoughts and beliefs regulate your patterns of health, any persistently recurring images and suggestions about illness will make you ill.   As long as you believe that external factors like germs, viruses, accidents or infection can make you sick, you will need an external agent like a doctor, a medical practitioner or a bottle of pills to make you better.   And because you believe that these outside influences can cure you, usually they will. Such cures, however, because they deal with symptoms or effects instead of causes, are rarely permanent.   And follow-up medical visits or periodic treatments   for recurring flare-ups are expected and encouraged.

Unaware that thoughts and beliefs create bad health, we continue to keep illness solidly in place as one of the given conditions of life.   Symptoms keep coming back or new ones appear as you keep returning to the doctor. While you may acknowledge that you can obtain only temporary aid that way at best, you seem to have no other alternatives. So you keep going back for more. The long-prevailing Western medical model, with its focus on and preoccupation with illness instead of wellness, supports you to play out this unsatisfying pattern. Until death do you part.

Fortunately, other beliefs and medical models are open to you whenever you are willing to consider them.

Most Chinese doctors, for example, are not paid to make you better. Their orientation is on keeping you well in the first place. Since their primary focus is on maintaining your health, they charge for their services with a monthly or yearly fee. When and if you ever do succumb to illness, your doctor feels that he or she has let you down and you do not pay for whatever cure may be required.

Because belief systems about health are so deeply ingrained and so strongly reinforced by our environment, I am not suggesting that you attempt to change your ways or transform your beliefs overnight. If you go to doctors now, don't stop. If you have medical insurance now, don't cash it in. If you have been using medication, continue to use it. For now. And, for your own good, consider the alternatives. The older you get, the better off you will be for it.

In my own experience, I am quite clear that just as I make myself ill sometimes, I can also heal myself. Nevertheless, at times, I know expert support is essential and so I have a medical support team that I can call upon as needed. At the present time, my medical support team consists of an orthopedic specialist, a dentist, a rolfer, and a general medical doctor who maintains an open mind and takes an active interest in my work.

Whenever I need assistance from one of them, this is what I do. I tell whichever one of them I am seeing what is wrong and describe what I have been doing to correct the situation so far that has not worked. After I have been checked out and I learn what the problem is, I ask to see a picture, chart, or model of a healthy whatever-it-is so that I can visualize exactly where to put my corrective work. With the exception of dentistry (which invariably involves fixing an old filling or finding a new solution to an old problem), nothing more than a touch or two to reinforce my healing processes is generally required. Then, I go home and make myself better.

Only once in the last 15 years have I required the services of an outside specialist. When that happened, one of the people on my medical support team referred me to the appropriate doctor. He was so busy and so much in demand that long before I could schedule an appointment, I took care of the situation myself.

If you would like to recruit your own medical

support team so that you can be your own doctor, here are some general guidelines to follow:

1.   Choose the types of medical practitioners you believe you are most likely to need and select at least two likely candidates in each area. (Be sure to examine the underlying beliefs behind your conclusions before proceeding any further.)

2.   Arrange to talk with each candidate personally.

3.   Tell each one that you believe that you are capable of healing yourself on your own, but for back-up and occasional consultations you would like to be able to draw on his or her expertise.

4.   Clearly state that you want no unnecessary medication or treatments, that you prefer and intend to take care of yourself on your own, and that if you cannot count on his or her support on that basis, you will simply find someone else to hold down this particular position on your team.

5.   At each visit, if necessary, remind your medical support person about your particular needs and ruthlessly hold him or her to the groundrules that you have set up for working with them.

6.   Be sure to always ask to see what a healthy whatever-it-is looks like in a medical textbook or chart. Then, get a clear description of what is wrong with your own whatever-it-is and how that differs from the reference picture. You will then have a workable visual image of what the problem is when you begin to correct it later on, using the techniques you will find in this chapter.

7.   Drop anyone from your team who does not respect and support your autonomy and your natural capacities for healing yourself. Also drop anyone who suggests that illness is a natural condition 'at your age' or who attempts to keep you coming back for visits and treatments that you do not feel you want or need. Remember that it is your body, so you get the final and only vote about who you will choose to let participate with you in maintaining its health.

8.   Be willing to devote enough time to monitor your own health and your physical condition on a regular

basis; never neglect to heal yourself whenever you need to be healed.

Setting up your own medical support team this way serves two important purposes.

First, it places direct responsibility for your health in your hands. You become the source and the instrument of your own wellbeing. And you get to have firsthand experience at measuring your own efficacy and effectiveness on a primary level of existence.

Second, it establishes balance and partnership with whichever medical people you choose to enroll for support if conditions beyond your understanding or capacity to handle should ever occur. Coming from a variety of belief patterns about susceptibility to random diseases or the hopelessness of inevitably developing a major illness or chronic condition, many people throw themselves at the mercy of medical specialists as if they were omnipotent high priests of old. Some medical specialists thrive on the power of the role in which they are cast and keep feeding their patients all the right lines to sustain the drama. You are involved in theatrics of this type if you notice that you deal with your doctor more reverently than you deal with your auto mechanic, your accountant, your insurance agent, or your Avon representative. None of it is healthy for anyone. Least of all, you.

The price you pay for taking control of your health and medical needs is small compared to the cost of letting yourself get on the wrong end of someone else's beliefs about the cause of whatever they think may be the matter with you. The most important thing you will have to do is to reexamine your relationship to symptoms of pain and your reliance on turning to drugs, medications and other medical treatment including surgery and hospitalization for relief.

Drugs and medications may suppress pain and alter body processes for the better. But unless you examine and transform your beliefs, you will either continue to keep bringing the old conditions back or you will come up with new and even better conditions to take their place.   That is why headaches and stomach distress can never be permanently cured by pills, tablets or other stuff, no matter how much you may consume.

Have you ever noticed how medication usually works for a little while? It works because you believe it will work. However, no matter how much you rely on it, you will need more and more because your beliefs about the underlying condition are always deeper and stronger than your beliefs about medication or any other external cure that you can buy or try for it.

I don't like or approve of the idea of hospitalization. So I don't have a lot to say about hospitals and the things that go on inside of hospitals except this: Avoid them. And do whatever it takes to do that. Even if what it takes is working over your list of beliefs about health and wellness for a couple of hours a week or setting aside some time to do the work suggested in this chapter for a few months.

Hospitals are not healthy places and what goes on in them can be extremely hazardous to your health. Built upon assumptions that illnesses, disease and infirmity are normal everyday conditions and that health can be achieved only through surgery, medication, struggle and confinement, there are few resources available in hospitals that support your natural capacity to take care of yourself or to make and keep yourself well.

Hospitals are also an end-of-the-line result of a deeply ingrained human belief that illness is bad, wrong or somehow essentially evil, rather than simply a useful indicator of internal events, which is all illness ever is in the natural world. A sick animal or bird never feels hopeless about its condition, never wonders how it got into such a terrible state and never turns to another animal for treatment. Instead, it makes its own evaluation of what went wrong and begins its own process of therapy to correct it.

From the very beginning, on the other hand, whether in tribes or more civilized communities, men and women have tended to view ill health as a possible source of contagion or danger to others. I am aware that reported plague cycles throughout history give considerable mass and substance to the contagion theory.

And I am not asserting that it is incorrect, although I wonder if it may not be just another interesting concept that has become locked in place or if it is something other than whatever we think it is. At any rate, how each particular group has handled this view about the dark side of disease generally has determined whether its aging members were cared for, abandoned or killed.

From my own research into metaphysics and discoveries about the nature of reality, it is apparent to me that, in basic terms, there is no evil. There is only experience, which we then evaluate and label 'good' or 'bad' 'beneficial' or 'evil'. Sometimes, the same experience carries both labels, depending on where the evaluator may be coming from or what he, she, and others may believe is right or wrong. For instance, a 58-year-old Jehovah's Witness and a college sophomore might not agree about the goodness or evilness of a torrid sexual encounter or a wild drug adventure.

Some experiences are a lot better than others, but everything that we experience is useful and informative. It is only when the evaluation of any particular experience becomes heavily charged with emotions and gets stuck or turned into a conceptual notion that it becomes the foundation for beliefs. This does not mean that you will never meet with events or experiences that seem bad or evil to you. It simply means that if you focus your consciousness inwardly, you will notice that all events and experiences represent either the seemingly positive or seemingly negative side of your own supreme creative effort to produce externalized action in a physically measurable form.

In terms of health, the applications are very specific. Everyday consciousness exists within a body of beliefs that materialize as flesh and blood. It is the primary function of your physical body to provide an external mirror that accurately reflects each of your internal network of beliefs, thoughts and emotions. In sickness, your body performs this function just as well as it does in health, even though it may not feel as good to you.

As an intricate and intimate biofeedback creation, your body is always in perfect condition. However it feels to you externally is a reliable frame of reference for however it actually is for you internally. That's why it makes no sense to get angry or depressed about a distressful symptom when the symptom is nothing more than a physical replica or model of your thoughts and beliefs.

On still another level, as I have already pointed out, whatever you experience in the physical world also offers you the same kind of feedback. For the same reasons that it is useless and self-defeating to be continuously upset about your environment, it is just as useless and self-defeating to complain constantly about your health. All of your experiences, those you think of as good and those you think of as bad, are purposefully designed to communicate something to you. When you get the message, the tone of the communication will always change for the better.

All of this may be just a little hard to swallow. Especially if you are in a transition period of life, and you are dealing with real physical problems or upsets about them. Actually, it does not matter whether you are in a transition from 25 to 30, 40 to 50, 70 to 75, 90 to 100, or 115 to 120. If you do not feel as well as you would like to feel, you definitely have alternatives. And you can use them to regain and replenish your innate capacity for health, energy, vitality and wellbeing.

Here are a few ways to go about it.

Start by making a mental list of three to five of your most unlikable and unwanted physical conditions. These can be any body conditions at all, from sinus headaches and excessive weight to heart disturbances, warts, high blood pressure or cancer. The only requirement is that you must be able to repeat each item and describe your direct experience of it in great detail, because that is what you will be doing for ten to fifteen minutes a day, every day for three months.

To set up the process, give each condition an original name that accurately classifies it. Do not use commonly accepted medical names. For instance, instead of calling your condition 'sinus headaches', you might call it 'painful throbbing in my forehead'. Overweightness might be called 'a band of fat under my ribs'. Try 'tightness in my chest' instead of 'heart attacks', 'nasty little growths on my eyelid' instead of 'warts', 'a feeling of near-busting in my veins and arteries' instead of 'high blood pressure', 'dense lumps in my lower abdomen' instead of 'cancer'. In each case, use your own description as a label and forget whatever the rest of the world might call the same condition.

Then, each day, sit quietly for at least 10 minutes and call off each of the unwanted conditions on your list by the name you gave it. After each one, describe in great detail exactly how that item feels to you on that particular day. You might cover as many of the following aspects as you can:

• Physical sensations and exact location of the item like 'Pulsing, throbbing, marble-size ball of pain about one inch above my left eye-brow and two inches into my head'.

• Feelings about the item like 'Right now I feel angry about it, like I'd like to punch somebody out. And I also feel a little sad that it hurts so much and I have to suffer in silence.'

• Thoughts about the item like 'I think it's migraine sinus headaches. I think I get them from pressure on my job. I think I need acupuncture treatments.'

• Beliefs and atitudes about the item like 'It runs in my family. What can I expect at my age? Everyone has things like this so who am I to complain.'

• Things that other people have told you about the item including anything your doctor, mother, friend, lover, boss, children or Cosmopolitan Magazine ever had to say about it.

• Images from the past that you somehow associate with your item like the time your brother threw a rock at you that hit you on your forehead just over the left eye. Or the pain you remember when a loved one left you. Or the first few times you noticed that particular condition. Or anything else that comes to mind.

This exercise will put you in touch with your capacity to create your own physical symptoms, to label them and freeze them in place, and to make them worse or let them go. It is an incredibly powerful tool for working with yourself.

If you like, you can do the following process along with it for any single unwanted condition on your list.

In your mind, build a three-dimensional model of yourself and, as you sit quietly, imagine that you are projecting it out a few feet in front of you where you can see it clearly. Then duplicate your unwanted item on your model so that it looks and feels exactly as it looks and feels right at the moment that you are experiencing it yourself. Notice everything there is to notice about that item as it appears on your model of yourself.

Next, visualize a chart or medical textbook picture of a healthy, perfectly functioning version of your item. (If you don't know what that looks like, look it up in a book or use your medical support team's illustrative material for reference.) When you have the picture in your mind, project it out so that it hangs directly in front of your model.

Observe the differences between the chart and the condition of your model. Then, reach out with your hands and gently massage your model on the affected areas of its body. After a minute or so, allow the chart to merge into your projected model and notice how the healthy condition replaces the unwanted condition as the two images slowly come together.

When the process is complete, enjoy your model's transformed condition of health for a few moments, acknowledge yourself for your good work, bring the image back inside of your mind and open your eyes. Be sure to notice how good you feel.

Two other exercises you can apply to health issues are the processes for creating and suspending beliefs found in Chapter 6. Do not, however, use both of them at the same time.

To create a nurturing and healing belief pattern, choose an unwanted physical item from your list. Chances are, the description you have given it is phrased negatively. It will be important to turn that around. For instance, if your unwanted item is 'recurring dull pains and discomfort in my stomach', in this exercise you will need to call it 'a stomach that functions perfectly and glows with health and vitality'. Or words to that effect. Do not refer to the condition that you want to produce as 'a stomach that feels better' or 'no more pain in my abdomen'. That will only reinforce your present condition and your existing pattern of beliefs about it.

Then, just as you did in Chapter 6, repeat the positively worded description of your item over and over, either silently or aloud for five minutes a day. Use visualizations too. See yourself able to eat and enjoy large dinners, pizza, hot dogs, mixed-meat deli omelettes, and other delights that you may have been avoiding. After five minutes of this, let it all go and forget about it. Later that day, allow yourself just one tiny indulgence like a half teaspoonful of some forbidden treat. And watch for results within three weeks.

If you prefer to do the Suspending Beliefs process instead, set it up exactly as you did in Chapter 6 by affirming your willingness to suspend all previously held beliefs about your bad health or physical problems for the next ten minutes. Using the previous example, add words to the effect that: 'Instead of my current beliefs, if only for the next ten minutes, I will choose to believe that I am filled to the brim with perfect health and vitality and that I can eat and drink whatever I like without discomfort. In fact, I can enjoy everything I consume as a completely natural process and remain slender, trim, and physically fit in every way.'

Reinforce your words with visualizations of yourself completely surrounded by wonderful things to eat, digging in without fear of pain or gastrointestinal reprisal, remaining your ideal weight, radiating good health and abundant energy. Stay with the exercise for at least three weeks to let all the appropriate inner connections link up.

Maybe you are still wondering how this kind of thing can possibly work. Particularly when it flies in the face of most medical and scientific theories and may very well antagonize your favorite family doctor or specialist.

I don't know how. All I know is that it does work and, unlike many of the widely-accepted contemporary medical theories, it will work for you. Remember, I am never certain that I have the right or the only answers for you. What I have are the right questions. And, in this case, the questions and the possibilities and alternatives that emerge out of them are designed to direct you to where the ultimate sources of power in the universe might lie. My experience so far indicates that it lies within each of us, unless we choose to give it away or delegate it to an outside realm of authority.

In my book Complete Meditation, I explore this premise in considerable detail. Exercises are included that enable you to experience the actual moment in which your power is both fully charged and fully available. That moment is always the moment that you occupy in time and space right now. And right now. And right now. And right now.

Furthermore, each of these moments in the immediate present does not show up as a single dot or isolated speck. Each one is more like a star or asterisk, with rays or lines of force that extend out in all directions into the past, into the future, and into all of the diverse alternative possibilities that exist concurrently and are open to you. These exercises lead to the conclusion that, in the most fundamental sense, anything and everything is possible. Because all of it exists simultaneously, any actual, possible or even theoretical experience can be accessed or brought forth at will.

As all of this relates to your health, the point is that every possible past, future, and present medical condition from perfect wellness to near death is available to you. And in each and every moment that you experience, you somehow trigger or cause the condition of health that is most appropriate for you in terms of your beliefs, your emotional state, and your inner conclusions based upon both.

When you alter or transform your beliefs about health and wellness in the present, new lines of force extend out in all directions, and you also alter or transform your own past and future. Newly awakened healing principles begin to modify the cellular memories that physicalize illness and hold it locked in place. Probabilities and possibilities are reshuffled and new variations emerge, creating a robust future from reversed patterns of disease and initiating new cellular memories that can support and maintain good health.

Realizing all this, you can choose your own alternatives to a wide variety of illnesses associated with aging. You also need never again be on the victim side of the scale, a prisoner of heredity, past events or circumstances over which it used to appear that you had no control.

When you begin to build on this foundation, many of the major health issues that relate to aging fall simply and matter-of-factly into place.

Consider The Great Vitamin Debate. With the FDA's minimum daily requirements on one side and Pearson and Shaw's *Life Extension* megadosing on the other, what and how much to take used to be hard to figure out. Now, vitamins can be as simple as choosing whatever you want and knowing why you are making that choice.

If you find that you accept such conceptual notions as declining immunization factors and natural protection from external disease sources, crosslinking genetic damage as a cause of wrinkling, agespotting and certain forms of cancer, and a general falloff of antioxidation agents and hormonal support in the body, you may want to take a heavy formula of vitamins, amino acid supplements and, perhaps, a few prescription medications as well. If you accept no such notions at all, you may want to bypass nutritional supplements entirely. And there will be nothing wrong with either position, unless you say there is.

Personally, I don't believe in vitamins. But I take them anyway in fairly large amounts because I am on a limited food intake program, which I will discuss later in this chapter, and I want to cover all possible nutritional bases. I also happen to like the symbolic act of popping vitamins every morning. It reminds my body that I take its needs seriously and that I care about it. My body and I, like good friends, carry on occasional conversations that usually tell me what I need to know about its processes, cravings and potential problems. It would serve you and your body well to do the same.

Just for the record, I am sharing my present daily vitamin formula with you in Table 2. Please note that I neither recommend it nor suggest it for anyone else who has not consulted with his or her body or medical support team or both. Also note that the 'reason why' column contains a number of medically off-the-wall personal beliefs and interpretations. So far, this latest blend works well for me; when I no longer get what I want out of it, I'll change it again.

It is largely a case of suiting yourself. I am open to the possibility that a solid conscientious regimen of vitamins could very well be a genuine Alternative To Aging, if only because it might strengthen the body's chemical processes and its systemic resistance to breakdowns. But because I tend to suspect the validity of any external substance as a primary reason for an internal process, I suggest that the main value of vitamins might be to serve as a positive reinforcing agent or a token daily commitment to well-being. And that's all.

TABLE 2. STEPHEN KRAVETTE'S DAILY VITAMIN PROGRAM.

WHAT	HOW MUCH	WHY
Multivitamin	1 Tablet	Balance to prevent overload from any excesses.
Vitamin A	25,000 IU	Vision; immunization system benefits.
Beta Carotene	25 mg	Vision; immunization system benefits.
Vitamin B1	125 mg	Healing; imunization system stimulation.
Vitamin B2	125 mg	Antioxidation balance; healing.
Vitamin B3(Niacin)	500mg-1g	Cholesteral reduction; antitoxidation; nice flush.
Vitamin B5	625 mg	Cosmetics and age pigment removal; healing.
Vitamin B6	75-100 mg	Stress reduction; relaxation; healing.
Niacinimide	500 mg	Mental stimulant; energizer.
Vitamin C	4-8 g	Healing; immunization; over-all protection.
Vitamin E	2000IU	Cosmetics; immunization; over-all healing.
Selenium	100 mg	Cosmetics; Vitamin E and C support; anticancer.
Calcium/magnesium	500 mg	Bone, muscle, tissue support.
Zinc	50 mg	Cosmetics; antioxidation; sexual support.
Lecithin	40-60 g	Mental, physical, memory stimulation.
Choline chloride	1 g	Mental, physical, memory stimulation.
PABA	1 g	Antioxidation.
RNA/DNA	1 g	Healing; support for cellular regeneration.
L-Cysteine	1 g	Healing; immunization; Vitamin C support.
Thymus extract	750 mg	Immunization system support.
Ginseng	500 mg	Protection; healing; sexual stimulation.
Bee Propolis	500 mg	Over-all healing; staph infection fighter.
Phenylalanine	500 mg-1g	Mental alertness and stimulation; antidepressant; dream intensification.

Another major health issue that could well stand to be observed from a new vantage point involves food, dieting and weight control.

We, in this particular culture, simply eat too much. We have a collection of beliefs suggesting that feeling full and overstuffed is somehow related to feeling satisfied. Charles Dickens family-style holiday dinners and 'All You Can Eat For $5.95' restaurant specials are based upon this largely indigestible belief structure. Do you buy it or reject it? You might take a few moments to check out your own beliefs about food, nutrition and sufficiency before reading further.

An enormous amount of evidence about alternative diet routines has been accumulating from sources as diverse as Dr. Ken Pelletier's investigation into the world's pockets of longevity where people live well into their 120s and 130s and Dr. Roy Walford's work with laboratory animals at the University of California. The results overwhelmingly indicate that a lot less food means a lot more years of life.

Where an average American consumes 3000 to 3500 calories a day, the average Georgian in the Caucasian Mountains and the average Vilcambambamian tribesperson in Ecuador consume only 1500 to 2000 calories a day. About half the food intake seems to just about double the lifespan. Georgians and Vilcambambamians reportedly live 50 to 80 or more years than we do. On a smaller scale, laboratory rats on similarly restricted diets live 36 months instead of 18 months or twice as long as their fat rat cousins. In theory, when you have less food to process, your body accumulates fewer toxins in its fatty tissues and your immunization system ages at a slower rate and therefore remains active longer. In addition, a body on a restricted food intake program has to work more efficiently, so it cannot support as many unnecessary, extraneous or malignant cells.

I am willing to go along with all that. And I suggest that you consider it too. Even if it is only a belief, it is the kind of belief that is worth having because it could protect and preserve you for a long time.

Lowering your food intake requires a gradual reduction in the quantities of food you consume to an average of 1500 to 1800 calories a day. Too rapid a reduction does not work for the same reason that dieting does not work. When you are too severe or too abrupt, your body feels cheated and begins to act crazed with cravings for food until you give in.

In addition, reducing your daily food quantity demands that you closely examine your beliefs about how much food you really need as opposed to how much you think you need or how much other people like your mother once may have said you needed. If you continue to believe old chestnuts like fat people are more lovable because there is so much more of them to love or that good little boys and girls eat everything on their plates or that anyone who works as hard as you do just has to have a lot of nourishment, you will find it almost impossible to successfully cut down. For example, I grew up during the late depression and Second World War years and I was a notoriously wasteful eater as a child; something within me to this day believes I have to atone for all that badness by consuming every last crumb on the table.

Once you clear away your own versions of that kind of stuff and you are really willing to begin a reduced food intake program, there are three ways to go about it.

(1) You can conscientiously count your calories every day and stop eating when you reach the 1500 to 1800 level.

(2) You can ease over to raw fruits and vegetables for your primary foods. To do this, eat only fruits and fruit juices until noon. Then prepare salads or lightly cooked vegetables for lunch and dinner. These can be mixed with your choice of: A meat, poultry or fish product. Or a starch food. Or a high-grained bread. Or a dairy product. But never more than any ONE of these at any given meal. This plan naturally reduces the amount of food you will choose to eat. After three or four weeks, you will no longer have the slightest urge to overindulge. You will probably also find yourself giving up sugar, caffeine, and other dietary killers that shorten lives instead of extending it.

(3) You can eat just about as much of everything as you want for five days a week and then fast, avoiding all solid food substances, for two days in a row.

Whichever way you choose, the idea is to ease into it. Over the course of six months, for example, you might knock off 50 or 100 calories a week. Or eat only fruit until noon without monitoring the rest of the day. Or slowly extend your fast from half a day to a full day to a day and a half to the full period.

I personally switch between the second and third approaches. I am not willing to measure out my meals drop by drop although many people seem to have no trouble with it. I now also find that even on anything-goes days, my once ravenous appetite is subdued and contented with reasonably small portions. Ordinarily, I rarely eat more than one-and-a-half or two meals a day.

All three versions of this limited food plan demand that you take nutritional supplements. While you can ordinarily afford to be slightly undernourished and hope to process whatever you need from normally excessive daily quantities of food, you cannot allow nutrition gaps while you are involved in this program. So you will need to find a hardline vitamin formula that works for you or customize your own blend yourself. If my vitamin and mineral preferances (in Table 2 on page 138) seem either too severe or too moderate for you, there are literally hundreds of books you can use to guide you in finding your personalized level of nutritional balance.

The statistic to keep in mind is this: People with reduced food intakes live 40 to 50 percent longer; people with malnutrition die 40 to 50 percent sooner.

As radical as it may sound, these dietary Alternatives To Aging have been around for more than one hundred years and have become fully proven lifespan extenders. All that time, they have also been steadfastly resisted. At the turn of the century, when portly men and Reubenesque women were believed to be beautiful, thinness and restraint were unthinkable. Today, limiting your food intake could well be an idea whose time has come.

If you have any question at all about the effects of less food on your health, consult with an appropriate member of your medical support team. If you don't have a medical support team yet because you are still tied to your belief in the ultimate medical authority of your family doctor, then by all means clear your participation in a reduced food intake program with him or her. The point is to respect your own beliefs, whatever they are. And indulge them responsibly by never, never pretending that you do not believe in something that you do believe in.

One of the nice things about lowering your food intake is that after a while you automatically handle the problem of excessive weight, especially the extra pounds and bulging midsections, so often associated with getting older. Slowly, gradually, painlessly, permanently, over the course of two to five years or so, you will find yourself weighing ten percent less than you weigh right now. And ten years from now, you could weigh as much as twenty percent less. You will enjoy the physical freedom of less weight and you will love all the extra energy that goes with it.

It is no secret that overweight people are always the first to fall off the statistical lifespan charts. It also is no secret, as already noted, that diets are hardly ever a legitimate solution. The best result a diet can produce is a temporarily thin person who believes that his or her natural condition is to be fat.

You see, everyone thinks they are overweight because they eat too much. Actually, it is the other way around. Everyone really eats too much to maintain an image they have of themselves as being overweight.

If you have a so-called weight problem, check and see if that is true for you. Then, examine what you believe to be the good things are about being fat. That's right. I said the good things about it. Say to yourself **'One of the good things about being overweight is...'** And finish the sentence with at least three different endings in your own words. Then you will know what some of the payoffs to your excess pounds are. When you weigh those payoffs against the personal, romantic and emotional costs of staying fat and then if you factor in all the years of life you are likely to lose, you may find that you will never have to consider dieting again. Instead, you simply will transform the image that you hold of yourself, which will immediately begin to transform the way you look.

You may have noticed that all of my concerns about the relationship between food intake and health and longevity involve only quantity and not quality.

I assert that a strongly positional preoccupation with 'health foods' and 'natural foods' is similar to the kind of belief that limits medical and healing skills exclusively to doctors. In both instances, external factors are arbitrarily given responsibility for your health. In both instances, you place yourself in a position of factually ungrounded and unnecessary vulnerability.

As related to food, artificial moral values are assigned and righteously proclaimed and defended. Good foods and bad foods show up at every turn instead of simply a wide variety of different types of things to eat for different reasons. Unfortunately, belief systems about morality issues tend to produce extremism. And in much the same way that many anti-war advocates are ready to kill for peace, a large number of health food proponents will clobber for cucumbers.

In reality, our bodies don't really much care what you feed them. When you have a particular need, you will soon find out what it is, especially if you and your body are in good communication. Often unfulfilled nutritional needs explain sudden midnight or midafternoon cravings for lettuce, camembert, meatballs, brown rice or M&Ms.

You can usually count on your body's miraculous ability to draw a sufficient level of life-sustaining nutrition from almost any edible substance. Over the years, my diet has wandered impulsively from McDonald's to macrobiotics while my health and vitality have remained extraordinarily high. I say, you are not what you eat; you are what you are. And you can be whatever you choose to be, as long as you are willing to commit yourself to creating the conditions that make it possible.

In addition to offering alternatives to many of the physical health issues that arise with aging, I want to deal with one final issue involving mental and emotional health and examine the widely feared, widely anticipated problem of senility.

On a superficial level, I do not consider senility as we commonly think of it to be a problem at all. Affecting less than five percent of the aging population, it is not nearly as widespread as we think it is. What is more, outwardly manifested senility symptoms usually tend to go away whenever there is the option of something more interesting to do.

It is on a deeper level that senility and everything that senility represents becomes worthy of consideration. On that level, it affects each one of us. Therefore a closer look will be well worthwhile.

I have already likened my view of the aging process to the procession of the seasons, in which each period of natural life on the planet evolves into the next in a peaceful orderly way, and the purpose and intent of each period is obvious and clearly observable.

In a similar manner, as our minds and bodies journey through life and time and space in physical form, a progression of appropriate and necessary functions are triggered into operation. These are like positive versions of the so-called biological timeclocks. Instead of shutting us down, they expand and nourish us. Because they promote and sustain health rather than diminishing it, accepting and participating in them on a belief level will enhance our health.

I assert that one of our most important seasonal periods of evolution and development spans the years from 60 to 75. A variety of mental and psychic accelerations occur that are intended to facilitate our movement from the late summer of life into the early fall, where at least 50 more years of active productivity are available.

The result of this major transformational shift is biologically designed to be similar to the growth and creative energy of adolescence, when each new day is filled with questions, preparations and learning

experiences that allow an entirely new personality to be
formed and to emerge.   But where adolescence and
transcendence into adulthood is supported and
encouraged, our next major transition into postadulthood
is all but totally blocked by belief systems that deny the
process and distort our experience of it.

Many of us are able to glimpse or intuit the
appropriateness and the underlying promise of
expansiveness which could lead to a period of potential
value as great as that of any other developmental stage.
Chronologically, it would represent a time of harvest and
fulfillment. But virtually all of us succumb, instead, to
prevailing beliefs that prevent or pervert any possibility
of crossing over to the next level of human awareness.

It is no wonder that our health fails during these
years as a direct result. Or that faced with a discouraging
absence of life-sustaining alternatives, we decide to shut
down, get sick, and die.

When this unusually rich and fertile time of breaking
free from the confines, structures and narrow focus of
our midadult existence occurs, there is a word we use to
describe our embryonic stages of expanded consciousness
and unfamiliar mental activity.

That word is 'senility'.

To the best of my knowledge, no one has yet
attempted to compare the subjective experiences of senile
people with representatives of other age groups who are
experimentally involved with altered or expanded states
of consciousness. One result of such research would
surely confirm that where younger people share their
enlightening new perceptions and sensations proudly and
are usually acknowledged positively by their friends,
older people suppress themselves for fear of senility
labeling, diagnostic tests or confinement.

What material is suppressed? All of the following.
And more.

Without the assistance of drugs, meditation, or self-
hypnosis techniques, waves and waves of new but latent
abilities are released from the creative right side of the
brain. When this occurs, each 60 to 75 year old individual
begins to see far beyond his or her previously-held ideas

about time, space, and separateness. Significant and illuminating insights are revealed and a variety of new experiences occur that cannot be recognized or communicated about from any previously existing conceptual base.

There is a shift of focus that would not be workable or even acceptable while holding down all the responsibilities and tasks of adult living. But because there is no system of beliefs to support this shift, our natural and innate inner physical and mental therapy resources cannot be activated to smooth out the period of transition and restore internal balance. Instead, drugs, tranquilizers and sedatives are given, which further mask or cover up the emerging clarity of what has already been labeled distorted vision. An event intended to result in a whole new cycle of creative accomplishment, celebration, and valuable new experiences is turned into a nightmare of uselessness, rejection, abandonment.

The playful, creative, explorative nature of advancing age is no secret. Comparisons with childhood are invariably made, but these are always stated negatively. Second childhood experiences ought to draw upon early childhood's wonderment, mysticism and unfettered sense of being tempered by the wisdom of adulthood. As you know, second childhood experiences never do.

You lose.

And humanity loses.

I will have more to say about exactly what it is that we lose and why you may not want to lose your share of it in the next chapter when I discuss the reemergence of physical desire and the regeneration of sexual capabilities. In addition, in Chapter 10, I will present many of the unusual perceptive shifts and new skills to watch for, and cover The Midlife Metamorphosis encountered during the years between 60 to 75 in greater detail.

For now, since what we lose relates directly to health, what I want you to know is that the results of selling out to beliefs that support a label called senility can be fatal as well as tragic.

It is a well-documented fact that whenever emotional or physical growth and expression are denied, suppressed or inhibited, symbolic and occasionally grotesque substitute forms of growth like ulcers, kidney stones and skin eruptions show up. Taking this one step further, I suggest that when the second growth cycle of postadulthood is thwarted , a direct linkage to cancer is formed and an intensified susceptibility to its effects results.

The vast quantity of energy released to propel an individual into the full potential of his or her prime of life demands a suitable form of release. When sexual, psychic, and other necessary avenues are closed and no legitimate outlet is permitted, all of that developmental energy remains convolutedly trapped inside, seeking actualization. The path of least physical resistance is found at the simplest of cellular levels where wild and uncontrollable cancerous patterns of growth appear.

And spread.

And spread. And spread and spread.

The vigorous physical and hormonal activity that was supposed to lead us to greater perceptive skills and wisdom unrestricted by adult standards of practicality leads us instead to suffering, pain and disaster.

Quite literally, it can be any way that you choose it to be. On every level and at every moment, your body is constantly creating and recreating itself. Unerringly following your direction like an advanced data processing system, it strives to achieve its ultimate form, renews itself wherever necessary, responds and reacts to your programming.

No matter what the present state of your health may be and no matter how much unconscious or unknowing harm you may have caused yourself in the past, it is important for you to now have alternatives.

It is equally important for you to begin to use them.

CHAPTER 8
THE SECOND TIME AROUND

Early one morning, little Sidney woke up and felt the first sweet forbidden sensations of sensuality.

The stirring and throbbing seemed to be centered in the small pee-pee thing he had between his legs, but a larger sense of excitement and adventure burned like liquid fire from his forehead down to his toes. It coursed through every vein and artery in his body, pushing sleepiness into the shadows, leaving only an exquisite sense of ecstasy in its place.

Sidney reached under the covers and touched himself. His shoulders and chest tingled beneath his fingers. His stomach shivered with an unknown anticipation. His buttocks and upper thighs were warm and alive, and felt a certain way they had never felt before. When his tiny hands grasped his rigid pulsating penis and closed tightly around it, he gasped loudly with joy.

Roused from dreams of homerun hitting and bowl after bowl of ice cream, Peter in the next bed woke up irritably and looked over. He didn't know exactly what Sydney was doing, but he knew that it wasn't normal to do whatever it was. So he began to chant the meanest thing he could think of, over and over. 'Hey, hey, Sidney's growing up! Hey, hey, Sidney's growing up! Hey, hey, Sidney's growing up!'

By the time that Sidney realized some kind of commotion was going on, several of the other boys had joined in and formed a chorus. 'Hey, hey, Sidney's growing up! Hey, hey, Sidney's growing up!'

Ecstasy abruptly turned into a more familiar mixture of fear, shame and guilt. Sidney's body now burned not with newly awakening lust but with embarrassment and dread. 'Oh God,' he cried to himself, 'Don't ever let me ever feel that terrible way again.'

It has always seemed wasteful that one of the most potentially valuable gifts we can give ourselves and those we care for is invariably so misused and misunderstood that it loses its joy and magic.

The gift is sexual pleasure or the art of creating ecstasy. And in its purest form, the gift is nothing more than a game with only one intrinsic rule: Any one, two, or more people can play so long as no one harms anyone else physically, emotionally or mentally.

All through life, we complicate that simple structure by adding rules, restrictions and expert opinions formed from dense, suppressive personal and cultural belief systems. The bottom-line result is we undermine our natural capacity to cause and to experience intense pleasure for no real reason at all.

Confused about what is right or wrong and stuck in a confining structure of religious, national or international, generational, parental and other generally mistaken ideas and thoughts about sex, we rush blindly back and forth between selfdenial and promiscuity. Given all that, on a cultural level, it should come as no surprise that we have produced some remarkably dangerous and deadly sexual diseases. At the same time, on an individual level, we have set things up so that sexual desire and the physical mechanisms for implementing it begin to shut down early in life and often disappear altogether before we reach 50 or 60 years of age.

The gift, misused and misdirected, goes away.

What you have just read is a short summary of more than 2000 years of civilized sexual history. You can readily observe the themes. They are played out all around you in movies, in television soaps, in novels, in locker rooms, in bed. And you can easily see how the effects of so much confusion on such a massive scale show up constantly in your own life.

For just a few moments, take out your belief list or notebook. (By now, if you are really into this, you may need a small notebook to hold all of your newly awakening thoughts and ideas.) Without pausing to analyze anything, jot down as many beliefs as you can about sex, sexuality, yourself as a sexual being, and your capacity to share yourself sexually with others.

Several interesting and useful things will show up. Not only will you begin to find notions that limit your sexual fulfillment and ability to enter into mutually rewarding relationships, you will probably also notice the incredibly large degree to which sexual issues are buried at the roots of all your relationships.

As part of this process, allow your imagination to run wild. In your mind, scan through a few of your favorite or most frightening sexual fantasies. If you don't have any or cannot think of one right now, make some up.

Pay particular attention to whatever emotions or feelings you discover as you read these instructions and as you view your fantasies. If you have any fixed ideas about what nice people should and should not do, you can expect to come up against them nose to nose. When you do, you will discover how much and in exactly what ways you manipulate other people and allow them to manipulate you, using sex as the big incentive and grand prize. As you watch your fantasies and become more aware of the beliefs that lie beneath them, you are also likely to see the actual workings of the internal machinery that runs all of your tensions, inhibitions and conflicts about sex.

This exercise is an ideal place to start. Whatever age you are right now, you can safely bet that you have something or other going on about sex. And there is only one thing you can do about it: Notice whatever it is and simply acknowledge it as what's so. As always, the one alternative you do not have is choosing not to accept that you feel the emotions you really feel, see things the way you uniquely see them, and have done what you have done. As you have seen, any pretense about any of these issues is deadening. And when the subject at hand is as highly charged and potentially enlivening as sex, the one thing you do not want to be is deadened.

You are already familiar with the consequences of avoiding these issues or of pretending you do not have any issues involving sex. Only, until now, you may not have thought of them as consequences because they seemed to be the simple and absolute facts of life.

These direct results of avoidance and pretense include such classic symptoms as a gradual falling off of desire, a loss of interest in making love, and a never-ending succession of short-term affairs with younger partners as an attempt to cover up the fear of losing interest and to avoid the depression associated with shutting down.

Moreover, since it is the nature of emotional issues to manifest themselves in physical form, the worst is yet to come. Women, after menopause, frequently begin to experience soreness, burning sensations and pain during sexual intercourse; many find they would rather avoid the whole thing than participate in an unpleasurable activity. Many men experience diminished ejaculatory capacity, less seminal fluid, more difficulty producing and maintaining an erection, and inability to have sex two or three times or more in a lovemaking session.

Those of the scientific, medical, and reportorial featurewriting communities agree that depressed sex drives in the 40s and 50s are linked to reduced estrogen production in women and a combination of declining testosterone and increasing prolactin production in men. For women, they say, it has been all downhill since 35 or so; for men, from the tender young age of 18.

Everyone agrees all that is true. But is it?

And even if it is true, would you care to venture a guess as to which came first? The declining hormone production? Or the declining sexual activity?

It might just be that a depressed sexual drive can be much more appropriately linked to depression. Period. And that the depression which commonly shows up between 40 and 50 can be directly linked to the hopeless feeling that it is all over and that no alternatives are possible. By now, I am certain you realize just how unlikely a possibility that is.

Alternatives have always been available.   In fact, many interesting and affirmative clues exist right in the Western civilized world's most widely read single book: the Bible.   Along with many of the premises responsible for creating sexual repression, alienation and disassociation in the first place are a few definitive clues about the way it may once have been sexually and the way it could be again.

Whether you view the Bible as fiction, truth, revelation, history or dogma, does not matter for the moment.   In the beginning, you will find some very unusual references on the subject of extended sexuality. Back in those early days, as you may recall, hardly anyone went forth and multiplied fruitfully until fairly late in life. Among the legendary longlivers of Genesis, Adam began to beget at 130, Seth at 105, Enos at 90, Jared at 162, Methuselah at 187, Lamech at 182, and Noah at 500.

With the shorter maximum life that followed the flood,   an unusual and notable phenomena occurred. Abram and his wife Sarai experienced a transformational rebirthing process and became Abraham and Sarah at the ages of 99 and 89.   Both were aged and barren, long past the other side of menopause, yet both experienced a profound regeneration of their physical capacities, fertility and desire for sex.   When Abraham was 100 and Sarah was 90, their first son, Isaac, was born.   Almost 40 years later, when Sarah died, Abraham remarried and had many other children before his death at 175.   This may have been the the first recorded case of reemerging and returning sexuality.   It is certainly not the last.

Throughout history, the dirty old man, the nasty old goat, the sexcrazed crone, the horny harpy, the orgiastic witch or warlock, and other immortal vampiric creatures and ageless goddesses who feed upon the vital body fluids of the young show up as recurring characterizations and symbols in folklore, fables, inquisitions and exposes.

All of them share certain fundamental attributes.

They are old, much older than you or I.   They are lustful and uninhibited, much more lustful and uninhibited than you and I.   They are immoral, scorned and feared, creatures of the dark side, and to take up their evil ways would surely damn or doom any decent, godfearing, shutdown, sexually repressed person like, for instance, you or I.

But whether fantasy, fact, or a combination of both, they all have two things that you and I don't seem to have. They have allowed some process of sexual regeneration to occur late in their lives. And they have wild, flamboyant, unabashed fun.

What is interesting to note is the extent to which we look upon that as being wrong. While I am in no way an advocate of the more unsavory sexual excesses and coercive tactics associated with many of these creatures of folktales and stories, I am definitely in favor of allowing my natural capacity for sexual regeneration to occur late in life. I think that fun is pretty good, too. As a conscious and well-considered choice, I am not willing to make those two things wrong because if I did, I would have to find some way to make sure I couldn't have any of them for myself.

All of the old myths and stories are pleasant ways to stretch the imagination. They are also useful tracking devices for determining the sources of current cultural symbols and themes. When the same characterizations keep appearing in the folklore of virtually every civilization and every country on the planet, even those separated by impassible barriers through which no ordinary communication could be possible, it begins to seem reasonable to assume a factual basis in reality for a common origin.

Is there evidence in the real world to support any of this? Maybe so.

All studies of the longlived peoples of the Hunza region of West Pakistan, the Vilcambambam region of Ecuador, the Soviet province of Georgia and the nearby Abkhasian region, and assorted life histories of other people over 100 years of age support the theory that sex is here to stay. In effect, it has a pattern that is as regular and incessant as the tides. Sexual awareness begins in early childhood, crests with puberty and the early childbearing years of young adulthood, fades briefly in a midlife period of transition, and returns again with renewed strength and vigor after 70.

Now you see it.

Now you don't.

Now you see it again. And again. And again.

The way it works follows a fundamental observation that is stated simply but eloquently at the end of every est training, a unique adventure in transformation that takes place over the course of two weekends and has had profound impact on the lives of more than 450,000 participants since its inception in the early 1970s. Everything you ever need to know about sex is boiled down to ten short words: When you're hot, you're hot; when you're not, you're not.

Apparently, the longer you live the truer that is.

It is worth noting that in addition to having active sex lives for more than one-and-a-quarter centuries, people in the world's isolated pockets of longevity are extremely tactile. They touch a lot. They hug. They stroke each other. They display affection openly and uninhibitedly. They ignore artificial social boundaries of gender and age. And they live a long long time.

Do they know something we don't know? Probably not. It is much more likely they don't know something that we do. Something, perhaps, having to do with our fear of rejection and judgments or our overriding commitment to avoid embarrassment at any cost.

Closer to home, there are two places to look for validation that extending your life includes extending your life as a sexual being. The laboratories of geriatric research. And the homes and institutions where many older people are sent to end their days.

All at once, the conclusions begin to appear almost painfully obvious.

Under laboratory conditions, rats and mice that live 50% to 100% longer lives than their born-free counterparts also keep reproducing and bearing young for a proportionally longer time. It seems reasonable to postulate that men and women who extend their lives to the maximum human potential or beyond could do the same.

Recent geriatric research suggests that as the average lifespan is extended, our physiological or functional ages will no longer match up with our pictures of how chronological age is supposed to look. The middle years will spread out to a large degree, so that a person with a 120 to 130 year life expectancy could have the same physical appearance, energy and sex drive at 80 that a person has today at 40.

Within this framework, even those scientists who support and defend the biological timeclock theory agree that menopausal and other hormone-related slowdowns would be postponed until much later in life. There is even speculation that child-bearing and family-raising functions might be postponed until 80 or 90 years of age. This may not be a radical new idea at all. It may simply be the beginning of official scientific acknowledgement of a long denied human possibility.

Just as interesting and perhaps even more relevant for all of us who are here today and unable or unwilling to wait for science to save us tomorrow are the records kept at residences claiming to specialize in the care of aging men and women.

Here, despite sedatives, restraints and other generally nonsupportive devices of that type, both the desire and the ability to perform sexually have returned to a surprising number of occupants. What is more, it has come back bigger, better and more powerfully than ever. With no known exceptions, the authorities don't like it at all. They wish it would go away. They try to make it go away. But it doesn't go away.

Thwarted, subverted, suppressed by outside forces as well as denied and misunderstood from within, just when everyone thought it was safe to go back to bed again, Sex II rears its disturbing head.

Older people who experience this sexual reawakening most completely are usually labeled senile and unmanageable. Actually, they are neither. What they are is unexpectedly engaged in a process of evolutionary change and biological growth that includes new and sudden bursts of sexual energy for which there are no outlets. In addition, they are confused and upset.

As part of the transformational package, they discover that they are losing what they consider to be their time-tested conventional sexual roles.

Almost all of us have noticed that people become less markedly differentiated as male or female and more androgynous as they age. However, we attribute this shift of physical characteristics to 'second childhood' and the fading out of sexuality. With convenient labels like these and inner pictures of sexless childlike beings to fall back on, we fail to grasp the true nature of the metamorphosis that is attempting to occur. Hardly anyone ever discusses this particular facet of the so-called change of life. Perhaps hardly anyone realizes what it is or knows how to communicate about it.

Nonetheless, from dimly remembered traditions of ancient Egypt in which a true balance of power was achieved by the joint rulership of male and female pharaohs to contemporary therapies like polarity balancing, acupuncture and kinesiology in which positive and negative body points and meridian lines are activated to promote better health, the dual nature inherent in men and women has been observed and utilized.

Carl Jung, one of the early pioneers in psychotherapy, wrote at length about the phenomena. In every man, he hypothesized, there exists an internal female essence called the anima, whose purpose is to counterbalance the dominant external male characteristics. Similarly, in every woman, an internal male essence called the animus can be found.

A constant tug of war is enacted throughout much of life to maintain equilibrium between these two complementary but not always harmonious forces. Thus, you find many commonly accepted contradictions. There are men who pretend to be strong and forceful when they are actually romantic softies at heart. There are women who practice coy feminine wiles when, in reality, they are powerful and dynamic leaders. There are ongoing 'battles between the sexes' in which the only enemy is ourselves. And there are hundreds of variations in between. Including your own particular one.

In issues about love and sex, each of us is most

158 Alternatives To Aging

compulsively attracted to the person who most closely mirrors our internalized opposite essence at any given stage in our ongoing process of personal evolution. We seek our anima or animus in externalized physical form. So, if you ever wondered why you are drawn to a certain type of lover, the answer is inside of you.

When I first caught on to this idea, I began to communicate with my anima on an active and continuous basis using a series of combined Gestalt-like dialogues and meditations that I devised for the purpose. The experience opened me fully to my androgynous male/female nature and forever freed me from having to live up to any stereotypic patterns of manliness. No longer finding it necessary to prove anything about myself to anyone, I discovered that I could relax and enjoy my relationships as a much more gentle, sensitive, vulnerable person than I had ever been before. Jennifer, my anima, and I have been conferring and collaborating successfully ever since.

A more lengthy discussion about the nature of androgyny and practical uses of your anima/animus is beyond the scope of this book. Indeed, it could provide the basis for a whole new guide to enhanced and enlightened sexuality. However, once again, a familiar and recurring theme reappears:

> Whenever I accept and acknowledge
> that which I may fear
> or question the most about myself,
> I can release the best that is within me.
> Moreover,
> whenever I focus my attention on
> my deeds and my results instead of on myself,
> I can produce
> the best I am capable of producing
> in any given period of time.

This is particularly true and becomes more necessary to remember than ever as we reach the period of our Midlife Metamorphosis between 60 and 75 years of age.

As I pointed out in Chapter 7 and will further expand upon in Chapter 10, when this vital shift of behavioral patterns at the chronological midpoint of our maximum potential life occurs, we complete the process of separation and individuation that marked our early years. In its place, we begin a process of reintegration and experience ourselves as being basic parts of everything that exists. Participating in this process expands our growth and development as individuals; denying or disowning it depresses our lifeforce and shuts us down.

Reawakened sexuality on powerful physical and emotional levels is a natural and appropriate expression of this voyage into the second half of our lives. It is intended to dissolve the labels of strictly male and strictly female that separate you from me and us from them, and to open up our experience of the true balanced nature of our beings. Strength can merge itself with gentleness, power and protectiveness with vulnerability, aggressiveness with the capacity to be tender and loving.

Let there be no misunderstanding. The labels that support separateness and individuation are not wrong. They are extremely useful conceptualizations that arise from an essential period of our development and that make growth and movement possible. Just as you cannot love another person until you first love yourself, you cannot enjoy the sense of yourself as an integral part of everything there is until you can first stand alone on your own two feet and enjoy the sense of personal satisfaction that goes with self sufficiency and responsible individuality.

Once again, there are seasons of experience that mirror the seasons of each passing year. Each has its own purpose and place in the mastery of life. Each provides a transitional passageway to the season that follows and cannot be made into a fixed place to set up a permanent residence.

The primary alternative that is activated here is this: Go with the flowing nature of your own experience. When you sense a time of sexual reawakening or the period of temporary sexual shutdown that may precede it, observe what is occurring on as purely an experiential

level as you can.   Be there for it in a role of active
participation. Suspend all noticeable belief patterns that
could block the process of personal transformation.
Trust the integrity of your being to keep you on paths
that are appropriate as well as expansive. Communicate
fully with friends and loved ones, sharing your
observations, needs and conclusions as completely and
caringly as you can. And remember that you have the
opportunity to choose between allowing this period to
become the middle of your life or the end of it.

While all this is going on, there are a few additional
alternatives that you can explore playfully and
adventurously. While they are not likely to make any
difference by and of themselves, they can certainly give
you physical and psychological support on a belief-system
level and become externalized gestures for facilitating
and reinforcing your creative process of new sexual
growth and development. They can also be fun to do.

First of all, you can step up your daily intake of
antioxidation supplements like Vitamins A, C and E and
the minerals zinc and selenium.   These will help you
maintain your physiological functions at an optimum
level.

For mental support, particularly as an
antidepressant over short periods of time, you can take
up to 1.5 grams of L-Phenylalanine daily. Reduce your
dosage if you notice headaches, irritability or insomnia.
And if you have high blood pressure that you have not
yet handled, start with no more than 100 milligrams a
day, monitor your blood pressure regularly and increase
your dose gradually.   If in doubt, confer with your
medical support team.

To simulate and also stimulate the pleasure and
tingling flush of sexual excitation, all you need is a little
imagination and as little as 100 milligrams of niacin
(Vitamin B3) on an empty stomach. Taken five or ten
minutes or so before making love, it is a high that also
offers highly beneficial side effects. Niacin can focus your
ability to relax yourself, widen your blood vessels, and
reduce serum cholesterol and other lipids.

Ginseng is another substance that reinforces your

intentionality to increase your sexual endurance and activity levels and stimulate the rest of your metabolism at the same time. Laboratory mice swim twice as long in ten-gallon tank tests when they are given ginseng regularly. Russian athletes can run a three kilometer race an average of 53 seconds faster on genseng than they can off of it.

Despite modern applications such as these, ginseng is an ancient herb. Both its root and leaves were used by Amerinds, classical Greeks and thousands of generations of Chinese people who knew about the magical sexually-restorative properties of ginseng and used it regularly. Try some in pill, tablet, powder or tea form, and see how it works for you.

If you really like the idea of using external agents to trigger internal change and if you have a sense of humor as well as a desire for sexual revitalization, you might also try shunamitism. It is an another ancient process that has somehow survived time's round file. In fact, King David and King Solomon of biblical fame, both of whom were known for their many wives, indulged in it frequently.

Openly used today in many of the more so-called uncivilized places including those inhabited by longlived people and secretly practiced where you might least expect it, shunamitism consists of sleeping with a young person of the opposite sex. A virgin is preferable, if one can be found. You lie together, face to face, in a nonsexual embrace. All night long, the older person inhales and absorbs the breath exhalation and body heat of the younger one. Later, he or she experiences the effects of sexual rejuvenation.

Equally ancient and long surviving, but designed to work from within, is the oriental discipline of Taoism.

Practitioners believe their supply of vital bodily fluids is limited and that to ejaculate externally during orgasm depletes their reservoir of sexual vitality and physical energy and shortens their lives.

Instead of ejaculating, they practice a highly controlled technique that internalizes the experience of orgasmic pleasure and sends orgasmic fluids on an internal path from the sexual organs to the brain. As orgasmic energy travels upward through channels on either side of the spine, it passes through each of the major energy centers of the body, recharging and strengthening the entire system.

Both western and eastern Taoists claim to have extraordinary sexual endurance, an excess of creative energy and unusually long lifespans. Traditionally, Taoist practitioners are men, and in China records of Taoists who have outlived a succession of five to ten wives are commonplace. However, I see no reason why the technique of charging the body with internalized orgasmic energy could not also be used by women.

I have practiced Taoism off and on for reasonably long periods of time, but in spite of its benefits I don't stay with it. With an internalized ejaculation, instead of experiencing the release of sleep-producing hormones that has followed the male orgasm since the dawn of time, I feel more creative stimulation and more highly charged up. I also can continue to make love for astonishingly long periods without needing to rest.

At the same time, I reject the notion of scarcity implicit in the notion that a person's vital bodily fluids are in short supply or that only a fixed amount of them or anything else for that matter is available. So the techniques are useful to me when I choose to draw on them but I have no philosophical anchor to hold me to the discipline itself.

When I used to teach yoga, I was acquainted with other yoga instructors who could argue vehemently for or against Taoism for days and days without stopping even to make love and practice it. To each his or her own.

Last on the list of sex-related subjects to explore for the purpose of preparing for or reinforcing the process of sexual regeneration and metamorphosis is an alternative to the widely-held belief that 'if you don't use it, you lose it'.

If that sounds at all as if it might be one of your beliefs, acknowledge it now. And pay attention.

It is just not so. Unless you say that it is.

At the same time, I suggest the reason we have bodies with built-in sexual organs is to experience the enjoyment of using them. I recommend regular sex for the same reasons I recommend regular exercise of any kind. In some basic, highly nurturing way, it is richly satisfying and extremely good for us because it keeps us constantly in touch with our powers of self awareness and self realization.

Even during unfortunate times when an appropriate partner is not available or you are alone for any reason, you do not have to give up your sexual nature. Not now. Not at any age. Not ever.

I invite you to take a moment to scan whatever beliefs you have acquired about masturbation. Run them by, noticing where they may have come from and when you may have decided to make them your own. Then be willing, for however long a period you choose, to suspend them all and to discover what you really feel like. Touch yourself. Caress yourself. Drive yourself wild. Without guilt or fear of judgment, condemnation or recriminations of any kind. And find out whether that kind of pleasure is permissible or not.

Masturbation is actually one of the nicest presents you can give yourself. If you don't know why that is true, take the time to discover why. Really, how can anything that is called 'playing with yourself' be bad for you?

There you have a variety of interesting new things to consider. What works in each of these instances, I assert again, is not the external idea, technique or substance itself no matter how reasonable or how outrageous it may appear to be. What works is the willingness of your body to respond to anything that supports its own natural processes.

Every body wants to bypass artificially imposed commands to shut down and close up shop. All anybody has ever needed to be able to do that are a few well-chosen alternatives.

CHAPTER 9

A COMMITMENT TO LIVING

Tommy, Teddy and Timmy all woke up one morning within five minutes of each other. The sun was shining brightly and it was well past ten, according to the hands on the Murray Mouse clock. In their younger days, they remembered everyone always wished that they could sleep as late as they wanted. Now that they could, it somehow didn't seem as good as they thought it would.

After a leisurely breakfast, they went out together to sit on the senior children's benches where they could watch all the younger kids play.

They sat and watched an exciting game of Capture The Flag and remembered how much fun it used to be to play it. They sat and watched King Of The Mountain and thought about how grand it once was to try and hold on to the king position at the top of the play pile. They sat and watched the smaller children as they went inside for lunch and a nap. They sat and watched them come out again for an afternoon swim in the little round pool.

Then they sat and watched them go back inside again for dinner and bedtime stories on the vidscreens. Wordlessly, they held on tightly to their memories.

When it began to get dark, they got up and went back inside. They helped themselves to some dinner from the leftovers that had been brought over. And then they went to bed.

Tommy, Teddy and Timmy woke up the next morning within five minutes of each other. The sun was shining brightly and it was well past ten, according to the hands on the Murray Mouse clock. In their younger days, they remembered everyone always wished that they could sleep as late as they wanted. Now that they could, it somehow didn't seem as good as they thought it would. But there was nothing they could do about it.

Since each of them was more than twelve years old and well over the hill, there was nothing they could do at all.

There is an unfortunate and widely prevalent view about the way things are in the world today that stems from a belief pattern known as 'This Is Not It'.

In its most extreme version, it takes the form that life is a vale of tears and suffering. If we grit our teeth and bear it patiently, and if we do not succumb to forces of badness that may be lurking here and there to tempt us away from our misery, we will die someday and go to heaven. And that will be wonderful.

In its more common everyday version, it goes like this: Imagine that you are a little child playing with your toys and suddenly you get a funny left-out feeling. Someday, you tell yourself, you will be older and go to school on the yellow schoolbus like the big kids and maybe then everything will get better. Time passes. You go to school on the yellow schoolbus like the big kids, only it is not as good as you thought it would be. Something is still missing. Oh well, you sigh, someday you will go to high school and drink and smoke and go out on dates and then everything will be terrific. Time passes. You go to high school and drink and smoke and go out on dates, but it is not as terrific as you thought it would be. Someday though, you will go to college and have a car and fool around and learn interesting stuff and that will be incredible. Time passes. You go to college and get a car and fool around and learn interesting stuff, but even that is not so incredible after all. It's a good thing that someday you will graduate and get a job and make money because then everything will finally get better once and for all. Time passes. The job isn't quite it either. Neither is the money; it's not enough money. Getting married isn't it. Or raising a family. Or buying a house and then buying a bigger house and then buying an even bigger house with two cars, a swimming pool and membership at The Club. But just wait. Someday you will retire and do nothing but take it easy and have fun. Then, for sure, everything will finally be better.

Guess what?

Retirement is not it either. Moreover, it probably could never be as good as anyone hopes because its real purpose is not to provide the ultimate cure for lifelong dissatisfaction.

The whole idea behind retirement is this: Somebody younger than you are thinks that you are too old to hold down the job you have, that you are out of date and out of touch, that someone younger can do whatever you do better than you can, so it is time to turn you out to pasture with the other old nags and has-beens.

If you have any question about whether or not that could possibly be true, remember that just as you reach the customary age of retirement, you are standing on the brink of a major period of growth and acceleration. According to even the most conservative present-day longevity research, you are at the potential midpoint of your life. And you are poised at the threshold of a creative new cycle. You can enter and enjoy it with renewed strength, vigor, vitality, health and enormously productive capacities if you so choose. Or you can pass it by and dejectedly fade away.

The first option requires work.

Virtually none of the many 100 to 140 year old people in the scattered longlived communities around the world have ever stopped, dropped out or bought condos in the Sun Belt. They continue to work all day in fields, in villages, in their local equivalents of childcare centers. It is interesting to note that the way they work is like a joyful celebration of life. Their physical movement is slow, graceful and deliberate, resembling a naturally aerobic, yoga-like process of coordinated breathing, bending, lifting, stretching. It is not what they do, it's the way they do it that produces all the benefits.

In our western civilization, bucking all trends of the past, the entire issue about retirement can be summed up in just one word.

Don't.

Don't do it.   Don't even consider doing it. Consider, instead, your alternatives.

Maybe you think you don't have any alternatives. Especially not at your age.   Notice what an illuminating thought or belief that is.   Then notice the facts.   Your company is set up the way it is. It has retirement policies, retirement rules, retirement programs.   You can't change any of that.   Therefore, one thing is clear.   Staying with your company is definitely not one of your alternatives. In fact, if your work is too comfortable, too unchallenging and too quiet or boring, you may have stayed there too long already.   So just take the retirement money and run.

Where can you run?   At 55, 60 or 65?

Lots of places.   You will soon see quite a few of them.   But I suggest that you start by looking first at some of the places to which you may not want to run.

Close your eyes for the next minute or two.   And imagine that for the next 75 years you will do nothing at all. That's right. Nothing. For 75 years it will be exactly the way it is now as you sit with your eyes closed doing nothing.   Maybe every so often just to break up the monotony you will eat, sleep, sit on a bench in the sun, go to the bathroom, play golf, fish, take up bridge or canasta, visit your family, or read the obituaries.   Really get into what all that would be like for you.   See yourself doing the same things that retired people are supposed to do.   Now see yourself doing those same things over and over, over and over, every day for three-quarters of a century.

Perhaps you were wondering why, if the potential maximum lifespan is 120 to 140 years, more people don't live that long.   Now you know.   Within the framework as it is currently set up, there just is not a whole lot to live for.

Naturally, there are alternatives to that framework. All you need to know is where to look for them.

Here's where:

Find a clean piece of paper or turn to a new page in your notebook. Stare at the blank piece of paper as you begin to think of all of your physical and intellectual abilities, your specialized training and knowhow, your unique gifts and talents. Then write them down. Write down as many as you can.

Also list any impulses you can remember ever having about involving yourself in any kind of activity whatsoever. Also list all the things you always wanted to do but never had time for. These might include piano playing, going back to school, photography, breeding cats or horses or flowers, learning to read tarot cards, tap dancing, painting, poetry writing, really getting rich, remarrying or exploring alternative forms of relationship, whatever comes to mind.

When your list is complete, look it over carefully. It is something very special, something to be valued.

What you have before you is a useful guide to the possibilities from which you can choose what to do next in life. You will find that any direction you choose to follow is wide open and completely accessible right now. And that any of the items on your list, when pursued, will open up considerably more possibilities for other paths to follow even further down the line.

During the early adulthood years of our lives, we become too fixed, too focused, too singlemindedly driven down the one path we then consider to be our one and only answer. We become singularized entities and identify ourselves completely with whatever label we attach to our one area of specialization. Instead of simply being an open field of possibilities, we limit ourselves to being a doctor, a lawyer, a housewife, a computer technician, a factory worker, a receptionist, or whatever the case may be. In doing so, we block out all of our other choices. From now on, you may not want to do that anymore.

Perhaps the only good thing about the notion of retirement is that it forces us out into the world of alternatives once again. Now that you are beginning to discover what some of your alternatives may be, here is how to organize them into a more usable form.

Take out six to eight blank pieces of paper. At the top of each one, write a heading that identifies each of the decades of the rest of your life. If you are approaching 60 years of age, your headings would look like this:

60 TO   70.
70 TO   80.
80 TO   90.
90 TO 100.
100 TO 110.
110 TO 120.
120 TO 130.
130 TO 140.

When all of your headings are written down, take out the list of possible things to do that you just completed. For each upcoming decade, write down at least one major goal that you intend to accomplish professionally and as many hobbies or secondary interests as you like. Later in this chapter, I will discuss involvement in transformative areas and personal causes like ending hunger, saving whales and porpoises, eliminating the threat of nuclear arms, safeguarding the environment of the planet for future generations of humans and other endangered species, or whatever other worldwide issue you choose to see handled or corrected during your lifetime. You will probably want to refer to your list of decade-by-decade goals again at that point.

I recommend that you carry your list of goals in your briefcase, shoulder bag or pocket. Or that you tape it to your bedroom mirror or place it under your pillow. This will remind you to keep part of your focus and attention goal-directed every day, which will energize the process of bringing each choice into being so you can enjoy the results. I also recommend, at this point, that you consider the goals of each decade to be a list of promises rather than a list of tasks or items to do. Promises have power; tasks and other interesting items to try do not. There is a staggering amount of difference between the two.

The main thing to remember about goals is they are simply an excuse or a reason to keep playing the game. Think of any game. Take, for instance, basketball. Ten grown men bounce a large orange ball back and forth across a wooden floor and throw it at metal hoops mounted to plastic boards over their heads. They get sweaty. And tired. And angry. And enthusiastic. And occasionally violent. And they are very very serious about it all. They train long hours so that they can play with skill and excellence. They play hard, put 100% of themselves on the line for the entire period of the game, and generally have a great time. Why are they doing it and what are they after?

That's right. Just one thing. Goals.

Without goals, basketball would be a stupid and pointless waste of time and energy. So would hockey and football. So would life.

Keep that in mind and you can avoid the biggest trap of all about goals: The mistake of believing that any goal is a solution to life instead of just another good reason for living. The trap closes tightly on your leg every time you think that what you have isn't good enough yet and will not be sufficient until you attain the goal you came up with to make your game interesting. You can tell whenever that is happening because you will catch yourself saying or thinking 'When I get (whatever that goal is), then I'll be happy.' You can also tell because the goal trap has very sharp, very painful steel jaws and you will be walking around feeling upset and hurt all the time.

Goals are not supposed to upset or hurt you. Designed solely as excuses for the game or reasons to get out and play, they are supposed to be enlivening, stimulating and fun. It is up to you to keep them that way.

In the most basic sense, any goal is a commitment either to yourself or to others. You give your word, implicitly or explicitly, that something will be done. Then, either you keep your word by doing what you said or you do not keep your word and you don't do what you said. It sounds simple that way, doesn't it? But one of the complications is that a commitment is a promise. And as you may already have noticed, we attach a lot of beliefs to promises. We do not give them lightly or easily because we fear the consequences of breaking them.

Why do we fear that? And why do we let that fear hold us back from making commitments that could produce miracles all around us?

I don't know why. It is another one of those characteristic patterns of behavior that makes no sense to me at all. We are all creatures of truly high integrity and at the same time, we are all human. This means it is inevitable that sometimes we will make promises that we cannot or do not keep. If we count on that to be the way it is, here is what happens.

I make a commitment to you that I will see to it that something will be done. I make that commitment with the full intention of doing what I said. Then, either I actually do it or I don't. If I do it, all is well and good. If I don't, what I must do instead is acknowledge to you that I did not keep my word; then, I can either revoke my promise and take it back or correct whatever went wrong and recommit myself to completing it.

Either way, that part of the game is then over, and the gameboard or videoscreen is reset for the next game or next playing period.

If we could only keep it on that simple a level, life would be as light and clean as soap bubbles riding a gentle breeze.

Instead, we get caught up in defending ourselves, justifying our broken words, blaming other people or external circumstances for our failures, and deciding never never to make the mistake of making a commitment to anything else.

You hear it all the time.

'I'm late because of the traffic.' Not simply 'I'm late.'

'The accident wasn't my fault.' Not simply 'I was there at the time and involved in it, so it is clear that I had something to do with it.'

'The devil made me do it.' Not candidly 'I am responsible for what happened. Now how can I clean up the mess?'

Where commitments and promises are concerned, whether they are between two or more people or strictly to ourselves, only two forms of behavior are appropriate. Either you acknowledge me for keeping my word when I have kept it. Or you acknowledge that I have not kept my word and you support me to revoke my promise or to push myself past the point where I shut down, to renew my commitment, and to get out and keep my word after all.

In both cases, the word of the person who commits or promises is treated with honor and respect. The person who gives his or her word is held fully accountable for keeping it within a specific period of time and invited to take responsibility for delivering the goods or for changing, modifying or canceling the promise or commitment whenever that time is up.

Notice how there is no wrongmaking, no namecalling, no emotional warfare, and no guilt producing behavior involved. All loose ends are tied up on the spot. Nothing is left written on some imaginary balance sheet and carried over into the dim and distant future. On rare occasions when the expression of strong feelings will forward the action, even they may be communicated with authenticity and discharged immediately.

Like this:

'Hey! I did it. Everything's all finished!'

'Oh boy! You really did. I am just delighted! You are truly powerful and magnificent.'

Or this:

'Well, I didn't get it done and time has run out. I feel that I've let you down.'

'Yes, you have, although that has nothing to do with the issue. I am disappointed and angry because I was counting on having that part of the project ready before my meeting with Pamela. What do you intend to do about it now? Are you still willing to keep your promise and set up a new time schedule or would you rather revoke your promise all together.'

As you can see, everything is handled in a manner that is clear and absolutely straightforward. An environment of this kind is a very high space to be in. Everyone is more willing to put themselves on the line. Productivity flourishes. Creative results show up at every turn. And things get done at an astonishing rate.

Still another way to look at commitment is to realize that it is considerably larger than the act of doing anything. It is the nature of a commitment to transcend whatever the thing is that you are committing yourself to do. In effect, it is a place to come from instead of a thing to do.

Things to do are burdensome. They take time and effort. They get heavy and make you feel tired and drained. As places to come from, commitments are nothing like that. In fact, whatever you may have thought a commitment was until now is probably not really a commitment at all.

A commitment, in fundamental terms, can be defined as a context or a way to hold circumstances. What circumstances? All of the circumstances that surround you. This means, a commitment holds a targeted goal with all the solid structural support of a box or a bowl. It also holds all the ways there are to achieve that goal and every possible obstacle, problem or consideration about it as well.

When viewed only as something to do, a commitment invariably involves pushing your way through or doggedly wearing down all opposition until you succeed. Viewed as a context, however, a commitment can have no opposition because it is the structure that contains the opposition along with every other possible attitude, position and point of view. Everything exists in it. And everything, including doubt and negativity, becomes as much an expression of commitment as the commitment itself.

Within the contextual framework of a commitment, all the considerations and obstacles can get handled. The power of your word creates a shift in the pattern of life in which everything turns around. Whatever did not work before suddenly begins to become workable. It is truly a magic place to come from and well within your reach any time.

How do you create a commitment as context? Simply by sticking your neck out and saying so. You see, only the act of taking a stand and giving your word about it can make it real.

A Commitment To Living 175

All of the following are commitments in contextual form:

- I will pay you back by next Thursday.
- By next July, I will have a $75,000 dollar-a-year job at CBS.
- I will meet you at The Lucky Dragon for lunch at 12:30.
- I will have it done by the time you get back.

All of the following are good ideas and possible things to do:

- I'll try to pay you back by sometime next week.
- I've just got to get a better job and make more money.
- I'll see if I can meet you for lunch by 12:30 or 1:00 or so.
- Don't worry, I think I can get to it today.

All of the difference between the two is in the language used to express yourself. In fact, languaging is what the art of giving your word is all about. Your word is language. So whether your word flies into existence powerfully and absolutely or weakly and conditionally is up to you.

The act of taking a stand through the language you choose to express that stand is one of the most awesome acts of creation in the universe. It is the only consistently available way to express who you really are and then to make the most of it. And it is the only possible way to break through to your next level of development.

Here is how and why it works.

Each time that you take a stand, you become the stand that you take. The context that you create holds literally everything that you are. Including all of your body sensations, your emotions, your thoughts, your beliefs, your attitudes and positions, your judgments, your evaluations, your circumstances, your talents and abilities, your memories, your images of the past and your fantasies about the future.

All that and more is held within the context of the commitments you make. This means: You can be afraid to commit yourself and you can bring that fear into your commitment with you. You can be busy and bring your busyness along. You can be doubtful, angry, bored, immobilized, overly enthusiastic, resisting, skeptical, or uncertain about the outcome. And, as a contextual space, each of your commitments has room enough to hold all of that along with all of the courage and vision required to be willing to make a commitment in the first place.

As you age, particularly as you find yourself seeking active alternatives to retiring and shutting down, the stands you take through the language that you choose to use will become the most important tools you have for building your future.

So far, we have been looking only at commitment to personal goals. It is extremely important never to lose sight of these. Everything you are, everything you do and everything you have begins at the level of self. Ultimately everything ends there as well, for that is where all of your chickens or your eagles will come home to roost. It is in-between that you can discover a lot of room for expansion. And what expands, of course, is yourself.

Take a moment to look inside and ask yourself: What is your dream? What is your vision for life on the planet Earth? If there was one idea or one ideal to which you could commit yourself, what would it be? Can you find the one serious blind spot in your neighborhood, your city, or your world that irks, saddens or enrages you so much that you would dearly love to illuminate and transform it?

Perhaps you would like to clean up all the trash and litter in the streets. Or put an end to the threat of rape. Or handle rush-hour traffic in a more civilized way. Or reestablish midwifery. Or remove graffiti from subway trains. Or eradicate the threat of war and nuclear destruction. Or put a stop to starvation on a countrywide or worldwide level. Or wipe out a certain disease. Or extend human life to its maximum attainable limits. Or preserve what is left of our natural resources and wildlife so future generations will be able to enjoy seals, elephants, fir trees, butterflies and wildflowers too.

There is an endless number of things to be done in the world, all in the name of life. Any one of them is larger than the confines of your own personal living space and your active involvement could well become a legitimate alternative to the quiet desperation and despondency associated with aging.

When each of us keeps asking 'What can I do?', we discover that we are all in alignment that something must be done. Whatever each of us specifically chooses to do then comes out of the context called 'What Must Be Done . This context expresses itself by producing measurable results and by your personal commitment to get a specific job done. At this level, who we really are is what makes the difference. So anything or everything we do makes a difference regardless of what it may be.

Can you make a difference? Can little you really have any noticeable impact at all on such a widespread far-reaching scale?

It all depends. It particularly depends on where you are coming from, how you choose to express your own good intentions and great expectations, and how hard you are willing to play.

Once, I used to think that becoming involved in any remote cause or burning issue outside of myself would require a large dose of self sacrifice. Actually, that could never be the case. Sacrifice is only possible when you believe that existing conditions are inevitable and that if anything could have changed, it certainly would have changed by now. From such a ground of being, all you can hope to see is that everything is stuck in place, no one can do anything about it, and even to try would only be a waste of time or other resources.

This is a very common point of view, by the way. It shows up whenever you attempt to take on an issue from its middle or from the point that you are already enmeshed within it.

You have to start fresh, using the stand you take by expressing your commitment as the point of embarkation. When you start at the beginning, your stand becomes the first step of the solution, and you can see resolution at every turn. When you try to start in the middle, all you can experience is the helplessness of getting stuck in the quicksand of something you already see as a problem. If you happen to be unusually perceptive, you may also notice that you are the one who is calling it a problem and that you are labeling it, defining it, and otherwise limiting it. If you were to call it an opportunity instead, just imagine how much space for action would open up.

It is always the fundamental positional belief that something is unworkable that keeps whatever you happen to be calling a problem locked in place.

Whenever you do not start at the beginning of an issue that needs to be handled, nothing works. What is even worse, anything you try to do about whatever has become unworkable won't work either.

Everything gets to be hopelessly frustrating. You find that you cannot make a difference. All you can do is make a gesture. Gestures are dehumanizing admissions that the problem is too big to solve but too horrible to be ignored. You have to do something. So you halfheartedly give up some time or some money and, as a compromise, you sacrifice them to the cause.

When you are participating in the physical manifestation of a personal dream or vision at a contextual level, it is not like that at all. What you are doing does not involve giving up anything. It involves only the act of expressing yourself on a transformed level of being. And whether you become transformed early in life by studying a discipline, meditating, attending a consciousness training or whether you just naturally grow into it when you turn 55 or 60 or 70, you now need to take that transformation out into the world and begin to express it actively.

Only active expression of your self can reinforce your process of personal transformation and make further growth and expansion possible. Not to do that, at this point in your life, actually holds back and diminishes the self, which can be looked upon as the ultimate form of self sacrifice.

Look at it this way. When you are an expression of your own transformation and you are choosing to share yourself on increasingly larger levels of reality, no sacrifice is involved because you have nothing to lose. In fact, if you are not literally getting more out of your participation than you are putting into it, you have a reliable indicator that you are in the wrong place. And you had better move on to another vision or another setting in which to express yourself and bring your vision forth.

You may be wondering where you will find the energy to participate in a major venture when you can barely drag yourself through the day as it is. Do you still believe in scarcity? Scarcity of anything? Including energy? Check around inside yourself and see.

Life possesses an exuberance that knows no boundaries and no limits. When you encourage and nurture your exuberance, vast supplies of energy are generated that are not ordinarily required in day-to-day living. This energy can be directed to other places in the world that may need it or it can be brought along with you to activities in which you would like to be involved.

Thus far, we have looked primarily at the problematic side of beliefs and thoughts. There is also a positive side that is rarely utilized. Clear, precisely focused thoughts and beliefs have a unique kind of strength and power. They can literally create events, not only on the personal levels that I have already discussed but globally as well. In case you are doubtful that thoughts and beliefs can produce anything as large as, say, world peace, ask yourself what it is that starts wars in the first place.

The same principles that produce our personal realities and practical experiences also produce positive or negative external conditions. Whenever you create a personal shift through a stand that you take and share the results outside of yourself, world conditions can also shift.

The whole idea is to plant yourself firmly in your own reality by being who you are, seeing what you see, knowing what you know, feeling what you feel, wanting

what you want.   And promising what you promise
independently of the rest of all that.   Acknowledge and
encourage your strength and vitality.   And then use your
strength and vitality to empower other people to
empower still more other people in everwidening circles
around you.   From this self-generated power base,
remember constantly to keep checking and validating the
stands that you take.   Watch for signs of righteousness
and wrongmaking.   Without them, there could be no
wars or conflicts of any kind.

Remember also that there is an immeasurable
distance between taking a stand to transform an external
condition and opposing something, rebelling, or otherwise
coming out against it.

When you take a stand, as you have already seen,
you create a context in which everything can be held and
used in a way that works to produce your desired result.
You operate independently of the circumstances involved,
and you are the complete cause in the matter.

When you come out against anything, whether war,
disease or cruelty to animals, you are merely one side of
the issue instead of a space in which all of the sides can be
held in totality.   Taking any side, for or against, always
creates the opposite side.   The opposition meets the
attack with a point of view that may be just as justifiable
and defensible as your own.   Everything quickly
degenerates into an angry struggle.   It is you against
them instead of you and them collaborating together to
get everything handled.   You are acting only in response,
or reacting.   If the condition were not there to begin with,
you would not be there either.   Instead of being the
causal agent and in complete control, you are at the effect
of external circumstances and therefore you are at the
effect of external circumstances and therefore you are
powerless.

Notice once again the power of the language you
use to set up your involvement and participation.   'I
commit myself to putting an end to the threat of nuclear
war on this planet by the end of the century' creates a
playing field that has infinitely more possibilities than
'Let's go get those lousy militarists and show them what

irresponsible creeps they are'.

After you choose a personal vision to be committed to and you set out to make your commitment real in the world, you may become interested either in forming or joining a group of similarly committed individuals.

Being primarily a do-it-yourselfer at heart, I used to be very strongly opposed to groups. I could see, with a lot of justification, that as an individual I had 100% of the vote all locked up. In a group of two, I would have to give up half of it, so I would have only a 50% vote. And in a group of ten, my vote would account for only 10% of the total. I could not imagine giving up control to that degree, much less becoming involved in even larger groups where my vote might count for only .001% or less. It did not seem worth it.

What I did not know then that I know now was this: All group dynamics are definitely not the same. Groups are either in agreement or they are in alignment.

Agreement means that everyone in the group is going in the same direction. As long as no disagreement alters that direction and enough consensus is maintained, the group will stay together. While it stays together, the power of everyone's vote is inversely proportional to the size of the membership of the group. The arrangement is volatile and unstable, and it is almost impossible to get everybody to agree to do anything the way that you would like to do it.

On the other hand, alignment means that everyone in the group is coming from the same purposeful commitment. What is important is that something gets done, not how it gets done. Alignment includes everybody's best way to do it and all of their positions and beliefs about the other ways. It even includes disagreement about how the results will be achieved. Because everyone wants to do the same thing you want to do, everyone's vote counts 100%, just as it would if everyone were working individually. But by drawing on the group's fringe benefits, which include synergy and high-level occasionally-ruthless support, each person's control and efficacy becomes infinitely more powerful.

A working group effort requires alignment, not

agreement. It gets the job done as a whole instead of trying to get everyone to agree to do it your way.

There is one other strong reason to consider aligning yourself with a committed group. A group can occasionally have more impact on more levels than you may be able to achieve all alone. It is a matter of applying lines of interactive force which radiate outwardly from the hub of an imaginary circle.

As an individual, standing at the center of this mythical circle, you can interact most effectively only at the next level of impact open to you which is in relationship with another person or with other people in a group. That may be all it takes, because your personal energy ripples out and can produce waves of global change all by itself.

But as a group, you can deal with elusive conceptual structures more directly than that. For instance, you can reach and interact effectively with institutions that are inaccessible to individuals. Only institutions can interact effectively with the ultimate conceptual structure, society, which is at the outermost ring of this particular circle. (Other similar circles might be extended even further to include the world, the solar system, the galaxy, and the universe.)

Using our circular model, the final interactive step is essential, because it is at the level of society that you can most accurately measure the results of your commitment, intention and action. It's not hard to do. One morning, soon after the time you said you would get the job handled, you wake up and observe that war has stopped or starvation is eliminated or the streets are clean or whales are multiplying, and your dream, whatever it might have been, was not so impossible after all.

And then it is time to take out your list of personal visions and commit yourself to taking care of the next one. Keep moving. Keep on playing. Do not stop to fall back into complacency or to wonder, even for a moment, whether this was really it or not because now it all seems to have been so easy and effortless. Just acknowledge yourself, experience the feeling of satisfaction that accompanies completion, and push out to whatever is next.

The point of this chapter, by now, is fairly clear. As you evolve through the seasons of your life, you need to be aware of what is going on, and you need to act appropriately. You can turn convolutedly inside, bury yourself in the tragedy that summer is over, and quietly wither away. Or you can put on an attractive new sweater, lace up a pair of brand new running shoes, and get out and crunch in the leaves.

Given that the process of living involves taking everything you've got and manifesting it in the physical world, only the second choice is a viable Alternative To Aging. It is also the only true commitment to yourself. You can evaluate how well you are doing in this respect on a special type of scale that comes with aliveness-measuring intervals from 0 to 100.

Consider this possibility. Contrary to most commonly held belief structures which assume that your life peaks in the middle and then runs downhill, on this special scale, the older you get and the more you know about the way things work, the higher you can reach.

During the early part of your life, you can often get away with living at a 0% to 30% level and still be happy and satisfied most of the time.

All the trouble begins when you continue to expand and grow to become 70% or 80% alive or more, but you continue trying to live as if you were still at a 30% level. When that happens, you can no longer experience exhuberance and joy because you are not living up to your actual capacity for life. Whenever you do not measure up to your true level of self, you will be unable to feel complete.

On this unique scale, you always know when you are really living because you will always feel alive and satisfied. This is not the same as doing your best or even going for it. It is nothing less than living your life fully every moment.

Using this same unusual scale, imagine how it would feel to live your life at a 100% level. It might not be easy and it certainly would not be comfortable. But it would be wildly enlivening for you and tremendously empowering for everyone around you.

There would be some risk involved. You could not hide from people with whom you did not want to deal or escape from circumstances you did not want to handle. You would have to be committed to having your life work at every moment and in every aspect. You would need to share yourself openly and honesty without pretense or phoniness. And you would be required to remember that you were bigger than your emotions, thoughts, beliefs, body sensations, judgments and memories. Every time you found that you were too scared or too tired or that you just didn't want to that day, you would just go out and live it up at a 100% level anyway. Just because you said you would.

As I said, there would be a lot of risk. But on a scale of life where the highest value consists of allowing yourself to make a difference in the world 100% of the time, if you are not living at risk, you are not living.

Maybe you can see all the immediate and longrange benefits of living 100% of your life 100% of the time. Maybe you would even like to do it, but you don't know how. Here is how: Just do it. Give your word that you will do it. Then keep your word.

With stakes as high as these, you will find that you cannot always keep your word. When you live in certainty all the time, keeping your word is easy. To live 100% of your life, nothing is certain except that you are fully alive. So, on those occasions when you fail, you need to remember not to make yourself wrong and not to shut down. Acknowledge your own courage and willingness to participate at the level you have chosen to participate. Also acknowledge that you failed. Notice exactly at which point the failure occurred, where you may have stopped short or sold out. Then recommit yourself to a retargeted goal, correct whatever requires correcting, and live some more of your life at the 100% mark.

When you choose contribution as the context of your life, you become the contribution. The only thing you have to share is what you are right now. You do not need to get better first or to wait until you have a degree, a facelift or the right clothes. All you need is exactly what you already have: Your self. And that is all you will ever need need.

You can prove that very quickly. Right now, try to change something in the past. Right now, try to change something in the future. Right now, try to be someplace other than where you are.

That's right, you can't. What's more, no one else can either.

This is the way everything turned out. This is the tomorrow we waited for yesterday. The way things are right now is the way things are. That's that. And that's just fine like that. Once we acknowledge how that is so, we begin to experience satisfaction. We also have a place to start whatever will come next.

The only way to get where we are going is to tell the truth about where we are now and to fully accept where we are coming from. Right at that point, all the possibilities begin to open up.

You see, after something has turned out, your only choice is either to be satisfied or not to be satisfied. If you are not satisfied, you are stuck. All you have to contribute is your dissatisfaction. When you are satisfied, you have the opportunity to contribute your satisfaction. Who can say when you are satisfied? And who can say when you are not? That's right, the same person. In fact, it is the same person who is responsible for saying everything you say.

Your satisfaction is your ultimate and only contribution. Share it lavishly and notice how other people come alive all around you. Once again, it is your choice. You can hold on to every moment you have had up until now and never be satisfied. Or you can make a commitment to have every moment count from now on and then experience each one as a direct source of satisfaction.

There is a curious paradox about life. It goes like this: Anytime something seems wrong outside of yourself, the way to handle it best is to look for the solution inside. Anytime you are confused, doubtful or upset about something that seems wrong inside, the place to look for the answer is always outside of yourself. It is when you are most confused, doubtful and upset that the act of becoming committed to something larger than you think you are serves to remind you of exactly how much you really have to offer.

Consider your own commitment to life. It is the only alternative that makes an extended lifespan worth living.

CHAPTER 10
THE MIDLIFE METAMORPHOSIS

Long before the dreadful change of life was due or even anticipated, little Diana began to lose interest in many of the wonderful things to do each day that made life so worthwhile.

The sweet sugar-frosted breakfast cereals tasted stale and dull. The morning Hide-And-Seek game seemed boring. The cheerful childish chatter of the other children was tiresome, and she caught herself only half listening most of the time. Playing House in the afternoon got to be just a little bit dumb; it was always the same. Even her dollies had become stupid, lifeless cloth and plastic things. The round above-ground pool no longer held the promise of adventure. She yearned for deeper waters to explore. The din at dinnertime was more and more annoying. And the bedtime stories failed to carry her off to the Land of Nod on broad wings of fantasy. Her bubbly little world had turned flat.

Diana ground her teeth, picked at her fingernails, smiled and pretended everything was still the same as it always had been. She never told anyone, not even Betsy, Peggy or Carl, about her increasing discontent and dissatisfaction with the way things were. If she had told them, she might have discovered that they felt the same way she did. But she just could not bring herself to talk about it. Everyone knew it was not nice to feel that way and the only possible reason for it was not only unmentionable, it was unthinkable. So no one acknowledged that something odd was going on.

After all, if it were not for breakfast cereals, endless games like Hide-And-Seek, cheerful childish chatter, House parties, wading pools, and the same old videotaped fantasies, what would life be all about anyway?

Life in a physical body appears to exist within a framework of space and time. This framework is fluid and flowing, not fixed or locked in place. Transitions occur each moment, endlessly. Normally, we do not perceive them until after they are complete.

We walk down city streets on sidewalks that have different textures from step to step. One building stops, another starts. But until we come to a curb or a vacant lot, we seldom notice the shifting patterns.

We fly across countries and oceans, noticing only where water and shorelines meet or where farmland begins and cities or deserts end. For the most part, we are unaware of the infinitely subtle points and spaces of transition in between.

We wake up one morning and see that the winter snow has melted and the air is warm and new. Or we see that one lone tree has burst into color. Or that all of the leaves have fallen to the ground. And we know that another season has arrived. The seasonal change was not spontaneous. It was no instantaneous creation. It emerged from day after day after day of seeming sameness, during which any number of almost imperceptible yet readily observable signs could have easily been identified and used to mark the passage into a new cycle.

Life draws heavily upon this endlessly recurring pattern of nature. Each pattern, each season of our lives slowly evolves into the next. And the next. And the next. Children know that they are continuously growing and learning. But as adults, we forget. We wonder who we are as if we were only a simple sentence that has already been spoken.

Actually, we speak or language ourselves as we go along. Each word or modifier we use, like mother, father, doctor, writer, fat, thin, goodhearted, is only one of many possible variations and alternatives available to us. We choose each phrase the same as we choose experiences we want to activate. And at those points where our transitions from one level to another are most obvious and most striking, the language that we use to bring ourselves forth and self-express becomes extraordinarily powerful and far-reaching in its implications.

If we only knew how to read and interpret the subtle signs that precede each transitional period and how to make the most of them, more and more of life would immediately become available to each of us.

In this chapter, I will examine some of the signs I associate with The Midlife Metamorphosis, cover in detail some of the major midlife opportunities that I have not yet discussed, and suggest ways to turn the entire experience of the transitional years between 60 and 80 into a blueprint for longevity and an absolute Alternative To Aging.

To begin with, the very idea of viewing your 70th birthday as the midpoint of your life instead of the end requires a major shift in belief patterns. The processes in Chapters 6 through 8 are necessary prerequisites to gaining the mental flexibility you need to accept it even as a remote possibility.

It is, of course, much more than merely a possibility. And examples of the highly transformed quality of life that can become available after 70 have been exemplified throughout recorded history from Abraham and Sarah to Grandma Moses and George (God I, II and III) Burns.

At this point, a look at a few fundamental questions would be appropriate and productive. For instance: What is the scale on which a midpoint can be determined? What human characteristics are metamorphosising anyway? What are they metamorphosising into? In which noticeable areas will the first signs of transformation show up? What, exactly, is that next level of being? And how does it fit into life as we know and understand it?

I have already touched briefly on answers to some of these questions. Now it is time to examine all of them in more detail.

As a species, one of the unique patterns of human

development involves the power to discriminate between self and others, between this and that, between these and those. Psychiatrists and researchers in human behavior refer to this phenomenon as the process of separation and individuation and consider evolution into autonomy as the primary goal of maturation.

Separation can be defined as the act of differentiating the self from the nonself or discovering the boundaries at which the self ends and everything else begins. It is learning to define where this thing stops and that thing starts and noticing why one thing is not the same as another.

Becoming proficient at separation is the major job of infancy and early childhood. Each newborn baby, thrust from a secure environment of wholeness and oneness, must learn to handle the physical world alone.

Individuation includes the acquisition of mental and physical survival skills that will provide a firm basis for autonomy. A strong sense of personal identity and a large capacity for inner direction are required to judge and evaluate external material as accurately as possible.

Beginning with birth, when a child is literally cut off from his or her life support system and must begin to function independently, each stage of life contains its own challenges and dangers as the circles of autonomy grow wider and wider. From interactions with mother, with family, with friends, with schools, with neighborhoods, with work and careers, with cities, with love and relationships, with nations, with new family circles and other group involvements, and finally with the world at large, life is an ongoing process of maintaining and expressing our own identities in increasingly larger and more stressful arenas.

At each stage of development and expansion as individuals, we are more or less appropriately supported by those around us who have already moved on to the next stage. Parents, teachers, mentors, and other channels of embodied information abound to assist us on the path from childhood and adolescence into adulthood. It is clear to one and all that each stage must be mastered or the next cannot be achieved.

When development is arrested or emerging needs are not met, we simply do not survive. Illnesses, frailties, accidents, infirmities and death appear whenever the quality of our lives falls below minimum acceptable standards for a long enough period of time. When newly emerging needs are only partially met, portions of a previous stage of development may remain stuck in place and our complete human potential may never be realized unless we consciously take a stand to the contrary. In the absence of such an active stand, a person may go through life as a big baby, a bad boy, daddy's little girl, a teacher's pet or a rebel without a cause, never growing beyond the point at which the blockage occurred.

Fully autonomous maturity is the goal of separation and individuation. It is not at all easy to achieve, but it is definitely the ideal towards which we strive during our early and young adult years of growth. With its attainment, we can step back and stand securely on our own. We can be alone and function effectively in our aloneness. We can independently perceive right and wrong, evaluate justice and injustice, assess external events and situations with complete objectivity and full conceptual clarity. We have arrived.

It is all well and good. And all very much part of the process of movement through life. However, we make the mistake of thinking that's all there is.

There is more. We should have known, even though there has never been any formal psychological behavioral study or laboratory evidence. We should have known because all through life there have been clues.

As each step of separation and individuation is successfully completed, a period of reintegration is required before stepping out alone again. After experiencing our separation from mother at birth, we reintegrate with her in a new form of relationship based upon loving care and nurturing. After experiencing how we are separate from father and family, we reintegrate with them in a new pattern of solidarity and wholeness. It is the same with school, friends, groups, relationships, working associations, and ultimately government, civic, national, and global issues, if we develop to that degree.

First we notice how and in what ways we are different from them and we feel separate, alienated and alone. Then, something clicks in place a new way and we notice how we are the same as they are. And once again we feel stabilized and wholly supported.

It takes about 60 years to master the ultimate separation and individuation of mature adulthood in all of its varied forms. It then takes another 60 years or so to master the second half of the cycle in which increasingly complex levels of integration and merging occur and, layer by layer, we return to the experience of our wholeness and our oneness with everything there is. In between the two is the transitional midpoint that I define as the midlife period, a time of readjusting, reconceptualizing, recreating and reemerging that can take 10 to 20 years to complete.

Because we are human beings and because one of our inherent characteristics as humans beings is choice, success at growth and transition is not guaranteed. Fearful, unfulfilled, dissatisfied or depressed, we can choose to remain stuck at any level and spend a lifetime as an emotionally dissatisfied child or teenager or young adult. However the price we pay is a costly one. Like a plant that is potbound or a pet rabbit kept in too small a cage, our development is stunted and distorted. We wither, age, and die long before our time.

Without a constant ongoing process of growth, there can be no life. Without life, there can be no life extension.

The notion of integration is occasionally confused with ideas like collectivism or collective consciousness in which the individual is merged into a larger group of beings and loses his or her identity as a singularized persona. I want you to know I do not mean anything like that at all.

While many benefits of merging and blending may occur in terms of expanded awareness and a diminished sense of aloneness, integration as the primary process of the second half of our lives does not in any way involve giving up our individuality or uniqueness. It is simply another form of growing up. In fact, it becomes one more version of using personal and personalized attributes as fully and completely as we can. Integrating ourselves with our environment and dissolving barriers that separate and alienate us could no more demand giving up our individuality than becoming a responsible grownup demands giving up our childlike sense of playfulness. Both transitions require that we bring all of the uniqueness of whoever we are into the process with us.

In doing so, as we travel from phase to phase and season to season, surrendering to the natural flow of life instead of resisting it, we acquire a lot more of ourselves in each experience we engage in along the way.

As the time of The Midlife Metamorphosis approaches, the pace of normal everyday living seems to slow down to support us in focusing on the issues at hand. And several unusually powerful Alternatives To Aging begin to appear. Like always, participation is a matter of choice. Your choice.

Only now, the options are bigger than ever before.

1. We can become more loving, more expressive, more willing to touch others, more in touch with the joy that giving and receiving love can create in the world. Or we will become cold and remote. Love is a natural byproduct of integration. As we observe that others are not really that different than ourselves, our capacity to give and receive love grows boundlessly and effortlessly. We begin to see that it will either be us and them together in a world that works for everyone or no one in no world at all.

2. We can become more gifted, more willing to use our natural and latent talents without self censorship or self repression, and much less fearful of evaluation or of deviating from conventional patterns of normalcy and self expression. Or we will become diminished in mental stature, blind to the futility of trying to stretch yesterday's talents to fit today's needs. As we notice that it is always the people with the lampshades over their heads who have much more fun at parties than the people who stand stiffly around criticizing them, it becomes easier to put more of ourselves into life. And to get more out of it.

3. We can become more psychic, more insightful, more open to impulses and hunches, better able to read people and events accurately. Or we will experience a great sense of loss and a fundamental inability to handle life. As we realize the falseness of the arbitrary boundaries we have always used to differentiate time between experiences and distances between each other, expanded communication skills and comprehension capabilities become available. Instead of merely thinking we know what we know, we find that we know what we know with certainty.

4. We can become more aware in ways we have never before been aware. Or we will cut off our newly emerging awareness and pretend that our senses are failing and fading away. As we experience what it could be like to suddenly become completely aware, our conceptualizations about ourselves expand and shift. For example, you might actually sense what it is like to be one of many individual experiential cells that make up the perceptual organs of some other being on a vaster scale. You might also become aware of other lives you can recall from the past, present and future. And you might see how each of these alternative lives, each reincarnational or possible you, contributes not only to your own direct experience but also to observations and data that add up to the life experiences of another far-reaching entity of which you are a vital part. Each of us could expect to have altered viewpoints of this magnitude about almost anything at all.

5. We can become emotionally open, willing to drift on the ebb and flow of our emotional tides without incapacitating our ability to produce our intended results, responsible for the role that our emotions play in forming both our experience of external reality and the actual events that we bring forth. Or we will be ravaged by our reluctance to open up and let go of the emotional baggage that holds us down. As we sense the curious fact that we are somehow always in the middle of things when they go wrong as well as when they go right, the true nature of cause and effect becomes obvious. At that point, it is possible for us all to become as joyous and free as transformed Scrooges on Christmas morning.

6. We can become our own role models instead of trying to be like someone else or attempting to conform to cultural belief patterns and behavioral standards that are not our own. Or we will perceive that we no longer fit, no longer belong, no longer have any reason or justification to be alive and well. As we perceive the price of trading off the power of our being, we can more readily reverse that pattern and discover how the acceptance we have been seeking naturally follows our willingness to be everything we are instead of small scaled down versions of ourselves.

7. And, as I have already observed in Chapters 8 and 9, we can become sexually expressive and able to assume leadership and take responsibility for making a difference on a large scale. Or we will deny our newly emerging creative powers and succumb to a label of senility. As we notice the intricacy of the balance between sex and power, we can responsibly begin to actualize 100% of our potential capacities in each area.

The point is that we cannot extend our lives unless we also expand our lives to a level that is appropriate for each phase of existence. Obviously, you would not expect to be successful in the working world if your developmental level was frozen at the age of seven. Not quite so obviously but for the same reasons, you cannot even hope to make it successfully past The Midlife Metamorphosis if your developmental level is frozen at the age of 37.   Life and the quality of our lives must expand or they dwindle away to nothing. There is no way that we can doggedly hold on to whatever we have, feel or experience right now without burning out the energy we require for growth and metamorphosis.

And there you have the ultimate issue behind each choice and each alternative.

It all gets down to this: You can extend your life up to as much as twice the time you are given by actuarial chartmakers and other authorities in the realm of geriatrics. But only if you remain open to new possibilities and new cycles of growth. Which means giving up the certainty of believing that you know everything that you need to know already.

There are times when your willingness to be completely open to new sensory data and new sources of knowing are particularly important. At these times, you will become increasingly aware of a shift in one or more aspects of your life that have always been considered permanently locked in place.

One such aspect is the nature of time. As I have already pointed out, the painfully long, almost endless hours and days of childhood and adolescence tend to speed up during the passage of early adulthood until, by the beginning of The Midlife Metamorphosis, six months or more can rush by before you even begin to read over your list of New Year's resolutions. At the same time that years begin to fly by, each moment of experience in the present opens as slowly and beguilingly as a fragrant multipetaled flower of rare and exotic beauty. And within each moment, even on an unclear day, you can see forever if only you choose to look.

Another aspect of life that inexplicably shifts during The Midlife Metamorphosis is sleep and your relationship to it. Most people between the ages of 60 and 80 do not sleep as soundly or as much as they did in their younger years. Most of them also think there is something wrong with that.

The most valid questions to ask are these. How much sleep do you really need anyway? And what is its biological purpose? I will examine each question in some detail since sleeplessness is to this period of life what pimples are to puberty.

To begin with, there is now fairly universal agreement among scientists who study biological rhythms that just as there is a marked low energy period in which people feel drained in the late afternoon, there is an equally obvious high energy period that occurs in the early morning hours. If you were consciously awake between 4:30 and 7:30 AM, chances are you would find it to be your most creative and productive time of the day. I do. And everyone I know who taps into that magic time of dawn, sunrise and reawakening tells me that they do too.

Over the past fifteen years, I have researched and experimented with different types of limited sleep programs and reached a number of somewhat unusual conclusions. I invite you to check out and validate each of them for yourself.

To begin with, I have found the human body requires no more than an average of four to five hours sleep a night to function at its maximum level of alertness, creativity, and efficiency. Sleeping for longer than six hours produces more fogginess, dullness and lethargy than sleeping for less than two hours. We may think we need more sleep than that. We may even strongly and seriously believe we need more sleep than that. And, sometimes, when we are healing ourselves, we actually do need more sleep than that. But for peak physical performance and mental clarity, four to five hours is the limit.

Strictly on the practical side, there is a major advantage to knowing this. Upon reaching a stage of life when you just don't feel tired when you go to bed or you wake up in the middle of the night and can't go back to sleep, now you don't have to worry about it any more. You don't even have to take anything or do anything about it.

Just do what your body is telling you to do. Get up. And find something more productive to do than trying to sleep when it obviously is not sleep that you need at that moment.

What you do need, and what you are giving yourself an opportunity to experience, is something you always wanted to have: More time. Two to six more glorious hours a day. With it, you can learn or finetune a new skill to prepare for a goal you have specified for this or the next decade of your life. You can catch up on all the reading you ever wanted to do but never had time for. You can write a novel, a poem, a journal, a memoir. Or paint a picture, compose a song or express your creative nature any way you choose. You can also start exercising if you have not done that yet. Or you can do utilitarian work like cleaning up the place in half the time because you are so much more efficient during your early morning high. Any of these activities will also free up more daylight hours for you to use and enjoy.

If you feel at all tired during the day, particularly during the first month or so of limited sleep, you can take a short nap (from half an hour up to two hours) or relax in a hot bath late in the afternoon or at the end of the day when your body rhythms have ebbed to their their lowest point.   By early evening, you will be fully recharged and ready to bounce back for more than ever before.

Staying on this strictly practical level, the whole idea is to follow your impulses and your own natural physical rhythms instead of trying to adapt yourself to an arbitrary cultural pattern that does not meet your personal needs. Sleep when you are sleepy. Rest when you are tired. Be fully awake and alive when you are fully awake and alive. What could be simpler than that?

On still deeper levels, limited sleep offers a variety of other benefits including significantly enhanced mental acuity, extraordinary perceptual clarity, and improved dream control and recall, which I will cover in detail later in this chapter.

Most important of all, sleeping four to five hours a night totally supports and facilitates the entire process of Midlife Metamorphosis. Perhaps that is why changes in sleeping patterns or problems associated with an inability to remain asleep all night are such common occurrences among people in their 60s and 70s. Only sleeplessness is not supposed to be a problem at all. It is nothing more than an evolutionary event designed to shift our perceptual base irrevocably from separation to integration.

Virtually every segment of the human race, no matter how civilized or isolated, draws sharp metaphysical and epistomological distinctions between day and night. The two are considered to be opposites, antagonists, opponents.   This cultural differentiation between day and night forms the basis for countless insidious and deeply-ingrained belief systems that reinforce and contribute to the notion of separateness and the fundamental incompatibility of our inner and outer experiences.

Some of the ways we unthinkingly accept this

notion include all individual and mass beliefs involving the following: Black and white. The light side and the dark side. The forces of good and the forces of evil. Fearlessness by day and fear of the dark. White people and black people. Gentle creatures of the day and monstrous creatures of the night. Salvation and damnation. Virtue and sin. Light cheerfulness and dark despair. Good guys in white hats and bad guys in black hats. Love and hate. Jekyll and Hyde. White magic and black magic. God and devil. Wedding white and funeral black. Safety and danger. Life and death. Summer light and winter darkness. And, yes, even youth and age.

Allow your own mind to wander through each pair of traditionally accepted opposites and check your own premises and conclusions about this issue. Notice how tightly the chain of beliefs is forged and how pervasive and apparently universal it appears to be. Notice also how your own beliefs and actions in the past have strengthened and heavily armored the chain, and how tightly it is coiled around you.

After you have been sleeping four or five hours a night for even a short period of time, that chain will begin to crumble.

Night and day will merge together for you as they never have before and centuries of superstition and well-meaning but incorrect assumptions will fall away. The light side of your life will take on rich new shades of color and deepen in its impact. The dark innermost portions of yourself where you have most feared to tread will shine with a glowing phosphorescent light and become more fully accessible, releasing an abundance of valuable gifts and buried treasures.

Through the simple symbolic act of participating in night and day on your own terms, powerful new creative resources will reveal themselves and illuminate the way to your next level of being. Foremost among these resources are your dreams.

If being awake is like tuning in to images of reality on your own biological tv set, dreaming is quite similar. The only difference is dream images are on another programming band. It is very much like the difference between regular network and cable television.

Dreaming, like cable programming, has a broader range of available shows and a wider spectrum of interest. You need to use a special tuning mechanism or the image and sound will seem unclear or distorted. In addition, unless your tuner is precisely focused you will get mixed images because there are so many channels and such a wide range of material to choose from.

When we are awake, we tune in our bodies and become the programming of the day as well as the viewers of that programming. It is the same with dreams. Because we have physical bodies even when we are asleep, dreams are physical events too, however different their format may be. Occasionally, in dreams as well as in waking reality, we become so involved in the show that we forget how easily we can switch to another channel or flick off the dial altogether.

Getting stuck in a storyline is a common theme of life. We choose one plot from the millions or so that are available and we usually stay within it. That's why, for some, life is an ongoing soap opera while for others it may be a gangster show, a quality drama, a medical saga, a war story, or a rerun of 'Friday The 13th' or 'The Wizard of Oz'.

Sometimes, we like the show that we selected so much that we stay with it like a favorite sitcom; other times we fear to try a new show or a new channel, thinking it could never be as good as the one we have become hooked on for so many years. It is when we prejudge all the new shows and all the other channels before we try watching and participating in them that signs of stiffness and rigidity associated with advancing age begin to appear.

A one-channel one-show television set will not entertain, enliven or empower you for long. Nor will a one-channel one-show life. Fortunately each of us can draw upon a built-in mechanism that prevents this from occurring: The mechanism of the psyche.

The psyche is a term I define as the whole of our being or all that there is to each one of us. It is exactly the same as what many call the spirit. It is never locked into one storyline or one show. It is much too big for that. In fact, it overrides all of the stories, all of the channels, and all of our notions about time and space. It cuts through arbitrary standards of separateness, bringing together all the dichotomous aspects of waking and sleeping, you and them, past and future.

The psyche's functions are to fully reveal and to open up the limitless possibilities of balance in our lives. These contributions are most clearly apparent in early childhood. Then the psyche submerges, only to reappear during The Midlife Metamorphosis when extremes of the early adulthood quest for separation create a crucial need for balance.

To grasp what it is that makes balance so essential to our wellbeing, imagine yourself talking in a steady stream of nonstop sound with no pauses between each word or punctuation between each phrase. Nowimagineapage ofwritinguponwhich allthe wordsran togetherlikethiswith nobreakswhatsoever youcouldnt doit becauseitwouldbe incomprehensible.

Just as language is as dependent upon the spaces in between the words as it is upon the actual words themselves, life also requires a balance of both. It is the pauses between words, the hesitations between sounds, the rests between activities that provide meaning and clarity.   On a day-to-day level, the balance involves waking and dreaming; in much longer-range terms, it involves life and death.

If the purpose of waking reality is to explore and achieve mastery of ourselves in physical form, the purpose of dreaming reality is to discover and utilize our psyches and to experience the availability of the vast multidimensional possibilities on all the other channels that are open to us.

Dreams can be said to be the language and communication media of the psyche. They seem surrealistic because they are. The psyche does not work in the same linear way that the mind and physical reality work. It is circular in nature very much like a cosmic wheel or spiral nebula with an infinite number of lines of force radiating out in all directions from the center, which is always the moment you are experiencing right now.

Within this wheel-like matrix, events of the past, present and future all occur simultaneously, instead of one following another as they seem to do in the conscious waking reality of the physical body. Incomplete experiences we have had and are presently having mix and merge with alternative possible experiences, allowing us to weigh various outcomes of action open to us before we have to actually act in our waking lives. Frequently, nightmares and unpleasant dreams are simply the psyche's way of tipping us off to possible danger and allowing us to experience it and discharge the energy involved on a level that does not include actual physical harm.

In dreams, in other words, we create and choose events from limitless possibilities. And in waking reality, we handle the events we chose.

It is another of the ways that dreams function as the language of the psyche. The process resembles the way in which we choose the words we will say in waking life.

Each time we start a sentence, we are never sure of how it will end or exactly what we will say. And yet, on some elusive level, if we did not know the ending of each sentence before speaking it, we could never put the beginning and the middle together so precisely.

Before it is actually spoken, a sentence can be expressed in any number of ways. We can often track alternative phrasing possibilities as they flash across our minds and evaluate which one best expresses each intended communication. In dreams, we find all of the sentences that we never speak as well as all of the events that we choose not to experience.

Physically tuned consciousness gives off dreams just as boiling water gives off steam. The same part of us that knows intuitively how beginnings, middles and endings of sentences will be strung together draws beginnings, middles and endings of later-to-be-experienced events from dreams and constructs the content of waking experience. Various endings drawn from future possibilities are previewed and body responses and hormonal reactions to each ending are tested so that the advantages or disadvantages of each possibility may be evaluated.

Dreams clearly dramatize all of this data. They transport each of us to the multifaceted timeless and spaceless domain of our psyches. That is why, in any given dream on any given night, you can appear in any setting in the past, present or future, meeting and interacting with long-dead relatives, still-to-be born children or grandchildren, old friends, new lovers and once-and-future companions. You can also access truly astonishing information about yourself and other selves who are part of you and your experience-gathering adventures in waking life. Finally, you can practice manipulating and manifesting the physical substances of dream realities and gain valuable insights into what the physical substances of waking reality are all about.

Ordinarily, even as neglected as it usually is, dream data is slowly but automatically processed by our conscious minds. It makes its appearance later in the form of impulses and hunches and sudden urges for action. These suggestions are true gifts from our psyches, designed to turn us toward directions that are most appropriate for our growth and expansion as complete human beings. When we don't trust ourselves, unfortunately, we can't trust our hunches and impulses either, and valuable material is suppressed, lost or ignored.

Knowing this, you can see how useful it would be to have open and free-flowing access to your dream material. There are two ways it can be done. By conscious programming. And by enhanced remembering.

Programming can be done just before you fall asleep at night. You choose an area of life that is troubling you and you ask for a dream that will provide an answer. Your programming might go like this: 'In my dreams tonight, I want to discover a solution to my problem with Alfred.' Or 'Tonight, I intend to dream of a new theme for a song.'

You can program whatever you want or need including creative ideas and inspiration, previews of physical pleasure, the subject of your next relationship, dress rehearsals for future events, the source of a sudden windfall, even improved health. Once, when I had an almost unshakeable cold in my chest, I programmed a healing dream and a group of dream doctors worked on me all night. Some of them I knew in waking life, some seemed to be familiar strangers. All of them were very good at their work. By morning, my cold was gone without a trace.

But programming is only half of the job. The most useful and practical suggestions will not do you any immediate good at all unless you can remember them the next morning.

Remembering dreams is no more difficult than remembering details of your waking life. It is also no easier. Ordinarily, we remember only peak experiences, highlights or heavily-charged emotional events of each waking day. Countless trivial details and just as many useful ones slip away. Quick, what did you wear last Tuesday? What did you have for lunch a week before last Friday? Where were you on December 11, 1988?

How fast we forget.

But you don't need to continue to forget your dreams just because you slept through them. From now on, you can use the following system to energize your dream memory cells and set up an information retrieval file.

• Keep a notebook at least the size of a stenographer's pad, a ballpoint pen or marker, and a small flashlight next to your bed where you can easily reach them.

• Each night, just before you begin to fall asleep, repeat this affirmation at least three times: 'Tonight I will remember my dreams. I will wake up after each one and write it down.' If you decide to program a specific dream, add your affirmation to the end of the program like this: 'Tonight I travel to Ancient Egypt in my dreams. I will remember each dream, wake up immediately, and write it down.' Don't worry about the difference in tense or incorrect grammar. Affirmations have grammarial rules all their own and work best when stated, at least in part, in the present tense.

• After each dream, do what you said you would do. Wake up. Reach for your flashlight, your notebook and your pen. Sit up in bed and write down as much as you can recall.

• Spend the next five to ten minutes sitting up in bed, doing anything that will keep you awake. When you lie down again and switch off your light, repeat your affirmation and also remind yourself that when you have your next dream, you want to become consciously aware that you are dreaming.

• Then picture your body asleep. And visualize yourself inside of the dream you just wrote down or any other dream, fully conscious and aware that you are dreaming. Stay with this visualization until you fall asleep again.

If you prefer to review and write down your dreams the next morning, use a cassette recorder at night instead of a notebook and follow the same steps. Be sure to play back your tape and review your dreams each morning.

You may experience a lot of heavy internal resistance at first. You will be too tired. You will pretend that it is too hard. Your bedpartner may not appreciate your new nocturnal explorations.

However, when you begin to remember and record your dreams conscientiously, your resistance will become less draining; it will even show up in a lot more interesting ways. For instance, you will probably have at least one experience of dreaming that you are waking up to record a dream when you are actually still sound asleep.

And that will be a sign of mastery.

Dreams within dreams, double dreams, and dreams about dreaming are all extraordinarily high-level experiences. As soon as you begin remembering that you are doing any of these, you can raise the stakes and fully participate in the power of your mind at play by shaping and directing the flow of your dream sagas as you are dreaming them. There are hundreds of exercises for strengthening your abilities in this direction. Here are a few of my favorites.

206 Alternatives To Aging

• When you are dreaming, suggest that the background of your dream will expand. If you are inside, observe the next room. If you are outside, widen the view to include more territory and more details.

• When you are dreaming, bring any other person or people you want to see into your dream with you and direct the action to proceed any way you want. You might have a favorite motion picture star, entertainer or singer that you have long been attracted to put in an appearance. Someone you wish you could make love with could show up and be with you. A local, national or world leader that you would like to communicate with might come and have a summit dream meeting with you. The possibilities are endless.

• When you are dreaming, carry a dream camera and bring back a photograph to record in your dream notebook alongside of your text.

• When you are dreaming, let youself take off and fly as often as you can. Flying dreams open up latent psychic abilities faster than almost anything else you can do.

Each of these exercises will strengthen your ability to bring your waking consciousness into your dreams with you and facilitate the integrative processes associated with a successful passage through The Midlife Metamorphosis into extended life. But that is only half of the story. The other half of the opportunity is to perfect your skill in projecting your dreaming consciousness into waking life. Then you can experience completely balanced integration and learn to manifest your thoughts volitionally into solid physical forms. Here are just a few more exercises that will facilitate this process.

• When you are awake, close your eyes and notice the first image or thought that comes to mind. Create a dream around it and later interpret that dream. Watch for hidden messages and write them down.

• When you are awake, close your eyes and imagine that the very moment you are experiencing right now is a

dream and that all of the events and people in your life
right now are dream figures. Interpret them accordingly.
Then ask yourself what kind of reality you will find
yourself in when you wake up.

    • When you are awake, choose any day last week
and trace the events you experienced with as much detail
as you can. Start when you woke up and review the day
as if you were watching it on a videotape monitor. When
you have finished the day and gone to bed, choose
another day and repeat the process, only this time choose
a day from next week. Start when you wake up in the
morning and follow each event that occurs until you
switch off your bedside lamp that night. In both cases, see
whether you can recreate your body sensations, emotions
and thoughts, as well as what actually happens.

    • When you are awake, focus all of your attention
on the present moment. Take it in as completely as
possible, fully noticing all the sights and sounds and
sensations of your immediate surroundings, Then, if you
are inside a room, imagine that you are outside. If you are
outside, reverse the procedure. And repeat the process of
opening up your awareness to each and every sight and
sound within your immediate perceptual range. Finally,
return to the first part of this excersise and once again
fully notice every sight and sound that is present in your
environment.

    These processes, like the first set, create a perceptual
shift that supports The Midlife Metamorphosis by
triggering your awareness of other alternatives and other
channels available to you on your consciousness tuning
dial. Also, like the first set, they open up new avenues of
personal growth and evolution. Notice whether you have
a fear of being swept away or overcome by inner voyages
of discovery like these. Or whether, even though you
mean to and want to, somehow you never get around to
trying them.

    Resistance is a direct byproduct of having placed too
tight a cover on your consciousness.

    Let me reassure you: There is nothing to resist and
nothing to be afraid of except that which you yourself

have put there to fear. When you open up alternative channels of perception, you will find that you have more than one standpoint from which to view reality. This can be extremely useful whenever you feel unsure or confused, or whenever you are engaged in a major period of transformational activity.

Truly, there is no reason for separation between your waking and sleeping lives. When you take your waking consciousness into dreams and invite your dreaming consciousness into waking reality, you can notice how you operate at both levels and observe the similarities in each environment.

Whether dreaming or awake, you are you. And as you open channels of communication between waking and dreaming realities, new depths of experience, flexibility and expanded awareness of your own being emerge. You are better able to acquaint your unconscious with present physical situations or needs and then draw upon unconscious knowledge and buried resources for solutions. Wisdom and innate abilities you may otherwise deny yourself are released along with untapped stockpiles of energy for practical everyday purposes.

Best of all, the entire process occurs automatically whenever you use the dream world for what it is: A creative environment in which all possible situations are instantly acted out and formatted in real or symbolic terms so that you can choose the most appropriate ones for actual physical expression.

Many primitive societies and once isolated cultures like the Aboriginal Australians and the Senoi Indian tribes are known to have fully understood the integrative processes of life and utilized dream data effectively in their everyday reality. Children were taught to remember their dreams and recount their dreams each morning. When issues were left unfinished, they were instructed to go back to the same dream the next night and complete their business. Thus, instead of waking up terrified by the sudden attack of a monstrous creature and suppressing the memory of the experience, the child returned and either dug a large hole for the charging creature to fall into or produced a large hamburger to offer the monster as a gesture of friendship. All types of creative play in dreams was encouraged and rewarded.

Several past civilizations are believed to have carried the notion of utilitarian dreaming to an even further extreme. The dream state was considered dominant over the waking state and people actually went to sleep to go to work. Each person's waking life was thought to be nothing more than the dreams of a larger self. And it may indeed be true that our waking hours are like dreams to other parts of our consciousness which normally focus in other directions or tune in other stations of experience.

It is certainly an interesting possibility.

Because dreams are the proving ground of possibilities and because between the ages of 60 and 80, they become just as clear and vivid as the dreams of childhood used to be, it is definitely worth investing the time it takes to learn to use them as proficiently as you can.

More dreams, less sleep, an altered perception of time and spacial relationships, new insights, and a strong sense that you are a part of everything and everyone around you are all strong indications that The Midlife Metamorphosis is at hand. These phenomena will come upon you just as slowly and strongly and surely as the sudden overwhelming urge to take up spinning comes to caterpillars. The process is bigger than you realized and it will take you further than you ever thought possible, if you do not deny it or repress it. The process is also a little scary.

One important thing to remember is this: caterpillars that choose not to evolve for any reason do not make it. Those that give in to transformation emerge flying high with beautiful new forms, exciting new powers and a new cycle of life that doubles the length of their previous one. In our terms, at the very least, that translates into an additional 60 to 80 years of glorious life.

The Midlife Metamorphosis is much more than a change for the better. It is the one psycho-biological Alternative To Aging that everyone has always hoped and waited for, never realizing that they had it all the time.

CHAPTER 11

A MATTER OF LIFE AND DEATH

Where do they go?

Ronnie began to wonder about it one cloudy morning in March, just after her eighth birthday. She sat bolt upright in her little bed and began having some strange and unusual thoughts. It was strange because she didn't think very much about anything, ever. The thoughts themselves were unusual because no one had ever thought them before as far as she could tell.

Where do they go?

She did not like what was happening. She tried to think about her dolls. She tried to think about Freddie. She tried to think about swinging on a swing, running across a field of small spring flowers, dipping her fingers into an almost motionless backwater spot in a swiftly flowing stream to see if the salamanders had come back yet. But all she could think about was them.

Where do they go? Why do they go?

They would be sitting out there on benches one day, way back on the edge of things. Then the next day, they would be gone and never seen or heard from or talked about again. New ones would take their place on the lonely and remote benches. Some of them were always sitting around there. But hardly ever were they the same ones from week to week or month to month.

Why? Where do they go? And what happens to them afterwards?

It all began to seem very important. A little poem about the mystery flashed through her head. It went something like this:

No one knows,
Where they goes.

That, she thought to herself, didn't make much sense. It didn't even sound right. It would sound much better if it went:

We don't know,
Where they go.

Except that way it did not make any sense either. It took at least two people to make a 'we'. And as far as she knew, there was not a single other person in the playground world who had the slightest interest in where those older children disappeared to anyway. At least no one ever mentioned it to her if they did.
But where do they...?
One last time the thought began to reappear. Then some of the other children woke up and began to throw a pillow around. Ronnie joined in.
By breakfast time, she had completely forgotten about the whole thing. Something had made her feel uneasy and scared that morning, but she couldn't remember what it could possibly have been.

Throughout the many centuries of western civilization up to and including the present day, two almost universal fears have dominated each generation. Fear of living. And fear of dying.

The fear of living, which I have already covered in some detail, manifests itself in holding back, not fully expressing ourselves, saving something of ourselves for someday when external conditions will be perfect enough to allow us to be fully and completely who we are. Behind this fear of fully participating in life lurks our own personalized versions of the belief that as soon as we let all of ourselves out, there will be nothing left. It naturally follows that when there is nothing left, we will die.

Which brings us to the second almost universal fear of humankind: The fear of dying.

Today, surrounded by the pervasive threats of everything from nuclear destruction and sexual plagues to religious Armageddon, global cataclysm, and the death-and-rebirth cycle at the edge of the Age of Aquarius, the fear of dying may be at an alltime high.

In addition, instead of the comfort of dying surrounded by relatives and friends as in days of old, we usually die alone in institutions or hospitals. Cut off from the support of our loved ones, death is all the more difficult to handle.

Finally, we do not accept death as a natural phenomenon so we do not deal with it as if it were just another experience of living. In its most extreme form, fearing and denying death or viewing it as an opposing antagonistic force drives people into medicine. This is one of the reasons why so many doctors and nurses are insensitive and remote. Not only are their own fears about death activated each time they lose a patient, they also feel as if they have failed or lost another round in an ongoing battle.

In ordinary life, there is very little opportunity for us to get clear about where we stand in relation to death and dying. Nice people do not discuss their fears, horrors, or apprehensions about it. And because our feelings are so deep and personal, we probably would not want to reveal ourselves on that level to not-nice people. No matter how much everyone always talks about whoever died recently and whatever the cause of death may have been, to expose how we really feel about it honestly and openly is not acceptable conversation material for coffee breaks, carpools or cocktail parties.

At the same time, it is absolutely essential for each of us to expose how we really feel about it honestly and openly. If only to ourselves. As you have already seen in Chapter 5 about emotions and Chapter 6 on belief systems, fear loses its power to control and debilitate upon exposure to the high-intensity light of focused awareness, particularly when any specific issue about fear is acknowledged and accepted as a not-so-interesting fact.

Here is how to get in touch with where you stand in

terms of your personal relationship to death.

Use the next five pages of your notebook or take out five blank pages of paper. At the top of each page, write one of the following sentence beginnings in the order that I have indicated:

1. When I allow myself to think that I will someday die...
2. When as a child I first encountered death...
3. If I could tell you about my fear of dying...
4. One of the ways I manage to avoid death is...
5. If I knew that I only had three months to live...

When you have finished setting up each page, return to the first page and complete that sentence with the first ten endings that come to mind. Don't think about it. And don't censor yourself or reject any thought you have because it makes no sense or does not sound right with the sentence stem. Just write it down. Finish all five pages of sentence completions without taking a break or getting up to do anything else.

Then read over your list and see what is true for you right now. The first three lists will reveal your thoughts, attitudes, judgments, evaluations, emotions, and beliefs. The fourth and fifth lists will enable you to assess the extent to which you are not fully alive. If you and I were not so afraid to die, we would not have to be so afraid to live.

Most of us experience a crippling and strongly internalized terror about death. It is never discussed because it is so deeply ingrained that we could never allow it to surface and appear in our conscious thought. And yet, its effects appear even in early childhood when the first defenses against death are erected and a variety of lifelong behavior mechanisms are constructed and locked in place.

These death-defying acts can include: Refusing to grow up and become responsibly adult. Hiding from the timeclocks of life by never entering the game. Keeping excessively busy so that there is no time to die. Building a well-buffered wall of relationships or possessions to keep death symbolically at arm's length. Engaging in compulsive sexual activity to prove how alive you are again and again and again. Taking excessive and unnecessary risks to demonstrate your invulnerability. Waiting to share with your loved ones how much you really love them, knowing that you would never check out while so important a message remained undelivered. Postponing major projects to keep a few significant reasons for living waiting around as coming attractions. Participating in elaborate life-and-death games with parents like 'You old folks better keep alive so that I don't have to move up to the front of the line' and 'Don't you dare grow up, sonny, because if you ever do then I will be old and I'll have to die' instead of simply creating meaningful relationships.

All of these diversions tend to block even the earliest of our journeys down the life-road of separation/individuation and integration. If we do not emerge and grow and transform and really live as well-defined entities, we will be less obvious targets for death when it strikes. Or so we tell ourselves.

Then we believe all that. And we hide out all through the long long early and middle years of life, hoping to avoid the end. We try to lose ourselves in the various processes of life instead of just enjoying our aliveness. Doing things like involving ourselves in a preoccupied, automatic, less than fully conscious way with work, children, personal causes, possessions, escape substances like alcohol or drugs, relationships, survival needs, or the quest for wealth takes the place of fully living and fully experiencing each rich new moment as it comes along.

Life happens all around us but not directly to us because we are not present for it. We just are not available. And when we do finally meet up with death it is indeed a tragedy because we have not yet lived. However it is a tragedy of our own making.

To accept the simple fact that we will someday die is an act of almost heroic proportions. But once done, it opens up a vast array of new possibilities, allows goals and priorities to be responsibly established and implemented, and supports a more complete level of participation in every available facet of life.

Signs that your own acceptance of death has been successfully handled include all of the following:

1. A constant commitment to the ongoing process of monitoring whether or not the work you are doing, the activities you are engaged in and the person or people you are with are really the way you want to be spending your life. And the willingness to take all necessary and appropriate corrective action whenever it may be required.

2. An up-to-date will.

3. Prearranged funeral plans or other afterdeath accommodations that will spare others the burdensome necessity of doing it for you.

4. An active intention to live 100% of each day of your life as if it was your last and to have a tombstone that reads 'Burned Out' instead of 'Saved A Lot, See Where It Got'.

Whenever you are not secretly afraid that you are not living right now to your fullest capacity, you will not be afraid to experience the passing of time and the certainty of death. Living with a commitment to savor each moment of life as you live it is a terrific way to get in shape for dying. In fact it is the only way to stretch your ability to savor each moment of whatever cosmic expansion will occur after life.

Which brings up the famous dichotomy of living now versus living in the afterlife. Who says it is a dichotomy anyway? Do you? If you do, it will indeed become dichotomized for you. If you don't say so yourself and you don't believe that it is so just because some expert or one of your favorite authority figures said so, a natural condition I call 'No Such Thing As Dichotomies' will prevail. And the issue will resolve itself very quickly.

My own experience supports two simple and self-evident, if somewhat circular, conclusions.

First, you cannot live well now if you are longing for an afterlife to come along and bring you all the happiness and satisfaction that you lack. You would not be longing for happiness and satisfaction nor would you be lacking any if you were creating it as you go along by living well now.

Second, you cannot live fully now if you are obsessed with death. You would not have become obsessed with death to begin with if you were living fully now.

Fear of death always involves fearing the loss of whatever degree of individuality we have attained during our personal journeys through the stages of separation and individuation. Ironically, I suggest there is nothing to lose.

If the purpose of life is to facilitate growth, learning, creativity, play and evolution within each of us as individuals, then the purpose of death can be no different. Even if life had no purpose and was simply a state of being, death would still be more of the same. After all, death is just another phase of life. And it is experienced individually by each of us, whether we are involved in separation, integration, or any other possible process.

Numerous civilizations in the past, including Ancient Egypt, developed and perfected techniques for crossing the curtain between life and death at will with completely operational communication and sensory capabilities. We assume that these abilities were shrouded in supernatural mysticism because movies, dramas, novels and much psychic writing promote and advance such assumptions. Actually, the techniques may have involved nothing more mysterious than fullscale cultural participation in another level of integration between dreaming and waking consciousness.

When we break through the strictly conceptual barriers of adulthood during The Midlife Metamorphosis and we reexperience the integration of early childhood from a new perceptual base, both sides of any issue become joined in a circle of completion. And anything is possible.

For instance: Instruct your imagination to wander playfully for the next few minutes. Lie down or relax in a comfortable chair. Close your eyes and pretend you are an actor performing on the stage of a vast multidimensional theater, bigger even than Madison Square Garden or the Los Angeles Civic Center. Each role you play takes on a creative vitality that far surpasses the skill and adroitness of any Tony-winning 'Best Of The Year' performance.

Imagine yourself cast in any setting or script that you like. Follow the action for a few moments. Then abruptly shift the setting altogether to another evening and another performance. Imagine yourself in an entirely different role. If you were the hero or heroine before, pretend you are now the villain; if you were the star, pretend that you are now in the chorus line or a small supporting role that might expand considerably if it were projected offstage. Notice how the characters you are playing have implicit backgrounds that began long before each particular performance and how they bring their backgrounds with them to establish their personalities and motivations. Just allow your imagination to wander and follow along wherever it leads you. And finally, when you are ready, come back to the room you are in. As you open your eyes, notice that it, too, is just another stage on which you can perform. Whenever you find that you are stuck in a pattern of holding on to your individuality, particularly in the form in which it is most clearly differentiated at the peak of your separation phase of development, you are like a one-role actor who refuses to read new scripts or to go on with his or her career.

In dreams, you can become aware of many of the other possible roles you have played or are currently playing. You can also experiment with the mechanics of the structural integration of mass beliefs, cultural conventions and psychological foundations that form the stage, set designs, lighting, costumes and props for your performance. There are no limits to your consciousness and in dreams you can directly experience all of its vastness in dramatic, inspiring, and highly entertaining multidimensional theatrical terms.

As I discussed in Chapter 10, your dreams provide you with a safe place to try out different reality scripts and work with different combinations of the data that is necessary for creating your life. In this respect, sleep is more than just the other side of consciousness. It is the process that makes waking life possible.

Similarly, death is more than merely the end or other side of life. It is the necessary and vital process that makes life possible.

You don't have to agree with this. In fact, it does not matter at all whether you think any of this material is really true or not. What matters is whether you are open to new possibilities or tightly chained by the arrogance of believing that you know everything there is to know already and that you can find a lot of other people who agree with you about almost anything you think is so. If you are in the latter category, you are not alone. For more than 10,000 years, people have been dying to prove that no other point of view other than theirs could ever be right. And most of them managed to do just that, long before their time.

As an alternative, I invite you to remain open to everything and to seek out and cherish whatever works for you.

In the rest of this chapter, I will take a closer look at many of the ways death and life are both fundamental choices and examine their relationship to our normal everyday sleeping and waking cycles. I will also suggest a more workable context in which to hold dying. In addition, I will support you in considering the possibility of folding whatever death drama you are now involved in and consciously setting the stage for a new role in a new longer-running production that can include longevity as well as any number of other Alternatives To Aging.

The big question about dying is always 'Why?'.

Why me? Why her? Why them? Why do certain people die when they appear to have so much to live for? Why does it seem that the good die young? Why do babies or children who seem to have no business dying at all have to die the way they do?

One of the strongest underlying themes of this book is that life is a process of choice and that extended life is one of the choices open to you.

Dying is also a choice.

If you are near death or you have recently been closely involved in a tragic death of a loved one, you may not like hearing that. You may even notice that you are angry at me for suggesting such a thing. If this is so, all I ask is that you notice your emotional reaction, identify whatever belief patterns have activated it, and then bring every bit of that along with you as you consider other possibilities and alternatives. If this chapter is upsetting to you in any way, facing that upset and not closing the book on it, could become a matter of life and death. For you.

Once again, dying is a choice. That means no one dies who has not chosen to die.

While I do not necessarily mean suicide in this regard, I do not exclude it either. Suicide is an obvious example of choosing to die and, in somewhat distorted form, many parallels can be drawn between suicide and ordinary death.

In both cases, an individual assesses his or her patterns of existence or progress through living and reaches one of the following conclusions. Perhaps a certain minimal quality of life required for continuation is lacking. Or whatever job there was to do has either been completed or cannot possibly be completed under present circumstances. Or the high adventure and excitement of dying outweighs the dreary day-to-day routine of living. Or a more powerful and lasting statement can be made by the act of dying than the act of living, in which case death for a purpose becomes preferable to life without one.

In suicide and nonsuicide cases alike, the personal assessment that triggers the event is based upon physical sensations, emotions, thoughts, attitudes, positions, judgments, evaluations, pictures from the past, and internalized belief systems. Because each of these factors is reactive and based solely upon a personal abdication to circumstances rather than the self-generated act of taking a stand, they are about as faulty and unreliable a source for a decision as major as the choice between life or death as you are likely to find. All together they are as solid a foundation for action as a structure built upon blocks of lukewarm oatmeal.

The differences between suicide and nonsuicide are obvious. In suicide, the choice is consciously made. The individual's conscious desire to live gives way to an even stronger conscious desire to die. And death is directly implemented by whatever device may be close at hand to dramatize or expedite the process.

In other forms of dying, this critical relationship between choice and implementation is not so clearly defined. There is always, however, a psychological shift on a deeply internal not-so-conscious level of being from a personal commitment to life ('I will live') to the relinquishing of that basic personal commitment to life ('I will live or die, whichever destiny, god, fate or circumstances bring about for me').

The dynamic and energizing affirmation of a fundamental intention to live is no longer present. Instead, there is the acceptance of a kind of readiness to embark on a journey to some other reality. In such instances, an implicit invitation to external implements of death is sent out. A condition of openness to death as a viable possibility is set up and maintained. And the likelihood of dying increases significantly because sincere invitations and openness to new experiences are always appropriately rewarded.

Everyone gets exactly what they ask for. In life as well as in death. No matter how clearly expressed or covert the request may be.

People who have relinquished their commitment to live will find convenient avenues of escape at every turn: An unexpected flood, earthquake, mudslide, fire, or hurricane will hit the old homestead when they are trapped inside. A draft notification will arrive and combat orders will follow immediately after basic training. An automobile accident, ax murder, terrorist attack, or other unfortunate circumstance will occur and escape will not be possible. A ticket for Flight #313 to St. Louis, the one that crashes right after takeoff, will be purchased and no unexpected telephone calls at the last minute will prevent boarding the doomed aircraft in time. Cancer, heart disease, pneumonia, gangrene, kidney failure, hardening of the arteries, sniffles, high blood pressure, AIDs, or some other rare new epidemic will claim another victim.

For the moment, forget about the issue of morality as it relates to one's individual choice to live or die. Such issues invariably involve cultural belief systems which vary considerably from nation to nation and century to century. Until recently, suicide with honor was the

highest attainable condition of life in Japan and many
other Asian civilizations. In our own culture, hospitalized
individuals with inordinately painful terminal illnesses still
do not have clear access to the plug they may dearly wish
to pull and 'Right To Life' bumper stickers outweigh
'Right To Death' bumper stickers by a factor of at least
8700 to 1. For the purpose of this discussion, whether we
think the morality of choosing to die is right or wrong is
not important. At best, it is a convenient way to avoid
confronting the possibility that indeed we do create our
own deaths just as we create our own lives.

When death actually arrives in response to the
invitation that was issued, it comes for many reasons.
Usually the least of these is the immediately apparent
cause. Many of us die simply because we believe old age is
so shameful and degrading to the body and the spirit that
we would no longer be able to meet our minimum quality
standards for continuing life. This belief affects every
part of the mind and the physical body. Believing that old
age affects the senses, we lose our vision or become hard
of hearing. Believing that it affects the joints, we become
arthritic. Believing that it affects sexual desire and
performance, we become impotent. Believing that it
affects our capacity for living, we die.

We get so lost in negative beliefs that we forget
how easily they can be transformed. All that is required is
the simple affirmative act of constructively asking
ourselves why we are constantly dwelling on whichever
issue we happen to be preoccupied with at the moment
and then allowing the answer to come spontaneously
from within. Instead, we play out each issue to its
ultimate form, creating physical and chemical alterations
within our bodies according to rigid, unexamined beliefs
about seemingly appropriate activities over various
periods of our lives.

Let this sink in. It will literally save your life. Time
and time again.

When you believe that it is time for you to slow
down and die, whether your belief is conscious or
unconscious, you will bring about the means that will
make it possible.

Human consciousness senses the willingness to die ahead of time and brings forth the cause of death that is most consistent with whatever is considered to be the 'right' way to go. Many, to whom the idea of a slow languishing death in a hospital is unthinkable, choose harsh but decisive circumstances like being swept under waves or consumed in fiery explosions. Catastrophe victims choose the drama of leaving in a blaze of glory and heightened perception, fighting valiantly for life, not giving in peacefully. Sufferers choose agonizing longterm illnesses and struggle in a sea of pain that is specifically created to eject the consciousness from the body, while nonsufferers simply close their eyes and drift away.

The end result is infallibly the same.

Since the choice is all yours, one of the alternatives I want you to examine is this: Will you continue to go along with commonly accepted and widely held notions about the nature of aging and death, and die when everyone thinks you should? Or will you investigate all of the possibilities for yourself, age at your own rate and extend your own life accordingly?

The choice involves being willing to reconsider a huge stack of beliefs and notions that everyone else may continue to keep around. For example, everyone believes that death is mysterious, a grim and capricious avenger, a product of chance, luck, fate, tragedy, destiny. You will have to let go of all that and begin to realize it is untrue anyway, unless you say it is true; in which case, by agreement, it then becomes true for you.

You will also have to be willing to take complete responsibility for using the relentless power of personal choice that dictates the time and type of your death.

You may become aware that your life-or-death choice is made many times and is either checked and reassessed at appropriate intervals or dragged faithfully and compulsively into each successive moment like an overweight suitcase for which you must pay penalty charges at the terminal. Your choice is usually made on a deep unconscious level. Yet no level is too deep to uncover and explore in dreams or too remote to probe in exercises like the ones in this book.

Take a moment get in touch with everything you

know yet pretend not to know about life and death by asking yourself about it. Use the following sentence stems and complete each one at least five different ways without thinking about your answers or trying to evaluate them:

- **One of the things that's so about dying is...**
- **If I knew how I was going to die, the answer might be...**

Listen uncritically to yourself. And remember that whatever you believe, no matter how traditional or farfetched it may seem, it is nothing more and nothing less than whatever you happen to believe. It is definitely not the rigidly cast truth about reality. In reality, a limitless supply of possibilities and alternatives is open to you all the time.

If your personal horizons are less expansive than that, you are caught in a trap of your own making, and choosing not to break free will someday be the death of you.

When you get right down to it, the major source of all of the resistance and fear of dying comes from inconclusive evidence and lack of any certainty about whether or not we will continue to exist in any afterdeath form. When we know that there will be a tomorrow, we are willing to accept and even enjoy the end of today.

While the evidence may not present itself in hard and fast form, the guidelines for certainty about life after death are just as solid as the guidelines for certainty about anything else that we commonly take for granted.

Viewed strictly experientially and cut off from our thoughts, beliefs and opinions about reality, there is no more evidence that we will wake up when we go to sleep than there is that we will not wake up when we die. Because we do indeed wake up every morning and are involved in an intimately balanced ongoing relationship between waking and sleeping, and because we can observe others doing the same thing we do, the integrity of the process becomes self-evident and we trust the certainty of it.

We go to sleep, we wake up. We go to sleep, we wake up. We go to sleep, we wake up. And we willingly participate in the fundamental rhythm of the pattern. It is natural, normal and universal.

On still another scale, the same kind of self-evident trust and certainty is involved in the process of breathing. If you think about it, there is no reason to assume that you will ever inhale again after you have exhaled. In fact, you can't even think about it without tensing up. Nevertheless, everyone breathes over and over again automatically so many times that we take the process for granted. We breathe out, we breathe in. We breathe out, we breathe in. We breathe out, we breathe in. And as each breath we took becomes our last one, each new breath we take becomes out next one. It goes on and on and on.

There would be very little agreement available if you were suddenly to become too afraid to exhale, thinking that you would never inhale again. Or if you were to become too afraid to go to sleep, thinking that you might never wake again. In either case, you would quickly become the target of an extremely unsympathetic label known as 'Mental Illness', which is generally associated with both of those acts.

So it is curious that living and dying, obviously the next cycle outward on the scale of being, should be so highly charged with denial, avoidance and panic.

We can easily observe the cyclical nature of physical reality. It occurs all around us, everywhere we turn. In our own body processes. In the motion of the planet and the everpresent progression of the hours and the seasons. In the surging peaks and restful valleys of our emotional expression.

It adds up to evidence on a massive scale that each ending is only the start of a new beginning in an unbroken chain of experience. And yet, because we do not live and die as often as we inhale and exhale or wake and sleep or observe winter merging into spring, we view the process as a fearful unknown, veiled and obscured in mystery.

Death, itself, is actually not fearful. Any fears that we associate with it occur only as ideas or beliefs in the conceptual realm of our thoughts. If you have ever been with someone at the moment of their death, you may have noticed how there is a release from fear rather than a heightening of it. Like riding a bicycle or swimming the English Channel or stepping onto the surface of the moon, the experience of really dying is nothing at all like we who are not really dying think it is.

Moreover, death is actually not unknown. We directly participate in the act and aftermath of dying all the time, although we may not be aware of it. Since we do not produce our bodies in one single version and then watch them fall apart piece by piece, our cells die and recreate themselves every moment, one by one. Our bodies are created continuously over the course of our lifetime and we literally replenish and replace ourselves all the time. It is one of the ways in which having a physical body is a primary learning experience for each of us. In this instance, the ceaseless cycle of life and death is the lesson to be learned.

Death is not even veiled or obscured in mystery although it sounds poetic to say so. It is just not possible to perceive it clearly from our present observation points. Whenever anything seems unclear from wherever we are standing, the simplest recourse is to stand somewhere else instead and change our point of view.

Therefore, like video camera technicians, we will first move in for an extreme close-up look at the process of death. After that, we will pull back as far as we can to enlarge the context completely. This will alter our perspectives and unravel some of the obscurity. As you will see, all of this is easier done than said. Especially if you keep your imagination loose, playful and flexible.

1. The Multicelled Point Of View.

To begin with, imagine instead of being you that you are only one part of you. You can be any organ or group of cells that you like. Whether you are imagining that you are your finger or your stomach, notice how you are made up of much smaller cellular components. Notice also that each of them is highly specialized and able to function individually, yet all of them work together as a team to make the formation of your finger or your stomach possible.

Imagine that each physical cell is like a miniature brain, complete with memories of its own functions and of its interactive role in relationship to the body as a whole. And just for fun, also imagine that the memory banks of each cell contain pictures of the complete history of your body as it is now, as it was in the past, and as it will be in the future.

To complete the fantasy, pretend this cellular consciousness can somehow assess its own blueprint for the future based upon the impact of your thoughts and beliefs on all the available possibilities. And also pretend it can make instantaneous adjustments, revisions and compensations to bring its projected blueprint and your thoughts and beliefs into alignment. This may involve quite a stretch for you, but it is only a small step for any one of your cells.

Each cell actually does have a life cycle of its own and draws upon its own unique memory patterns to perform its role within an organ. When each cell dies (and cells live for an infinitesimally shorter time than you or I), another cell replaces it, drawing from the same unique chromosomal memory pattern and continuing to function exactly as before.

As a complex multicelled organ, you are ordinarily not aware of the constant life and death activity of each of your tiny components. You continue to go about your own physiological business as usual. Yet that business would be quickly terminated without the ongoing cooperation of each individual cell and the inherent cellular memory framework that makes the way you work possible.

2. The Self Point Of View.

Moving outward along an ever-widening spiral of existence, you will arrive at another level of experience: The one in which you normally function in everyday life. So imagine yourself just the way you are right now in physical form and notice how you are a collection of individual organs, parts and subassemblies that work together to support your life processes.

From the perspective of you-as-a-whole, tune into your cellular levels once again, and become aware of the enormous flow of energy that is released as each part of you continues to die and recreate itself over the entire course of your lifetime. Notice how, unless there is a serious problem, your everyday consciousness is never aware of all this constant vital activity. Continue to allow your imagination to flow and meander through each part of you and notice how you would be unable to function without the ongoing cooperation of each individual organ and subassembly of parts that make the way you work possible.

3. The Multiselved Point Of View.

Moving still further outward along our hypothetical spiral of existence, you will arrive at still another dimension of being. On this level, everything is much larger than it is in everyday life. To get the feel of it, imagine yourself just the way you are once again, only see yourself functioning as one individual cell within the structure of an altogether larger entity that transcends any commonly-accepted notion of time and space.

Imagine all the days of your life are but a single day, a single dream, a single hour or minute to the entity of which you are a part. And that your larger entity requires your experiences to survive just as you require food and water. Everything that you experience is essential to the wellbeing of your entity, including all the good, the bad, the ugly, the glorious. Everything experienced by each of the other cellular beings that form the same entity also contributes to the same vital lifesustaining activity.

Like simple single cells, you live and die and are constantly recreated anew with all of your biological and psychological memories in tact and fully available upon demand. Since death is as much of an experience as life, in either format you continue to contribute to the survival of the entity by maintaining your own integrity as a solitary individual and by creating and participating in all forms of experience to feed your entity.

Let your imagination carry you through each part of this gigantic multidimensional being and notice how your entity would be unable to function without the ongoing cooperation of each single cell, organ, part and personality that makes the way it works possible.

4. A Final Interlude.
While you are still playfully exploring these alternative notions, direct your imagination to still another channel altogether. This time, imagine that life and death are no more than the next wider level of waking and sleeping or inhaling and exhaling. On such a level, death might be a well-deserved chance to rest and refresh yourself. Or an opportunity for expanded dreams, in which you can try out new possibilities before actually bringing them forth in physical form, and meet with other beings you have known in this and other lives for the purpose of choosing up roles and sides for the storyline of your next life experience.

Close your eyes and imagine that you have died. Where were you when it happened? What was the theme of your life? What did you leave unfinished? Where are you now? What is the setting? Who do you see there? What are you and they talking about? What are you doing? Who else would you like to see and what will you say to them when they appear? Who are you when you are in your imagination and not in your body? Where will you be when you awaken once again? What will be the next theme of your life?

When you open your eyes, take a few extra moments and just be with yourself. Then, think of someone you would like to talk with for a little while. Call them up or invite them over and share any new insights or observations that you may have just discovered.

Unless you are willing to open up to new alternatives and new possibilities, aging will be the death of you. These exercises will separate your present conceptual packaging in which aging and death are tied together with the same cord. They allow you to see that you can have one without the other. They also demonstrate what it might be like for you to die, without the risk of the real thing. As you do each one, you will be expanding the limits of your consciousness and allowing new personal data to displace old files filled with assumptive belief patterns and second-hand conclusions.

The only beliefs and conclusions that can possibly

serve you in the long run are the ones you form yourself. I cannot repeat that often enough.

The basis for many of my own conclusions began with my first encounter with death in the autumn of 1977.

My friend Carolyn Coulter and I were driving home from Wakefield, Rhode Island, late at night. We had just come from a heavy dinner and an even heavier emotional experience with two beloved friends from my college days who had reached the terminal stage of their 20-year marriage. For four or five hours, the atmosphere had been crawling with unexpressed longing, fear, depression and despair. To make matters worse, I had found no way to crack the tightly impacted communication barriers or release the tension and strain.

From the moment we pulled out of their driveway, a dense cloud of sleep energy filled the interior of my small imported sedan. Carolyn began to drift away almost immediately, and by the time I pulled onto the dark deserted pavement of Interstate 95, wave after wave after wave of desensitizing zzzzzzzzzzzzs were swirling around my shoulders and neck.

A deafening thud and blinding flashes of light abruptly restored me to an acute state of consciousness. Carolyn and I were on our hands and knees on the ceiling of an enormous upside-down room that resembled an oversized high-school gymnasium or bus-station waiting room. Actually, it was difficult to tell whether the room was extremely large or if we were just extremely small. But I somehow knew that the size and spatial relationships were extremely important and had to be maintained just the way they were.

Intense golden light streamed from the far end of the room which merged into a large tunnel-like structure and an odd yet strangely familiar musical tone filled the air. It was altogether wonderful, tantalizing and compelling beyond words. In the passageway, bathed in light, I could see dimly remembered figures waving to me and beckoning gently. It felt like the end of a long journey home. Except, I realized sadly but surely, I was not ready to go home yet.

At the end of the room nearest us was a regular door with a lighted red and white exit sign over the top. Even upside down and very small compared to the rest of the setting, it quickly oriented me towards what I considered to be the real world.

Taking Carolyn's hand, I led her across the floor of the ceiling. We crawled on our hands and knees in a dreamy slowmotion rhythm. As we approached the door, it began to shrink away. I could see it becoming smaller and smaller. The knob did not work and I had to reach through the door in some indescribable upside-down way to open it from the outside in. I crawled out, dragging and pulling Carolyn along behind me just moments before the shrinking doorway would have become too small for her to pass through.

Suddenly we were by the side of the road on Interstate 95. The car had flipped over at least once or twice and was lying on its roof with its wheels in the air, smashed so flat that its hood and trunk lids were flush with the surface of the road. Every window was broken and shattered glass littered the road. The steering column was poking through the back of the front seat. Every door but the one on the driver's side was inoperably bent out of shape and sealed shut.

Carolyn and I stood quietly in the roadside brush. We were shaken but completely uninjured. Neither of us was even scratched. We watched as other cars began to stop. Finally the police arrived and bewilderingly began to search for the missing bodies. At first, they refused to believe that we were the bodies they were searching for.

The next day when we went to visit the ruins of my car, I could barely fit my arm inside to get the registration certificate out of the glove compartment. What had been a compact vehicle to begin with had become a thoroughly compacted pile of demolished rubble.

Even now, when I think about the experience, I have the distinct recollection of successfully manipulating the spatial dimensions of our bodies to keep us safe and of altering the flow of time long enough to allow us to return to this plane of reality. Since then, on several occasions I have become aware of the sensation of subtly shifting the content of space or time when some unusual or potentially dangerous circumstance required it, but never again on so grand a scale.

From that time on, my personal relationship to death and dying has never been the same.

Transforming your own relationship to death is a lifelong commitment of the highest order. An extended life is possible only when first you are willing to die and able to deal with death issues openly and honestly.

You can't run away from it. You can't hide from it. You can't even deny it or resist your feelings and beliefs about it and expect to come up with viable Alternatives To Aging and premature death.

All you can do is live as if your life depended on it. And watch what happens next.

CHAPTER 12

ALTERNATIVES TO AGING

There is a place where no one lives much past the age of twelve.

It is a playground kind of world. Populated by children. Run by children for children.

Every morning, the children leave their houses and go out to play. They play with trucks and erector sets and small machines and balls and electronic games and guns and shovels and doctor kits and marbles. Some of them play house.

Snacks and meals are provided automatically. So are clothes, sneakers and other necessities of life. No one goes without. No one lacks.

It is a well run economy with centuries of stability behind it, although no one seems to know how or why it works. In many ways, it is a better world than yours and mine. In many ways, it is somewhat the same.

The most important difference is that no one lives much past the age of twelve.

You know what happens when you turn twelve, don't you?

Your glands pulse with strange new secretions. Your biological clocks shift to a different rate of ticking and propel you down new developmental paths. Your body begins to lengthen out. Your proportions change. You grow hair on places that are not your head. Physically, you no longer appear childlike. Your emotional needs rise to unaccustomed levels of wanting and longing, and you are led in new directions by new dreams and new ideals.

Your mental perspective expands along with your metamorphosising body and emotions. So you see things in ways you never saw them before. And your intellect processes material differently than it did one or two or five years before.

Even time flows at an altered rate of speed than it did when each day stretched out like an eternity and each night became an endless struggle with shadows and terrifying hidden forces of adversity.

You know what happens when you turn twelve.

You change.

And when you change, the other children do not like it one bit.

They don't like it when you begin to think differently and look differently and act differently than you used to think, look and act. There is some scary substance that sticks to the notion of change.

At first, they good-naturedly make fun of you. They kid around about how your child-styled playclothes don't fit you so well. And how your hands are too big to manipulate the child-sized controls on the games. And how your mind no longer tracks clearly on childish chatter.

At first, it is so good natured that you even join in and make fun of yourself. But that stage passes quickly. Soon it is no longer funny at all.

The closer you get to the other side of twelve, the more serious a problem it becomes in the playground world.

The children will not allow anyone in the play areas at all past the age of thirteen. There is a special isolated section of benches where thirteen and fourteen-year-old people have to sit, if they live that long. All they can do is watch and wither away.

Those who live to the ripe old age of fifteen look and act so grotesquely that they cannot come out in public at all where the children can see them. They are shut away in dark rooms because they are so close to death.

Naturally, they die there. Where the children don't have to be around them or deal with them. Naturally, it is better that way.

And in that merry little place of eternal spring and summer, sheltered and securely set in their youthful patterns, the peachfaced cherubic children play on and on and on.

Or do they?

The alternatives are clear.

Throughout this book, I have presented a variety of new ways to look at the process of being alive as something separate and distinct from the process of merely staying alive. And I have shown how the experience of aging presents different choices, depending upon which of the two processes you happen to be engaged in.

Each choice is an alternative that opens up the possibility that aging does not have to be the sad, demoralizing, and debilitating problem most of us are conditioned into believing that it is. Since that possibility may not have existed for you before, each alternative has already done its job by creating a shift in your fundamental approach to the future. In this case, the intended shift has been from aging as you used to think it had to be for everyone, to aging as it now can be and, if you so choose, will be. For you.

Just knowing that alternatives exist can launch your life down eight-lane freeways that once were invisible, obscured or unavailable.

Some of the Alternatives To Aging that you have read about involved a technique or exercise. And when any of these particular alternatives was presented, I suggested that the technique or exercise itself was not the answer to a problem but merely a way to explore another point of view and transform whatever position you had consciously or unconsciously chosen to take about a specific aspect of your own experience of aging.

Still other alternatives offered guidelines for an intimate and thought provoking self-examination of the way you are and how you got that way, along with my view of the probable consequences in age-related terms. Again, each time, I suggested that while examining yourself can be useful, interesting and informative, it can only be viewed as a way to understand what has happened in the past. This is not the same as a transformational shift in the present nor does it have much, if any, impact on the future.

Don't get the wrong idea. All of the exercises, techniques and guidelines are truly powerful alternatives to the unworkable ways that most people spend the second half of their lives. Their effectiveness has been proven time and time again in my own experience and in the experiences of others. Each one can give you an edge on aging that can serve you by preserving your body, your mind and your spirit, right up to your maximum potential lifespan. However, none of them is really the reason why you will age at a different rate than statistical standards claim you must or why you will not shut down prematurely.

That reason may well turn out to be philosophical rather than experiential, psychological or even physical.

As you may have noticed, all through this book I have dropped fragments of philosophy for you to find along the way. In this chapter, I will tie enough of all those philosophical threads together to make a rope for traversing the years to come. It will be a rope that can hold you up instead of hang you up. Obviously, the kind of philosophy I am talking about is not a dry textbook dissertation but a living, breathing, active, self-generated pursuit of reality.

Once again, I invite your openness and request that you consider all of this and everything yet to come strictly as a possibility.

Consider, as a place to start, that the world as we truly know it begins and ends with each person who inhabits it. Imagine each of us is like a central axis upon which the world revolves. If you were not doing what you are doing right now, and if I did not do what I did today, the whole world would not be the same.

Like our external communications, our inner communication radiates outward in all directions. Using a broad, far-reaching, internally-sourced frequency band, we can contact our own psyches, touch our capacities to be fully who we are, and reach out to every other psyche as well. The problem is, no one can contact his or her psyche by thinking of it as a separate thing, an unknown to be feared and avoided, or a spiritual treasure locked away in some vast eternal attic.

We can only experience the strength and vitality of the psyche by exploring the subjective reality that belongs exclusively to each of us. Only voyages into those still uncharted interior regions will lead us to the greater part of our beings that transcends time and space.

Actually, it is a smaller world than it seems. And also a larger one.

Just briefly, imagine what it would be like if all past, present and future events and all identities occurred at one and the same time and if they existed all together for the duration of each moment. Each event would rub up against every other event. Action taken in the present could alter the past, and deeds yet to be done would have impact on everyone in the present. It might be very much like it is now, when any given event implies the existence of the possibility of other events which were not or have not yet been chosen, created, or communicated by our psyches.

It is our birthright as natural beings to possess an everpresent reservoir of inner knowing, vitality, peace and power. To draw upon it, all we need to do is to rely on immediate sensory data pinpointed in each moment of the present and based exclusively upon the way things are. This requires avoiding secondhand data, including our own and other people's thoughts, attitudes, beliefs, judgments and evaluations, as a basis for choice and action. Firsthand sensory data, anchored in the present and drawn entirely from our direct experience with the integrity of nature, can transcend time and carry with it all of the intuitive possibilities that are in the process of coming to be. It is the stuff that creativity, inspiration, resourcefulness and mastery are made of.

At one level of being, when we each set up our own reality from an infinite array of available possibilities, we also form the way in which we will perceive our experience of it and others within it. Meanwhile, at still another level, each of us also lives in an all-too-solid reality of hardcore substance and content which included all of the already created material that has already turned out the way it is. Our primary balancing act involves spanning these two dimensions and navigating freely between them. And for this purpose, we each possess a unique stance in time and space that is individually and exclusively our own.

Only when we come from our own stance can we serve and contribute to ourselves and others to the best of our abilities. If we become preoccupied with fantasy dangers that have not yet emerged or take on what others perceive to be problems, we diminish the very energy that enables us to deal effectively with dangers and problems that may be very real and much closer to hand.

The highest order of affirmation to life, and therefore to longevity, is one simple statement:

This is it.

'This' means wherever we find ourselves, wherever we are coming from at each actual moment of perception. 'Is' means existing right now as a presence in the present. 'It' means how everything has turned out so far in the external world that we can see, sense, touch, measure and feel all around us. Those three little words, eight little letters, simply mean everything is so just the way that it is with nothing added and nothing left out.

When we use our experience and acknowledgement of 'This is it' to orient ourselves solidly in the present reality, our minds can then be disengaged to handle future possibilities like an automatic pilot, a function which the mind is able to perform better than any computer. In the process, various unused portions of the brain become activated and the nature of future possibilities shows up in more consciously available ways. Aging versions of ourselves can then be created in fully actualized and dynamically alive form. The connective link is the fact that it is always you in the present who eventually emerges as yourself in the future.

Finally, consider the possibility that our lives are miniature and gigantic, mortal and immortal, existing on many levels simultaneously. Also consider that each of us might be able to open dimensions of reality that are unavailable to anyone else until we ourselves open them up as new and untried alternatives.

It is indeed possible.

No one but you can be you. No one else shares your place as the central axis of everything that is occurring all around you. Accordingly the universe leans in your direction, resounding with vitality and abundance in which you could never be lost, forgotten, dismissed, ignored or forsaken, unless you chose to be. No flower or tree has ever had to ask for life support from the sun and the earth. Neither do you.

Believing that you may be unworthy of life support does not stop the process. It only uses up more energy than would otherwise be required for the simple creative act of life and makes a maximum lifespan more difficult to attain.

I suggest that you reexamine your entire list of beliefs and let go of any that may be to the contrary. Then look within yourself for hidden or suppressed thoughts and feelings of exhuberance and joy, and become willing to engage in events that will actively support and release them.

In this book, a lot of space has been invested in the subject of beliefs. That is only because so much of your life has been similarly invested. Beliefs automatically mobilize emotions and lock them into fixed patterns that dominate one or more areas of your experience to keep you stuck. As you have seen, if you are stuck in a belief pattern about aging, you have no alternative but to create self-fulfilling difficulties, problems, and tragedies. When such beliefs are released, your imagination steps in to play a larger and more creative role. Teaming up with your newly-freed emotions, it forms an expanded basis for alternatives involving reality, events and even the material objects that surround you.

Take a few moments at regular intervals to notice where and when your thoughts or feelings are leading you. Whenever you are stuck, you can always shift your imagination to another directional path by pretending to have an emotion at the opposite end of the spectrum from the one you are having.

That's a useful alternative to remember.

But there is another alternative that may become even more useful. Choosing it, you can directly experience a shift in reality simply on the strength of your words. In fact, there is no trick or tip or process to it whatsoever.

Whenever you are stuck, in or out of an aging issue, find the one thing that needs to be done and promise to do it. Phrase your promise precisely by saying exactly what you will do and exactly when you will have it done. Say your promise out loud to yourself and then, if you think you will need support to keep your word, tell it to as many other people as you can. When more than one thing needs to be done, isolate the elements and promise either to do them all sequentially or to handle just one item at a time, whichever you prefer.

Two important points about promises: 1. Be very specific when you make a promise. The more specific you are, the more you will feel the earth move beneath your feet. 2. Making a promise is not the same as keeping it. Making a promise means only that you will live out of your promise for as long as you said you would. You may not know how you will possibly keep it. Finding out how is what always gets to be the exciting part.

Because the act of promising is such a practical Alternative To Aging or anything else that has not been going well for you, it will be useful to explore the dynamics of why and how it works.

It works because it automatically places you in a philosophical domain where workability itself is created. A domain is merely a box or a contextual space containing all of the possibilities appropriate to that space. Without being aware of it in everyday life, we constantly move from one box-like philosophical domain to another. This means we flow from one space in which certain distinct possibilities are contained to another space in which certain other types of possibilities exist. And on and on and on.

Being in a box does not mean you are stuck there. You can choose which domain you wish to operate in just as you choose anything else. You can even arrange to be in the box that best suits your purposes at any given time. Or you can take whichever box you happen to end up in by default. Either way, you are always coming from one philosophical domain or another.

There are many volumes of work on this subject and my short definition is intended only to provide a minimal framework for a lifetime of effective interaction with reality as the final Alternative To Aging. It is actually very simple:

Be sure that you are in the right box at the right time.

Many people are in a conceptual box. There is nothing wrong with that. In fact, it can be very useful for many kinds of activities like thinking, organizing, putting ideas down on paper, evaluating, judging, weighing decisions, and following instructions.

The conceptual box is the domain of your thoughts, your beliefs, your fixed emotional reactions, your attitudes, your defenses, your chronic fears, your justifications, your positions, your opinions, your habitual behavior, your relationship with time, space and distance, and all the various other tangible things that show up in life.

It is where you keep your voice over, the little ongoing commentary you hear in the back of your head about everything and everyone, and your internal monologue about what you should have done instead of what you did or what you are going to do the next time whatever it was happens again.

It is also where you set up a blueprint for aging and the space from which you then proceed to implement that blueprint down to the last tiny detail, exactly the way you thought it out.

The biggest problem, when you live in the concept box, is deciding whose concepts are right and whose are wrong, so you know which side to be on and what to share with people as your considered expert opinion about any conversational topic at hand.

Here is why you need to be extremely careful with conceptual material: If you buy into a wellmeaning but mistaken concept about aging, for example, or you are taken in by an outright ideological fraud which you then proceed to justify, defend and internalize as your own conceptual base, you could die long before your time. The cause of death would be thinking. Or, in this case, thinking that death was either the right or only appropriate action open to you.

242   Alternatives To Aging

It is worth noting once again that premature aging is only one of the possible causes of premature death. The concepts that you hold have more than a little to do with it. In fact, every war that was ever fought, every bomb that was ever dropped, every act of violence that was ever perpetrated began in this particular philosophical domain. But then, so did every intelligent decision, every moral position and every reasonable answer to any problem.

The conceptual box is one of the places in which humans differentiate themselves from other forms of animal life. It is where the mind and the powers of the mind are undisputed and supreme.

Separate and distinct from the concept box is the experiential box. Everyone enters this philosophical domain regularly. But few people live in it because that would require letting go of all of the virtues and vices associated with conceptual mental activity.

To remain purely in the realm of experience, you must give up your thoughts, your beliefs, your fixed emotional reactions, your attitudes, your defenses, your justifications and your positions. You must be willing to experience everything simply and directly, using only your moment-by-moment physical sensations, impulses, insights, imagination, observations, and emotional flow as your guides.

In the experience box, the nature of things as they really are is absolutely clear. Objects, events and actions show up as direct presences, unfiltered and undistorted by labels, definitions, or preconceptions. You can see the forest as well as the trees, the entire lawn and every blade of grass in it. You become intrinsically aware of your precariously balanced relationship with time, and you can participate in your own process of aging as an interested, impartial observer. As a result, you will age in a way that is consistent with what is possible for human beings as a species instead of whatever way anybody happens to think is so.

In the domain of experience, life is not very complicated. You notice that you are alive when you are living and dead when you die.

That's not so bad either. Because you could easily
live up to the 120 to 140 year maximum potential age
available to us all. And you could expect to live most, if
not all of that time, in a state of health, vigor, vitality,
and physical and mental wellbeing. That possibility is
definitely within the realm of experience.

The experiential box is where we discover that we
are a part of life and that the passage of our lives is no
different than the natural flow of the hours, the seasons,
and the tides. Being, just pure passive being, is
undisputed and supreme.

There is a trap however.

The trap exists because we can pass freely between
the boxes whenever we choose. While we live primarily
in the conceptual box, it is only by default. More
accurately, it is like the start-up setting of a computer. It
feels natural and seems right. However we also live in the
experiential box a good deal of the time, particularly
whenever we try something new. With no firm personal
judgments, evaluations or conceptual props to fall back
on, a new experience is always fresh and keenedged.
Then we evaluate it and form a concept so that we know
what to expect next time or what to compare it with if
we try it again.

And that is the trap.

If we believe it was a bad experience, all future
recurrences will be tainted by that belief. If we decide it
was a wonderful experience, all future recurrences will be
weighed against our conceptual memories of it and found
lacking. Our beliefs and decisions, or our concepts, will
have turned a freeflowing experiential act into something
that is rigid, predefined, and unlikely ever to be as good,
bad, thrilling, wonderful or difficult as it used to be or as
it should have been.

In truth, whatever we think may have happened is
probably nothing like whatever actually did happen.
Memories lie. That is why, as you may have noticed, any
two or more people can share the same experience and
have widely diverging opinions about how it was or even
what it was. Consider the experiences of sex, public
speaking, warfare, broccoli, and stealing and you will

quickly get the point.

What happens is that experience becomes subverted and lost on a vicious circular path between two boxes.

Everything is either better than it was before or worse than it was before. Everything is either more or less, the same or different as something else. Everything is no longer simply just whatever it is. In our own experience, nothing in our lives has the fresh keenedged clarity, sharpness, and distinctly aware focus inherent in each new event or action as it is actually unfolding. Major confusion obscures our ability to differentiate between action and results or the doer and the deed itself. A condition of flat, dull emptiness or a feeling that something is missing surrounds us. And we become hopelessly stuck.

There is only one way out.

That way is to choose still another distinct domain, a third box: The creation box. There is nothing in this box. Nothing at all. Except the power to bring something into existence where nothing existed before. In this domain, we encounter the raw primordial power of pure creation.

Everything that exists as a presence or as a concept is in the other two boxes. Literally everything. None of it has any validity or purpose in the creation box. Objects, events and experiences which have already occurred or are presently occurring have no purpose in this space. What you think or feel does not matter here. Neither does anything you have ever experienced up to now. Body sensations, fear, sadness, rejection, beliefs, attitudes, habits, past successes or failures do not count in this realm and do not belong here.

The only thing you can get out of this box is creation itself or the power to bring something forth out of nothing. To do that, the only tool you have to work with is your word. You say you will do something and then you do it. You take a stand that something will be done and then you become the stand that you took. You become, in other words, the focal point around which everything else moves into alignment to enable you to keep your word.

There is no safety and no comfort in creation. You

never know exactly how you will get what you said would happen to actually happen. All you can know is that you have taken a stand that something will be done. Therefore it will be done.

Each realm, as a contextual domain, is a space in which possibilities can be found. The creation box contains all possible choices, including the choice not to choose. The experience box contains all possible degrees of action, including no action at all. And the conceptual box contains all possible results that can be observed and measured, including no results. Under normal circumstances, we pass freely from domain to domain and use the contents as we need them.

Creation is followed by action or lack of action. Action is followed by results or no results. Either of these requires a recommitment to creation, which completes one cycle and immediately begins another. The cycle is designed to be an ongoing one. Stopping at the level of results or the lack of them only keeps us trapped in a conceptual space where other possibilities found in other domains are denied and unavailable.

Results mean that you have kept your word. Your choice to create or the stand that you took showed up in experiential form as action leading to concrete and observable achievements which are now memories of a successful venture.

No results mean that you have not kept your word. Your choice to create showed up in experiential form as a sensation or a feeling instead of elemental action. It too has now become a memory, the memory of a good try or a bad try, a near miss or a dismal failure.

Since all memories are concepts, they live strictly in the concept box. If you do not want to live in there along with them, what is required is your constant recommitment to creation. At the moment you give your word to be recommitted, POW! There you are, back in the creation box again.

The question is, 'What for?'

Why would you or anyone else for that matter want to venture into the only box that is not an easy and comfortable place to be?

For two very good reasons.

First, as serious as all of this may sound, it is no more than my version of a description of a playing field for the game of life. Descriptions of tennis courts or baseball diamonds will never capture the fun and excitement of actually playing on them. Because descriptions are conceptual, like all explanations, they are poor substitutes for actually being out where the action of the game is going on and giving it your best shot.

Second, it is much bigger than any ordinary playing field. It is the site of the only game in town. And you cannot possibly win if you don't play.

When we live primarily on a conceptual level, we have more than enough products and notions of conceptual thinking around to prop us up and provide fallback positions, justifications and reasons why everything is always someone else's fault. That is an easy way out of life. Western civilization thrives on it and holds it to be an appropriate standard for living.

The only problem is the price. All those conceptual products and notions that we get usually get us, too. Think of all the people you know whose lives are no bigger than their checkbook or stock portfolio or home or job or partner or car or religion or stamp collection or any other thing like that. Take away that conceptual thing or group of things. Their lives are over. Threaten that thing, and their lives are thrown into a state of panic and dread. They react to the content of their lives rather than initiating life itself. Quick, imagine that a motorcycle gang has just surrounded your car and that they are beginning to pound it with axes, chains, sledgehammers, rocks and steel pipes. You get the idea.

But it is even worse than you think.

Conceptually-oriented people age according to whichever external concept about aging is the currently accepted one. It seems to be the only appropriate possibility. They have their actuarial statistics and externally based opinions to prove their points of view. And the prevailing statistics and opinions have them: in the form of all the conceptual attitudes, positions, beliefs and justifications that they are literally willing to defend to the death. They age on schedule. They die on schedule. Usually years ahead of their time. And because it is all a process of reaction, it all takes place in the passenger seat of reality.

When we live purely on an experiential level, we live with all of the far-reaching experience of each and every moment to support us. That's easier than it sounds. All we have to do is to be present and to participate in life as it unfolds all around us. Eastern philosophies are built along these guidelines and, instead of thinking about what might have happened yesterday or what may happen next, moment-to-moment experience is held as the appropriate standard for living.

The only problem is, here too, there is a price. Life has a tendency to become too passive an experience if we are simply going along for the ride or even if we are participating fully but aimlessly in the present. There may be yearning, seeking, striving and wanting. Or there may not. Either way, there are no voting privileges and no direction, no goals and no regrets. Each of those requires nonexperiential data drawn from conceptual projections about the future and assessments about the past or from the creation of intended promises and the taking of a stand.

To live completely in the moment, each moment at a time, puts us almost completely at the effect of the flow of events and experiences that emerge and open up around us. There is nothing to do about anything except to experience and process whatever comes along.

We take what we get and agree to like it that way. We live while we are living and die when we are dying at our own rates and in our own time. But, once again, it all takes place in the passenger seat of reality.

When we live on a purely creative level, on the other hand, we live on the edge. We find ourselves at the source of it all and totally responsible for whatever comes out of it. Here, too, there is a price. We must give up the safety and comfort of the known because there is nothing here to know. We literally have to create everything.

To work in this realm, you must create your life and your experience of life by taking a stand. What stand?

Whatever stand you choose to take. Nothing precedes it.
And there is no path in front of you. There is not even a
certain way that you have to be in order to do it. You
simply take a stand. Then, the stand you took becomes
the initial act of creation. It elicits action and produces
results. All on the strength of your word.

In the creation box, your word becomes the
language of life instead of idle chatter. You discover the
immense power inherent in being who you are and using
the language you use to express that power. In fact, you
can directly link the reality you create in your languaging
to the experiences that you have and the conceptual
material that you later derive from those experiences.

Four questions will always lead you back to your
power of being in the domain of creation.

1. What is true about you and your power to be
who you are?

3. Where and how does that show up?

4. What makes it real?

Use these questions like any other questions. First
ask yourself each one. Then answer each one as precisely
as you can. Support yourself to tell the truth and do not
settle for an answer that sounds incomplete or shifts
responsibility to any external source.

Your internal dialogue might sound like this:

You: 'What is true about you and your power to be
who you are?'

Yourself: 'I am a person who tries to get things
done but has trouble seeing the results of that.'

You: 'Who says so?'

Yourself: 'My boss.'

You (pressing for the real answer): 'No. Your boss
may have said so in the past or in your memories. Who
says so?'

Yourself: 'My mother and father.'

You (still pressing on): 'No. They may have said so
some time ago. Who is saying so right now?'

Yourself: 'Uh, I don't understand.'

You (not buying that, knowing better): ' Listen, it's
easy. Who says so? Who says what you are saying? Who
says what you are saying right now?'

Yourself: 'Oh! I see. Me. I say so.'

You: 'Where and how does that show up?'

Yourself: 'I can see it at work. I can see it in my personal relationships. I can see it in my undone projects at home. It shows up all over the place.'

You: 'What makes it real?'

Yourself: 'All the unfinished things and confusion in my life.'

You (pushing for the truth): 'No. That is what is made real in the future or what has been made real in the past. What makes it real now?'

You (with a sudden burst of insight): 'I get it. My saying so makes it real Ohmigod!'

Try it yourself, playing the roles of questioner and answerer. Or if you prefer, ask someone else to work with you. Either way, hold yourself to answering the questions exactly as they are stated with ruthless precision. You will immediately see why things may not have been working in your life and who is responsible for it.

If aging has been an issue for you in the past, approach it from the creative box right now. This is the contextual space in which miracles originate, including the miracle of a longlasting, healthy, active body and mind. Use this unique space of creation from now on as an alternative to experiencing your age passively or playing out your aging process as an internalized version of someone else's beliefs, opinions, or other conceptual positions about it.

For instance, take a stand about your own process of aging. The stand you take might be to live to see your 135th birthday in good health, and to have a wonderful time each year along the way. Promise yourself that is what you will do. Then keep your promise. And watch what happens.

If you are still not sure about all of this, ask yourself the four creation questions but add the following variation to focus your insights:

1. Regarding aging, what is true about you and your power to be who you are?

2. Who says so?

3. Regarding aging, where and how does that show up?

4. What makes it real?

You will get the idea very quickly.

Alternatives To Aging have always been available to each of us. Until now, you may not have noticed how close at hand they actually were or how much control over them was within your grasp. Validating them requires no endless series of laboratory tests, no FDA approvals. Your life is the best proving ground of all. And your word is the highest authority available.

My Alternatives To Aging include all of the following. You may be able to come up with even more of your own to add to the list.

• Avoid stereotypic blueprints by being willing to venture out on your own and find out what is really so.

• Create your life each step of the way, using language and responsible promises to set up and color your experiences. Remember that things will turn out the way you say.

• Use up each moment of your life. There is nothing to save yourself or anything else for.

• Be willing to participate actively and to share yourself externally at a 100% level all of the time.

• Declare your satisfaction with what has already turned out in the past. It is already done so there is nothing further that you can do other than to accept it, acknowledge it, and use it as a foundation for corrective action in the present and future.

• Notice the natural clues all around you like the never ending transitions from day to night, the movement of the tides, the flow of the seasons. Interpret them consciously and draw your own appropriate conclusions from them.

• Set priorities that will allow you time enough for physical excercise, development of relationships, self-examination, personal exploration and growth, committed promises and anything else that actively supports your life.

• Establish decade-by-decade goals from now to your 140th birthday and don't shut down until you attain them.

• Express your aliveness and use it to empower others to bring forth and express their aliveness in everwidening circles. You will be starting a chain of life that cannot be broken.

• Promise to keep your mind in the conceptual box, your body and emotions in the experiential box, and your lifeforce and energy in the creation box where they all belong.

• Live each day as if you only had three more months to live.

Handle all that, factor in the certainty that lifespans of 120 to 140 years or more are physiologically possible and presently available, and you can keep yourself alive and well for as long as you like.

Alternatives To Aging, as you can now see, are not an issue involving lifestyle. Nor are they a process, a technique, or something specific to do or to take internally. Your lifestyle and whatever you include in it may support or detract from your capacity to reach your maximum age with all your vital parts working effectively. But it is not what will make the ultimate difference.

Alternatives To Aging are not a state of mind either. Your mind can only do what it is designed to do. It computes, stores, processes and evaluates data. The products and concepts of your mind may or may not support your intended longevity goals. They may even cloud your experience with enough secondhand negativity to keep you from attaining them. But by and of themselves, they lack the power to bring you to your 140th year in robust health and vitality.

Alternatives To Aging are a state of being. Just a pure and simple state of being fully operational and fully alive for as long as your biological heritage allows, which means for a lot longer than you ever thought possible. Each alternative requires only your willingness to be completely open to all of the possibilities available to you. And to be committed to stepping out and living your life as an exhilarating and exuberant game of creation.

By now, you understand the rules of the game.
Don't you?

First, you choose what you intend to create (from a phone call to a friend to the end of starvation to a 132nd birthday party for yourself) and you give your promise to bring it forth.

Then, you act consistently with that promise, and you either do what needs to be done to keep your word. Or you don't.

Either way, you acknowledge your results and find a way to be completely satisfied with them, whatever they were. (The easiest way is just to say 'I'm satisfied with the way it turned out' or 'I'm satisfied with not liking the way it turned out' and state whatever you intend to do about it.)

And finally, you reset the game board and start again.

Whether you are 30 years old or 130 years old does not matter. The only difference is in the profundity of your direct observations as you notice that you are engaged in a major experiential shift.

Stereotypic patterns of the past will fade into astonishing new alternatives. That certain quality of life you used to seek in vain will no longer be so fleetingly elusive or beyond your reach; it will surround you like a powerful new aura. And as each year passes, instead of putting up with the slowly diminishing faculties many people have chosen to associate with aging, you will be able to draw upon ever-increasing grace and beauty, power and dignity, wisdom and new skills, physical stamina and mental clarity, vigor and abundant energy.

You will no longer just be staying alive. You will be creating aliveness.

And that is the only alternative you can live with.

AFTERWORD AND ACKNOWLEDGMENTS

Somewhere near the beginning of all this, I recall a conversation with Norma Kravette, a friend who was once married to me. Norma commented that life was like waiting on line to die. 'When you were born', she said, 'you went to the end of the line. The older you got, the closer you got to the front of the line until finally there was no one left ahead of you. And you died.'

I began to notice how many people lived out their lives as if this were so, approaching their 40's, 50's, and 60's as if time were running out and nothing could be done, caught in a destructive belief pattern known as 'inevitability'. Then I noticed how a lot of other people who may not have shared this particular point of view still lived their lives coming from other beliefs that were even more harmful and destructive, beliefs that lacked even the small barbed bite of satire.

Finally I shifted into my observation mode in which, passively and spongelike, I take in everything around me that has any bearing whatsoever on any issue I am engaged with. Everywhere I looked, suddenly all that I could see were signs of aging, decay, decrepitude, shutting down. Everyone looked like a mill town after the mill has closed. It was terrible. What, I wondered, was the point of even holding on to a place in line if this was all that there is to look forward to.

Then, a long way off in my tunnel of hopelessness about aging, a ray of light appeared. Instead of only noticing what was lacking, I began to become aware of occasional exceptions to the downhill slide of advancing age. At first, these exceptions seemed almost accidental. But soon, other possibilities, other alternatives began to emerge at almost every turn.

Fifty-year-old women like Joan Collins and Vikki LaMotta suddenly showed up as national sex symbols. Eighty and ninety year-old entertainers like Fred Astaire and George Burns developed new skills, broadened their talents, and emerged as powerful and inspiring performers. Seventy-year-old political figures like Ronald Reagan demonstrated that age was no barrier to effective leadership. And ninety and one-hundred-year-old creative people like Irving Berlin and Eubie Blake demonstrated that their artistic gifts remained available to them on an ageless basis for all to enjoy.

I finally got the message that led to this book. Each of these and hundreds of other exceptions like them opens up and reinforces the possibility that personal choice can determine each of our personal destinies and that circumstances are never more than we say they are or what we make of them.

Each new Olympic record creates the space for all athletes to better their performance within newly opened possible boundaries. Each Albert Einstein creates the space for all mathematicians to transcend existing intellectual limits. Each Beethoven creates incredible new space for serious composers to explore. Each Shakespeare or Dickens or Bradbury opens new creative paths of possibilities for other writers. And each aging breakthrough by any human being that you see, hear about or know personally creates a space of new alternatives for everyone. In each case, what was once thought to be impossible suddenly becomes possible and what was once only a crazy dream becomes commonplace reality.

Aging breakthroughs of the type I am writing about exist all around us. So in my list of acknowledgements, I am including the names of those who provided me with most striking and inspiring examples of successful aging while this book was in process, along with the names of those who empowered me intellectually and supported me on emotional, physical, or intentional levels. First, I want to acknowledge Jo Dorr. She listened to my concepts from the very beginning and has validated many of my conclusions in her professional work. Second, I express my appreciation to Betty Dunlop for her concept for the cover design. Then for all of their contributions to me and to this book, I sincerely thank:

Shelby Allen
Fred Astaire
Irving Berlin
Nathaniel Branden
Amanda Burgoon
Tom Burgoon
James Cagney
Douglas Congdon-Martin
Carolyn Coulter
Mabel Daum
Plunkett Dodge
Jan Dragin
Ella Fitzgerald
Fr. Charlie Flaherty
Dorothy Fuldheim
Maria Fulton
David Glowacki
Michael Glowacki
Lisa Goldberg
Cary Grant
Fr. John Hall
Louise Hay
Lena Horne
Bob Hope
Charles Katz
Christine Kravette
Ellyn Kravette
Norma Kravette
Sanford Kravette
Vikki LaMotta

David Alpern, MD
Bartholomew
Eubie Blake
Lori Bruno
John Thomas Burgoon
George Burns
Joan Collins
Stavros Cosmopulos
Joanna Daum
Maharaga DiAndhi
C. Jo Dorr
Werner Erhard
Patrick Flannigan
Jane Fonda
Buckminster Fuller
Rosanne Glickman
Lois Glowacki
Bill Goldberg
Linda Goodman
Valerie Greene
Mary B. Hall
Wini Hedrick
Harry Houdini
Stan Kaplan
Anna Jillian Kravette
Edna Kravette
Jesse Kravette
Randolph Kravette
Maggie Kuhn
Shirley MacLaine

Jacque McLellan
Ann Miller
Laurence Morehouse, MD
Jack Nathan
Sir Laurence Olivier
Ramtha
Jane Roberts
Robert G. Scharf
Leonard Schwartz, MD
Sandy Shaw
Merlyn Sheehan
Nancy Straus
Milton Traeger
Mae West

James McLellan
Joan Mooney
Edith Mula
Daphne Weld Nichols
Durk Pearson
Ronald Reagan
Mickey Rooney
Peter Schiffer
Seth
Joseph Sheehan
Frank Sinatra
Mel Torme
Roy Walford, MD
Sally Williams

And, also, everyone else who is truly committed to growing as they grow older and thus, through their own direct experience, enriching the pool of possibilities for everyone else on the planet. I am certain that you know who you are.

Stephen Kravette
January 1989.